Inclus

Inclusive Aid

Changing Power and Relationships in International Development

Edited by
Leslie Groves and Rachel Hinton

London • Sterling, VA

First published by Earthscan in the UK and USA in 2004

Reprinted 2005

ISBN: 1-84407-033-6 paperback
      1-84407-032-8 hardback

Typesetting by MapSet Ltd, Gateshead, UK
Printed and bound in the UK by Cromwell Press Ltd
Cover design by Ruth Bateson

For a full list of publications please contact:

Earthscan
8–12 Camden High Street
London, NW1 0JH, UK
Tel: +44 (0)20 7387 8558
Fax: +44 (0)20 7387 8998
Email: earthinfo@earthscan.co.uk
Web: **www.earthscan.co.uk**

22883 Quicksilver Drive, Sterling, VA 20166-2012, USA

Earthscan publishes in association with the International Institute for Environment
and Development

A catalogue record for this book is available from the British Library

Library of Congress Cataloging-in-Publication Data

Inclusive aid : changing power and relationships in international development / edited
by Leslie Christine Groves and Rachel Barbara Hinton.
      p. cm.
Includes bibliographical references.
    ISBN 1-84407-033-6 (pbk.) — ISBN 1-84407-032-8 (hardback)
    1. Economic assistance. 2. Poverty—Developing countries. I. Groves, Leslie
Christine, 1974- II. Hinton, Rachel Barbara, 1968-

    HC60.I418 2004
    338.91'09172'4—dc22

                                                                            2003021889

To the late Barbara Castle, who inspired us all to make a difference

Contents

Part One: Challenges and Opportunities

Part Two: Power, Procedures and Relationships

Part Three: The Way Forward

List of Figures, Tables and Boxes

Figures

Tables

Boxes

About the Contributors

Robert Chambers is a research associate at the Institute of Development Studies (IDS), University of Sussex, UK. His work in development has been mainly in sub-Saharan Africa, South Asia and the UK, including an exploration of participatory methods, behaviours and attitudes for workshops, teaching and training. His books include *Rural Development: Putting the Last First* (Longman, 1983), *Challenging the Professions* (Intermediate Technology, 1993), *Whose Reality Counts? Putting the First Last* (Intermediate Technology, 1997) and *Participatory Workshops: A Sourcebook of 21 Sets of Ideas and Activities* (Earthscan, 2002).

Rosalind Eyben is a development social scientist with a career in international development policy and practice. She has had long-term overseas experience in anglophone and francophone Africa, India and most recently in Latin America. She was the first chief social development adviser to the Department for International Development, UK, from which she resigned to work for DFID in Bolivia before joining IDS in July 2002. Current interests include human rights and citizenship, the politics of policy-making, implementing poverty reduction strategies and the sociology of donor–recipient relations.

Clare Ferguson is a social development adviser at DFID, UK. Her responsibilities have included helping develop DFID's policy on human rights and piloting ways of operationalizing rights-based approaches to development. Her doctoral research was on reproductive rights and citizenship in Zimbabwe.

Leslie Groves is an independent social development consultant who has worked with DFID, the International Labour Organization (ILO) and a range of non-governmental organizations (NGOs). She has worked on development issues in Tanzania, Vietnam, Brazil, Honduras, Guatemala, Ethiopia, Bangladesh, Senegal and Burkina Faso. Her PhD research explored the issues of power, procedures and relationships in development organizations.

Rachel Hinton is a social development adviser at DFID, UK. She worked with Bhutanese refugees for her PhD in social anthropology from Cambridge University. She currently holds an honorary fellowship at Edinburgh University where her research interests include refugee children, child rights and social inclusion within education. These interests have taken her to a number of countries including Ghana, India, Kenya, Nepal and Zimbabwe. Her publications cover issues of child labour, participation in development programmes and methodologies for social research.

Jean Horstman is an organizational consultant working with individuals or groups engaged in innovative problem-solving or confronting issues arising from or generating a call for systemic change. In Jean's 25 years of working in the public, private and social sectors, she has partnered with multinationals, government bodies, universities, foundations and not-for-profit organizations. As former Managing Director of the Society for Organizational Learning (SOL), she worked extensively with organizations such as BP PLC, Ford Motor Company, Global Business Network, Hewlett-Packard, Shell Oil and the World Bank. Jean is a member of the Corrymeela Community of Reconciliation (NI).

Katja Jassey is a socio-cultural adviser for the Swedish International Development Agency (Sida). Her main areas of work are policies for poverty reduction as well as participatory approaches in development. Previously, she worked with the Food and Agricultural Organization (FAO) in southern and eastern Africa in a programme aimed at connecting agricultural research and extension with farmer realities.

Margaret Kakande is head of the Poverty Monitoring and Analysis Unit in the Ministry of Finance, Planning and Economic Development, Uganda. She has been involved in poverty work with government, dating from 1994 when she was social policy adviser to the Programme for Alleviation of Poverty and Social Costs of Adjustment. Margaret has participated in the development of the Poverty Eradication Action Plans, the enhancement of pro-poor budgeting and the formulation of the Poverty Monitoring and Evaluation Strategy. She has observed the development of partnerships between government, donors and civil society in the design, implementation and monitoring of the Action Plans. She holds a Bachelor of Statistics, MA in development economics and certificates in monitoring and evaluation; strategic communication; participatory research methods; development statistics; and manpower planning.

Ruth Marsden is a freelance researcher. She graduated in social anthropology (MA) from Edinburgh University. She worked as an information officer with ActionAid, a large international NGO in Nepal for one year, through a training placement supported by the Overseas Training Programme, a volunteer programme run by Voluntary Services Overseas in the UK. During this time she carried out research into how voices of those in project communities were listened to and incorporated in written reports. She later returned to far west Nepal for independent research work (supported by the Arkleton Trust and Edinburgh University) exploring one community's experiences of participation and social change.

Charles Owusu is an independent consultant specializing in organizational learning, monitoring and impact assessment. Prior to this he worked with ActionAid in the Impact Assessment Unit in London and was programme manager and monitoring and evaluation adviser for ActionAid Ghana. He has wide-ranging experience in community-level monitoring and evaluation systems.

Between 1995 and 1997 he was country coordinator for a DFID-sponsored study on participatory impact assessment methodologies and approaches in Ghana. Charles has played a lead role in ActionAid's efforts to pilot its new Accountability Learning and Planning System; leading to the development of a Participatory Review and Reflection Process (PRRP), which is helping ActionAid to promote downward accountability to local people and improve their participation and representation in local development processes. Charles received his academic training in rural social development at Reading University and has recently completed a Masters programme in management of development organisations at the London School of Economics (LSE).

Katherine Pasteur is a research officer at IDS, UK. Her present interests include participatory monitoring and evaluation, organizational learning and organizational change. Much of her work has involved relating these issues to the sustainable-livelihoods approach adopted in parts of DFID and by some NGOs.

Jethro Pettit coordinates research and communication projects with partners and networks in Asia, Africa and Latin America through his work with the Participation Group at IDS, UK. He is interested in power and rights, organizational learning and change, participatory teaching and learning, community-based development and social movements. Previous experience includes working with NGOs, community organizing and campaigning for peace, social justice and the environment.

Caroline Robb is a social development specialist at the International Monetary Fund (IMF), where she is responsible for developing a greater poverty focus for fund-supported programmes and opening up the macro-economic dialogue and policy debate. Previously, she spent five years in the private sector as a commercial manager and then five years in The Gambia, first as a VSO volunteer business and community development worker, where she lived and worked in a small rural village. She then worked as an NGO field director in The Gambia, and then on an assignment with the United Nations Development Programme (UNDP) to assist the government to develop a national strategy for poverty alleviation. Before joining the IMF, Caroline worked for the World Bank with a focus on how to include the poor in the policy-making process, poverty analysis and participation, and analysing the poverty and social impacts of the East Asian financial crisis. Current interests include combining different disciplines to improve understanding of poverty; poverty and social impact analysis of macro-economic and structural reforms; political and social analysis of policy-making and participation; and how to include poor people in policy dialogue and poverty analysis.

Patta Scott-Villiers is a member of the Participation Group at IDS, UK, working on organizational learning for participation with DFID, Sida and ActionAid; and the facilitation of multi-stakeholder processes with government, customary institutions and development agencies in East Africa. She started her career in development in Sudan in 1984 and spent 13 years in East Africa working on participation and community development with NGOs, government and bilateral agencies before joining IDS in 1997.

Everjoice J Win is a Zimbabwean feminist activist, a consultant to the Participation Group at IDS, UK, and regular contributor to newspapers in Zimbabwe and southern Africa. She has been a women's rights activist throughout her career, which started with the Women's Action Group in Zimbabwe, moving on to the regional network Women in Law and Development in Africa. Her work involved training, popular legal literacy, lobbying government/s on women's human rights and media liaison. Besides formal employment she has been an evaluation and training consultant for a number of international donors including Oxfam GB-Zimbabwe, Hivos, the Asia Foundation, USAID and UNICEF. Most recently, Everjoice was an adviser to the Commonwealth Fund for Technical Cooperation, attached to the Commission on Gender Equality of South Africa. She studied economic history at the University of Zimbabwe.

Preface

This book is about how bureaucratic procedures and power relations hinder poverty reduction in the new aid environment. Rapid and profound changes are taking place in international development that demand closer attention to the social and political context. New aid modalities have redirected resources away from discrete project funding to macro-level policy change and direct support to national budgets. This has increased the significance of the quality and nature of the partnerships among key development actors. Yet, major decisions that affect people's lives continue to be made without sufficient attention to socio-cultural realities and political incentives. This volume reveals the need for greater awareness of the dynamics of power and relationships among actors, and that shifts in attention to personal attitudes and behaviour are a missing link in enabling institutional and professional commitment to such change.

The past two decades have also seen a rise in the ideals of participation and partnership, and attempts to enable the voices of the poor to be heard. Despite this, embedded traditions, vested interests and bureaucratic inertia mean that old behaviours and organizational cultures persist. In spite of the rhetoric, planning continues as though it were free of chaotic interactions among stakeholders. The mounting concern during the early 1990s about the rigid implementation of centralized procedural tools, such as the logical framework, failed to dislodge the dominant paradigms. Meanwhile, donors have been slow to embrace recent institutional innovations that recognize the complex non-linear nature of development assistance. These include rights-based approaches that support the development of multiple accountability channels and mechanisms for citizens holding government to account.

Key individuals from various bilateral and multilateral donors, non-governmental organizations (NGOs) and academic institutions came together at the Institute of Development Studies (IDS), to debate these issues.[1] The experiences, ideas and case studies that emerged in this workshop have been further developed through various intellectual inputs and discussion with complexity thinkers into the material presented in this book.[2] The authors bring together and analyse recent experiences of institutional learning and change that respond to the new demands in development. Through case studies from around the globe they identify ideas and options for constructive change. The book argues that aid practice now requires a shift from linear planning for predetermined outcomes to supporting strategic change that recognizes development as a complex system. Only in this way can the well-being of poor people be truly improved and can there be any chance of successfully attaining the Millennium Development Goals, including halving world poverty by 2015.

This book is aimed at researchers and practitioners who work with or in international development organizations. Its lessons transcend the boundaries of professional groups and sectors. Through the case studies it exposes the agency that all actors have to make a difference.

Notes

1   Power, Procedures and Relationships Workshop, 8–12 May 2001.
2   It also draws on the IDS policy briefing paper that developed from the workshop (IDS (2001) *The New Dynamics of Aid: Power, Procedures and Relationships*. IDS Policy Briefing. Issue 15. August 2001).

Editors' Acknowledgements

We are indebted to many people who have helped us embrace the new developments in the process of making this book. We thank all the participants of the Institute of Development Studies (IDS) workshop who brought energy and experience to the lively debate on 'Power, Procedures and Relationships'. These co-authors have provided enthusiasm and encouragement through various iterations of their chapters. In particular, we thank Robert Chambers for his belief that these experiences had to be captured and recorded and his unending support and energy to continue to enlarge on the debate.

We gratefully acknowledge the time and intellectual input provided by those who reviewed and provided significant contributions to chapters: Bella Bird, Martha Caddell, Beth Cross, Alan Fowler, Liz Goold, Matt Pearce, Shiona Hood, Rosemary McGee, Garett Pratt, Caroline Robb, Patta Scott-Villiers and Jan Webb. Particular gratitude is due to Jethro Pettit and Rosalind Eyben for their professional insight and intellectual rigour – they have been a constant source of support for us both – and to Philip Groves for the cover design idea. We are grateful for the patience and professionalism of Jane Stevens and Dominic Glover at IDS, and to Jonathan Sinclair Wilson, Ruth Mayo, Frances MacDermott and Rob West at Earthscan.

In addition, we have personal debts that have made this book possible.

While it is impossible to name all of the individuals who have provided ideas and inspiration in far-flung places, I would like to give particular thanks to Ganga Neupane, Pingala Dhakal and the Bhutanese refugees who continue to demonstrate courage and commitment to change. To my friends and mentors for their encouragement and my family for their faith in me. To my loving and patient husband, Yadvinder, and our imminent new arrival, who has kept the whole project in perspective.

Rachel Hinton

I would like to thank all of my friends, family and mentors who provided support, inspiration and encouragement during the journey that is now this book. Special thank you to Mama Kuku and Mushi in Tanzania, all at SCP-DN in Vietnam, the Comunidade das Pequenas Profetas in Brazil and the many children with whom I have been privileged to have worked over the years and who have kept the twinkle of hope and joy alive in my heart. Thank you also to my parents, my brothers Stephan and Philip, Elizabeth Silvani, Beryl and Eric, and Marcelo. My extra special thank you is to Rachel Hinton: our friendship and work relationship has grown stronger with each twist of the journey.

Leslie Groves

List of Acronyms and Abbreviations

ADN	a political party (Bolivia)
ALPS	Accountability, Learning and Planning System (ActionAid)
APMSS	Andhra Pradesh Mahila Samatha Society (India)
ASPNSD	Association for the Promotion of North–South Dialogue
BWI	Bretton Woods Institutions
CBO	community-based organization
CDC	community development corporation
CDC/ARI	Community Development Corporation/Arts Resource Initiative
CDF	Comprehensive Development Framework (World Bank)
CDRA	Community Development Resource Association (South Africa)
CGIAR	Consultative Group on International Agricultural Research
DAC	Development Assistance Committee (OECD)
DDC	district development committee (Nepal)
DFID	Department for International Development (UK)
EDP	Exposure and Dialogue Programme
ESAF	Enhanced Structural Adjustment Facility
FAO	Food and Agricultural Organization (UN)
FAWEZA	Forum for African Women Educationalists Zambia
Finnaid	Finnish Department for International Cooperation
G7	Group of Seven (developed countries)
G77	Group of 77 (developing countries)
GNP	gross national product
GTZ	German Agency for Technical Cooperation (Deutsche Gesellschaft für Technische Zusammenarbeit)
HIPC	Highly Indebted Poor Countries (Initiative)
IAU	Impact Assessment Unit (ActionAid)
IBRD	International Bank for Reconstruction and Development
IDA	International Development Association
IDB	Inter-American Development Bank
IDS	Institute of Development Studies
IFAD	International Fund for Agricultural Development
IFI	international financial institution
ILO	International Labour Organization
IMF	International Monetary Fund
INGO	international non-governmental organization
INTRAC	International NGO Research and Training Centre
IRDP	integrated rural development project
ISDP	Integrated Social Development Programme (Nepal)

IT	information technology
LDC	least developed country
logframe	logical framework analysis
MCG	Manchester Craftsmen's Guild
MDG	Millennium Development Goal
MIR	a political party (Bolivia)
MNR	a political party (Bolivia)
MTEF	Medium-Term Expenditure Framework (Uganda)
NGO	non-governmental organization
NIEO	New International Economic Order
ODA	Official Development Assistance or Overseas Development Administration (UK, pre-1997)
ODA	overseas development assistance
OECD	Organisation for Economic Co-operation and Development
OPEC	Organization of the Petroleum Exporting Countries
PEAP	Poverty Eradication Action Plan (Uganda)
PLA	participatory learning and action
PPA	participatory poverty assessment
PRA	participatory rural appraisal
PRGF	Poverty Reduction and Growth Facility
PRRP	participatory review and reflection process (ActionAid)
PRS	poverty reduction strategy (World Bank)
PRSP	poverty reduction strategy paper
PSIA	poverty and social impact assessment
RIPS	Rural Integrated Project Support Programme (Tanzania)
RRA	rapid rural appraisal
RTA	Retrospective Terms Adjustment
SAF	Structural Adjustment Facility
SAL	structural adjustment loan
SDA	Social Dimensions of Adjustment programme
SEWA	Self-Employed Women's Association (India)
Sida	Swedish International Development Agency
SMUWC	Sustainable Management of the Usungu Wetland and its Catchment (Project) (Tanzania)
SWAP	sector-wide approach
TCO	Technical Cooperation Officer
UCS	a political party (Bolivia)
UNCTAD	United Nations Conference on Trade and Development
UNDP	United Nations Development Programme
UNICEF	United Nations Children's Fund
UPPAP	Uganda Participatory Poverty Assessment Process
USAID	US Agency for International Development
VSO	Voluntary Service Overseas
WDR	*World Development Report*
WHO	World Health Organization
ZOPP	objective-oriented project planning (*Ziel-Orientierte Projekt Planung*)

Part One

CHALLENGES AND OPPORTUNITIES

1

The Complexity of Inclusive Aid

Rachel Hinton and Leslie Groves

Inclusive aid

We will spare no effort to free our fellow men, women and children from the abject and dehumanizing conditions of extreme poverty, to which more than a billion of them are subjected (United Nations Millennium Declaration, September 2000).

The arrival of the 21st century heralded a new sense of optimism. At all levels people came together in a concerted effort to address world poverty. Advocates from 189 countries signed up to the United Nations Millennium Declaration, ready to fight for the rights of poor people. This declaration commits countries to fight world poverty and its main thrust was the setting of the Millennium Development Goals (MDGs), including halving the numbers of people living in extreme poverty by 2015. Poverty reduction has thus become the overarching goal of international development with a call for the adoption of more pragmatic and people-centred policy that takes on board the local knowledge and priorities of the poor.

Despite the expertise and energies of so many, the MDGs are unlikely to be attained within the agreed time frame. Far greater trust, accountability and responsibility must be developed within and among all actors, at all levels, as a condition for success. This requires a new focus on the socio-political dynamics of aid and an understanding of development as a complex system. Until this shift occurs, poverty elimination through aid programmes will remain elusive.

This book begins with a conceptual and historical analysis of aid to set the context for the proceeding chapters. The analysis reveals the major challenges and opportunities facing the aid community today. In Part Two, Chapters 4 to 10 look at the issues of power, procedures and relationships from a complex systems perspective. Each chapter represents a different voice in the development system: the donor; the government; the international non-governmental organization (INGO); and the Southern activist. Each author shows how entrenched procedures work to preserve and, indeed, are sometimes used to justify the status quo. These examples contrast with cases of recent procedural innovations in Africa and Asia that embrace significant cultural and political influences. The case studies illustrate how achieving inclusive aid requires new understandings and ways of thinking about the complexity and dynamics of the entire development system.

Part Three explores ways forward for aid agencies in changing their political, institutional and personal ways of working in order to better meet their commitment to the MDGs. Chapters 11 to 15 examine how organizations can build more-equal relationships with partner countries and create an environment conducive to personal change. They also look at how development practitioners can adapt existing participatory approaches to facilitate the involvement of poor people in holding governments to account for the decisions that affect their lives and for ensuring that governments deliver on their commitments. As a consequence of the systemic approach, the authors argue for greater sensitivity to local and global dynamics. They demonstrate that inclusive aid requires practitioners to re-evaluate and understand the extent to which the changing political context affects the outcome of the development agenda. This necessarily demands scrutiny of different lines of accountability. Crucially, the authors show how translating rhetoric into practice relies on changing the attitudes and behaviours of individual actors, and on the role of personal agency in creating change.

The new dynamics of development

Recent years have seen fundamental changes in dominant aid paradigms. The failure of development policy and practice to raise the standard of living of a large proportion of the world's poor has prompted a radical rethink of development policy and practice. There has been a dramatic shift from a belief in the importance of projects and service delivery to a language of rights and governance. Among policy-makers there has been an evolving sense of the need to involve members of civil society in upholding their rights and working to promote transparent, accountable government.

At the micro level, this has led to an increasingly sophisticated understanding of the benefits of local participation, and the development of approaches that prioritize the perspectives of poor people. Participatory rural appraisal (PRA) and related methods of participatory learning and action (PLA) revolutionized the way of thinking of many development practitioners, and enabled many primary stakeholders to have a voice in decisions about how project funds were utilized. The World Bank subsequently introduced participatory poverty assessments (PPAs), in part with the hope that they would enable poor and marginalized people to influence policy (Norton et al, 2001). At a macro level, there has been a shift from service delivery to supporting citizens' entitlement to services. Donors are emphasizing the need to work in partnership with national government rather than create parallel structures for service provision.[1] The

1990s witnessed a gradual increase in the flow of aid delivered through governments, as support for democratic national processes grew. The World Bank's poverty reduction strategy (PRS) process attempts to provide a direct link between grassroots assessment and development of strategies at policy level. It requires the participation of civil society and a move from government-owned to country-owned processes.[2] In this new environment policies take a central place whereas projects, from being central to the development process, become one element in a wider development agenda.

These shifts require new approaches and procedures that stress partnership and transparency. But embedded traditions, vested interests and bureaucratic inertia mean that old behaviours and organizational cultures persist. Hence the gap between rhetoric and practice remains wide. The contributions show that the way forward is to seek greater consistency between personal behaviour, institutional norms and the new development agenda. This will require a shift from linear planning for predetermined outcomes to understanding change from a complex systems perspective.

Development actors and the complex aid environment

For international development to move beyond the new and ambitious rhetoric of aid to a reality where the well-being of poor people is truly prioritized, there needs to be a far clearer understanding of the uncertainty, complexity and dynamics of the entire aid system.[3] International development practice is currently based on a linear outcome-oriented perspective, which focuses on individual institutions within the system to a degree that excludes attention to the relationships among actors. Thus, many development efforts fail to recognize the significance of cultural and political influences, and the potential of well-placed individual agency and leadership to effect systemic change.

This section argues that the way forward is to adopt a complex systems approach to understanding the aid system, and its outcomes.[4] This requires stepping back from the intricacies of individual projects or programmes and gaining an understanding of the relationships that link the various actors. It necessitates thinking beyond Newtonian modes of analysis (Uphoff, 1992). A central insight from complexity analysis is that the interplay between rules and agents lead to emergent outcomes that are not simply predictable from understanding the individual actors alone. We suggest that adopting a complex systems approach involves two elements. On the one hand, it is essential to understand the choices being made by individual actors and their position and power within the system. On the other hand, it is equally important to understand the wider context – the relationships and networks between actors in the system as a whole – recognizing that the system has its own emergent dynamism and internal logic.

The emergence of certain behaviours are the complex products of interdependent choices made by actors under dynamic conditions. Key actors include non-governmental organizations (NGOs), bilateral donors, international finance institutions, national governments, regional and local governments and 'poor people' who are the 'client group' of poverty reduction initiatives. Figure 1.1 highlights the extent to which actors in the aid system may be positioned differently. The choices being made and the behaviours displayed will shift at different times and in different contexts. For example, organizations may prioritize contrasting philosophical approaches and procedures at various moments in history. Building relationships with certain actors in the system may be emphasized at the expense of others, often in line with the perceived balance of power. Different significance may be given to different methodologies, values and accountability issues. Shifting organizational and resource pressures will also influence the choices being made. The diagram highlights the importance of recognizing the implications of where individuals and their organizations are situated on the spectrum; as well as of where various actors would assume other organizations to be located with regard to each dimension. The spectrum approach reveals the dangers of classifying organizations into one fixed category. It also points to the problem of programme operations that are based on predicted outcomes planned with only partial knowledge of the system and without constant review and reflection. Such generalizations hide the fluid and interdependent nature of organizations over time and space and the consequence of this is poor programming and policy design, based on inaccurate understandings of the behavioural dynamics of the system.

Figure 1.1 provides a simplified illustration of some of the choices that characterize the different aid actors.

We argue that if the new development agenda is to succeed, then new behavioural traits and capacities need to be prioritized. In the past, organizations have emphasized bureaucratic conformity, upward accountability and meeting financial disbursement targets. We suggest that these behaviours are inappropriate to the needs of the new environment, which requires greater emphasis on flexible, innovative procedures, multiple lines of accountability and the development of skills for relationship-building, such as language and cultural understanding. Internally, new organizational norms based on learning, growth and mutual respect would encourage teamwork and innovation. Leaders would need to provide a sense of clarity of the organization's mission and values and guide and inspire the team to meet their objectives while remaining reflexive.

Having explored the behavioural characteristics and choices taken by the development players, it is also essential to understand the interdependence and power dynamics of the different actors and how these in turn influence the choices being made. The schematic diagram in Figure 1.2 attempts to provide an example of such networks and power dynamics. Presenting power and relationships as an entire system reveals the extent to which development is complex and dynamic. Conventional flow charts generally present organizations as boxed entities, an oversimplification of the fact that organizations are at least as complex as the individuals that constitute them. A complex systems diagram illustrates the diversity of relationships as well as their fluidity and interdependence. It is also important to note that with each interaction, relationships evolve and all parties to the relationship are changed.

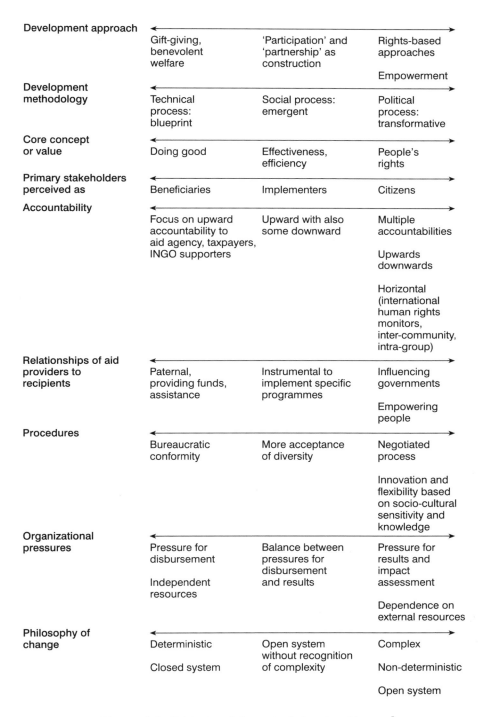

| Development approach | Gift-giving, benevolent welfare | 'Participation' and 'partnership' as construction | Rights-based approaches

Empowerment |
|---|---|---|---|
| Development methodology | Technical process: blueprint | Social process: emergent | Political process: transformative |
| Core concept or value | Doing good | Effectiveness, efficiency | People's rights |
| Primary stakeholders perceived as | Beneficiaries | Implementers | Citizens |
| Accountability | Focus on upward accountability to aid agency, taxpayers, INGO supporters | Upward with also some downward | Multiple accountabilities

Upwards downwards

Horizontal (international human rights monitors, inter-community, intra-group) |
| Relationships of aid providers to recipients | Paternal, providing funds, assistance | Instrumental to implement specific programmes | Influencing governments

Empowering people |
| Procedures | Bureaucratic conformity | More acceptance of diversity | Negotiated process

Innovation and flexibility based on socio-cultural sensitivity and knowledge |
| Organizational pressures | Pressure for disbursement

Independent resources | Balance between pressures for disbursement and results | Pressure for results and impact assessment

Dependence on external resources |
| Philosophy of change | Deterministic

Closed system | Open system without recognition of complexity | Complex

Non-deterministic

Open system |

Figure 1.1 *Critical and dynamic choices for aid actors*[5]

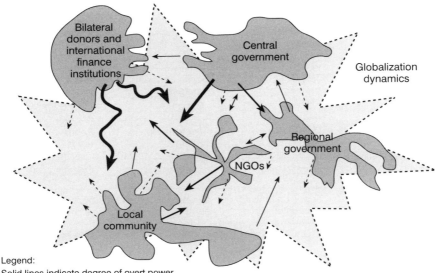

Legend:
Solid lines indicate degree of overt power
Broken lines indicate less visible forms of power
Shapes of bodies reflect the extent to which relations impinge on or influence each other's identity and capabilities
Source: developed by Beth Cross, University of Edinburgh[7]

Figure 1.2 *A complex systems illustration of power and relationships*[8]

The diagram takes us beyond common assumptions of power as simple, discreet and unidirectional. The arrows illustrate different degrees of power, which can be exerted through different means, can be two-way or one-way, and can be overt as well as covert. The backdrop to all of these relationships is the global political system, which plays a key role in determining the development agenda and its effectiveness in reducing poverty. In Figure 1.2, each organization is represented as an organic, fluid shape. Contours are determined by the relationships that actors have with other actors. The relationships are neither static nor predictable. Certain actors in particular organizations may have closer relationships with certain actors in other organizations (where the shapes move out towards each other), whereas others may not prioritize relationship-building with those outside their organization (where the shapes are introverted).

Building effective relationships is key to understanding and addressing power relations and developing mutual respect and communication, all essential to ensuring effective aid practice that is sustainable in the long term. It is important for organizations to provide incentives for staff to develop inter-organizational links, recognising how these impact on the professional choices being made. This is no easy task and great efforts are required to develop relationships of trust, even between 'like-minded' bilateral organizations who have many behavioural features in common.[6] It is clear that even greater attention will need to be given to ensure cooperation between organizations from different parts of the system. Through taking a complex systems view, the multiple relationships become apparent. Rather than being between two actors (either donor–NGO or donor–recipient government), as has traditionally been the focus, other significant actors are placed clearly in view – most significantly, the primary stakeholder.

In summary, this section has explored behavioural patterns to highlight the extent to which individual actors and organizations prioritize and adopt different behaviour types and choices. This reveals the complexity of a system, where generalizations are dangerous and where understanding difference is key. Building effective and ethical relationships is central to breaking down power imbalances, opening up communication channels and developing trust between actors. We suggest that these elements are fundamental to developing an aid system that recognizes complexity and which evolves accordingly into a system that will be more effective in reducing poverty.

Transforming procedures: a focus on cultural and political dynamics

Transformations in the procedures employed by donors have not kept pace with the rapid changes in development thinking. In Chapter 2, Caroline Robb reflects on Cornwall's (2000) work on the new language of aid and development, encompassing such terms as empowerment, ownership, partnership and participation. Organizational cultures from an era when the reductionist thinking dominated development have proven ill suited to the demands of dynamic people-centred development. This is despite increasing evidence that attention to local (citizen) analysis often reveals a more complex understanding of why a programme has succeeded or failed and can heighten progress towards reaching development goals. Yet, the persistence of old habits in the new development context has pernicious effects. Existing structures continue to reduce the effectiveness of interventions.

In Chapter 8, Charles Owusu provides an innovative example from ActionAid, which has sought to radically transform its planning and reporting procedures in an attempt to balance power relations, develop more effective relationships among stakeholders and promote downward accountability. The new system is known as ALPS or the Accountability, Learning and Planning System. Much less attention is given to the formats and needs of the donor; instead, energies are placed on learning and downward accountability to the poor and to ActionAid's partners. Owusu argues that procedural flexibility results in more honest reporting of successes and failures and, hence, a more accurate assessment of programme impact.[9] Unlike the traditional logical framework (logframe), discussed by several authors including Robert Chambers and Jethro Pettit (Chapter 11), Ruth Marsden (Chapter 7) and Katja Jassey (Chapter 10), use of local representations and reporting formats appears to encourage greater openness and understanding of socio-cultural dynamics and political constraints to success (see Gasper, 2000, for an analysis of the logical framework).

In Chapter 7, Marsden highlights how procedures often exclude those who don't have knowledge of how they are used. Yet, this is quite contrary to the intentions of donors who believe that the use of logframes improves the efficiency of planning and helps them to ensure that each stage of the programme has been logically thought through. This has been eloquently argued to be the case for their use by donors. Once a procedure is established within an organization, its use can be a time-saving device as familiarity with the procedure increases. However, even donor staff tend to require 'training' before they are confident about completing the logframe matrix with accuracy. It is essential to recognize that the development of such procedures stems from a particularly Western approach to planning, which is often incompatible with the distinct cultural and political environments in which they are employed. Furthermore, such procedures are often used in a top-down manner, used ritualistically as a necessity for funding to be granted. As Chambers and Pettit suggest in Chapter 11, such ritualization may lead to the loss of a valuable process of discussion and debate with primary stakeholders that should be part of good programme cycles. The most appropriate procedures are usually those that are developed jointly with the primary stakeholders.

Addressing power, politics and rights

In addition to adopting a complex systems approach and to developing more flexible procedures, it is important to address issues of power, politics and rights. Despite the current rhetoric of ownership, participation and partnership, the present system is based on entrenched patterns of dominance, hierarchy and control. The authors in Part Two of this volume reveal that these patterns of exclusivity are to be found throughout the aid system, both among and within the different groups of actors. Even the increase in the language of 'rights' hides the reality that much practice continues to revolve around entrenched beliefs in the welfare models.

In addition to aiding our understanding of relationships, a complex systems approach also enables us to gain a better understanding of power. The *Oxford English Dictionary* defines power as the:

- ability to do something or act in a particular way, especially as a faculty or quality;
- capacity or ability to direct or influence the behaviour of others or the course of events.

These definitions imply that all actors are potentially subject to external power and influence and therefore may not have the ability to act freely. Understanding where the power lies, and how it may be used, is thus essential to understanding the functioning of international development, a prerequisite to bringing about change.

Power is embedded in the system and in the terms and conditions of the relationships between the actors. In some cases, it is exerted overtly through the direct provision of financial resources linked to donor country political interests. For example, the Pergau Dam project in Malaysia was linked to an arms deal and was set to cost more than the UK had spent on all water and sanitation aid in five years; and economic aid packages were offered by the US to key countries during the preparations for war against Iraq in the spring of 2003. Many countries still tie aid to their domestic requirements, which means that funding decisions are often based on the needs of the donor rather than of the recipient country. There have been moves to redress this in some countries, such as the untying of aid in the UK, which happened in April 2001.

Power is also exerted covertly through actions taken outside of the aid system. Historical trends show how Western countries' domestic policies influence poor people's lives (see Chapter 2). For example, trade restrictions imposed by rich countries to imports from poor countries, especially on higher-value processed goods, such as clothing and chocolate, cost poor countries UK£64 billion a year, twice as much they receive in aid (World Development Movement, 2003). The dependence of many poor countries on rich nations means that they are in a weak position to contest unfair trade provisions. Adopting a systems approach to aid demands that aid is not separated from the wider issues of donors' domestic and foreign policies.

Often the impacts of political decisions overshadow those of development interventions. Donor countries invest significant resources in establishing international agreements with the aim of protecting their particular global interests. The power of veto is observed when the most powerful players refuse to participate. For example, the US government refused to ratify the Kyoto Protocol, aimed at controlling emissions of greenhouse gases into the atmosphere, although 190 other countries have ratified or acceded to the protocol. The US is the most significant polluter of greenhouse gases, with its 4.6 per cent of the world population accounting for 20 to 25 per cent of global emissions (Population Reference Bureau, 2002; Malhi et al, 2002), and its non-participation undermined international attempts to limit climate warming. Meanwhile, donors are providing a massive investment of energy and resources in flood-prone areas such as the delta regions of Bangladesh. Yet, it is likely that rising sea-water levels will ultimately drive millions of Bangladeshis from their homes, and many livelihoods will be lost. There is thus a need to counteract the increased trend toward unilateralism and undermining of United Nations (UN) credibility and clout, as was seen in the 2003 Iraq conflict.

It is important to note that less visible forms of power and resistance are also at work throughout the system. Hidden forms of power, embedded in ideology, discourse, religion and cultural norms, may also serve to exclude and discriminate against poor people (Lukes, 1974; Gaventa, 1980; see also Chapter 11). Such forms of power may be less manifest in actors, institutions and overt forms of decision-making, and more deeply rooted in social norms and conditioning. Understanding these dimensions of power and exclusion has important implications for developing effective strategies for addressing poverty, rights and inequality; and it is vital for encouraging and supporting alternative sources of power (VeneKlasen and Miller, 2002). Many useful frameworks and approaches have been tested for the analysis and balancing of power relations in the development context, and these could be more widely adapted by aid agencies concerned with pro-poor political change (VeneKlasen and Miller, 2002). The challenge of political participation is not only a question of who is sitting around the table, but of whether the table even exists, and whether the language and terms of debate are accessible to those whose voices need to be heard.

Power and influence flow through different forms of communication. These can be textual, oral or embodied and occur, for example, through the issuing of policy statements, application of procedures, provision of finance and face-to-face meetings. These may be used in the interests of poor people; for example, government actors can leak information to the press or citizens can engage in the informal economy. Relationships are formed through communication and become the enabling space through which communication does or does not occur.

While donors continue to hold access to finances, they also maintain significant control over the agenda. This dynamic can be traced back to colonial times and the concept of 'gift-giving'. Margaret Kakande's explanation of donor behaviour in Uganda (see Chapter 6) argues that this pattern continues and that it is through this practice that donors retain power and continue to dominate over gift recipients. Poor people rarely have a strong voice in determining policy directions. Thus, aid continues to be based around a series of fashions that can be argued to have as much to do with strong personalities and their political affiliations as with addressing the priorities of poor people (see Groves, 2001). Sector-wide approaches (SWAPs),[10] poverty reduction strategy papers (PRSPs) and direct budget support are aid modalities heralded as changing the balance of power in favour of governments and their citizens, stressing local ownership and local socio-cultural understanding.[11] New partnerships, forged in many countries around the PRSPs have, in places, resulted in better communication and cooperation among the international community, although few studies provide convincing evidence that the process has resulted in a stronger voice for the poor (see Chapter 4).[12] In many countries governments do not even have a seat at the donor PRSP table, giving weight to the claim that PRSP donor groups have shifted the power away from governments and further in favour of donors, as their voice increasingly represents the weight of a consortium rather than the objectives and budget of a single agency.

Despite the ideological arguments for increased government ownership, there is increasing evidence that direct budget support may not alter the balance of power in favour of the poor. This is of particular concern where a country lacks a track record of citizen participation, and has little evidence as to which programmes will truly improve the livelihoods of poor people. Direct budget support has been spearheaded primarily by economists, many of whom have significant power within their organizations to push through the approach, in some countries against the advice of the sociologists or anthropologists within the organization. In Chapter 5, Leslie Groves argues that the hasty implementation of this new policy may be seen to have neglected the needs and priorities of the poorest people.

In Part Three the authors examine ways to move forward in the context of the new agenda. In Chapter 12, Rosalind Eyben and Clare Ferguson argue that a rights perspective challenges the categorization of poor people as passive beneficiaries of aid. Until recently, donor governments have been primarily interested in human rights as an aspect of good governance, resulting in a narrow definition of rights related to civil and political liberties. However, rights-based approaches are generally understood to be broader than this because all rights – including economic, social and cultural rights – are considered indivisible, interrelated and interdependent. This approach reflects the complexity of the system and a holistic understanding of the nature of well-being (Eyben, 2003a). A rights perspective implies that poor people have entitlements to political voice, equal treatment and a basic level of services. The authors show how this places responsibilities on donors to manage and make explicit their different lines of accountability. They argue that there are five lines of accountability for bilateral aid agencies: taxpayers in the donor country; government in the donor country; government in the recipient country; poor people in the recipient country; and the international human rights framework. It is no longer a matter of those at the top of the hierarchy holding beneficiaries to account.

An inclusive system of aid would ensure that public funds are correctly spent and accounted for, and citizens would have the capacity and means to hold governments accountable for expenditure. Rights to participation are linked inextricably with rights to information, a position upheld in recent donor policy. Yet, it is recognized that these increases in transparency are unlikely to occur without broader social change (see Lipsky, 1997). In reality, this is rarely achieved, and those who are powerful keep the current dynamic in place. This is mirrored within organizations, as Owusu describes in Chapter 8, and junior staff can also reinforce patterns of control. The perceived expertise of those higher up in the hierarchy reinforces the view that senior staff must actually know better. Challenging the organizational culture is difficult and often junior staff fear repercussions. These fears are exacerbated when transparency is poor and access to information within the system is not freely available. Fear of losing favour is a particular issue in development where the job may demand repeated overseas placements and senior support can be critical in obtaining the posting of choice. Is there any scope for the individual to have agency in such complex organizational environments?

From organizations to individuals

The new policy environment demands that donors change roles from managing development programmes to becoming responsible and self-aware co-players in broader political processes. Yet, resources continue to be invested in organizational change with a focus on intra-organizational improvement. The drivers for change have tended to be internal efficiency and improved performance, with the focus on outputs rather than processes. This could go some way to explain the relative neglect of inter-organizational issues, despite the recognition of the importance of partnerships and a realization that the new environment implies changes in relationships and power structures that challenge well-established patterns of individual behaviour.[13] Many organizations are currently restructuring in an attempt to improve practice through internal change (for example, the Department for International Development, ActionAid and the Save the Children Alliance). Yet, an understanding of the inter-organizational relations remains limited. For instance, Scholte's (2002) recent study concluded that very little independent research exists on the relations between civil society organizations and the International Monetary Fund (IMF), just one of the key sets of relationships in the development system.

The changing policy environment has also altered patterns of interaction with primary stakeholders. As Eyben and Ferguson highlight in Chapter 12, donors are placing emphasis on government partnerships; yet, they struggle to establish new ways of relating to recipient partners. They face contradictions and tensions between their expressed desire to increase local ownership and 'hand over the stick', and the inherently political nature of the relationships, conditionality and policy influence. Simultaneously, opportunities for donor–citizen communication have drastically dropped as project resources have been subsumed within new aid modalities. Some donor offices have instigated rules that limit staff travel beyond the capital in the hope that this will provide more time for attention to wider policy debates. There is also evidence that the shift of resources has negatively affected civil society's ability to be an active player in the new environment.[14] Rather than the new era bringing more opportunities for citizen–government relationships to develop, there is now less support for poor people to build partnerships with the national and international community.

We suggest that one way to overcome the dilemmas presented above is to encourage individual reflection and change. To date, development initiatives have focused on intra-organizational change. This has involved changing organizational policies and procedural tools on a regular basis.[15] We argue that these types of change alone will not lead to the transformations required by the poverty reduction agenda. What is needed is a profound shift in the personal practices of individual development actors. Reflexivity can help in the complex world where learning is a critical component of taking on the current aid agenda with all the ambiguity, paradox and unanticipated outcomes that are encountered (Eyben, 2003b). This shift needs to be facilitated by organizations. Individuals must be encouraged by their organizations to act flexibly and creatively in ways that promote relationship-building and the breaking down of power imbalances.

Everjoice Win (Chapter 9), Ruth Marsden (Chapter 7) and Katja Jassey (Chapter 10) give three insightful accounts of interpersonal dynamics and individual quest for change. Win reflects on patterns of dominance of her counterpart who, over the years, has continued to gain power and influence, and no longer appears to respect the cultural context in which she is working. This is juxtaposed with the example from the representative of the Swedish International Development Agency (Sida) who struggles to ensure that its programmes are underpinned by cultural understanding, but whose intentions are regularly misinterpreted. Marsden provides an example from Nepal of how one donor worker relinquished her traditional role of domination, attempting to speak the local language, and hence enable Nepali villagers to state their own priorities. Despite such positive examples, however, patterns of dominance are difficult to shift and the majority of people with power are often resistant to losing it.

Individuals' desire to adopt new ways of working is difficult to assess; but there is a great deal of literature to suggest that people do not change their attitudes and behaviour quickly (see Hewstone et al, 1992). Organizations have an important role in providing incentives for change. Individuals only change if they believe that it is in their best interests and consider the idea to be important. For this reason Wheatley (1994, p148) argues that:

> *Both individual and organizational change start from the same place. People need to explore an issue sufficiently to* decide whether new meaning is available and desirable. *They will change only if they believe that a new insight, a new idea or a new form helps them become more of who they are [emphasis added]*.

People are often reluctant to examine their own attitudes and behaviours with regard to other cultures and their own organizational culture, preferring instead to remain in familiar social environments. Such risk averseness is widespread at all levels. For example, many development staff tend to socialize and work with those whom they know and can identify with, to the exclusion of those with different socio-cultural backgrounds or language. In Chapter 4, Eyben reveals that social structures in Bolivia enabled international development cooperation professionals to be rapidly included in the elite of Bolivian society, easily developing relationships through social events. While this forged the bonds for strong and supportive relationships in the working environment, contacts primarily with one sector of the community may provide a partial and particular perspective on the country. The confidence generated by 'inside' knowledge of local perspectives can also mask concerns of the wider heterogeneity of primary stakeholders.

Listening to the diversity of views is only part of the problem. There are also language barriers to building partnerships, including both verbal and non-verbal communication. When powerful donor groups operate in a dominant Western language, they exacerbate the sense that governments feel of not being in the 'driving seat'. In addition, donors share a more familiar non-verbal communication style, which can create a communication gulf and a dichotomy between 'us' and 'them'. Despite recognizing the problem, the commitment of donor organizations to supporting language learning among their staff still remains weak and, at an individual level, there may be resistance to invest in learning local cultural skills when work placements are relatively short term. Building socio-political awareness and verbal and non-verbal communication skills[16] would inevitably require a shift for most donor agencies as they reflect upon the nature of incentives and staff career profiles. It would also lead to more serious assessment of the potential resource and expertise that local staff bring, such as new networks of relationships (although these are often with an elite) and the ability to share cultural understanding and local knowledge of programme risks and assumptions. There are increasingly diverse staffing patterns in many development agencies. (The greatest socio-cultural diversity is typically found among the junior staff.)[17] Such change is essential to breaking the cycle of patronage.

In Chapter 13, Katherine Pasteur and Patta Scott-Villiers illustrate the positive consequences of organizations taking individual change and learning seriously.[18] They reveal how organizational learning can be improved through encouraging staff to take time to reflect on their experiences, as well as their values and behaviour, in order to reframe the problem and gain relevant insights, leading to improved future action and performance. Their chapter highlights how, as individuals, development practitioners have agency to address political issues both within and beyond the organizations where they operate. In assuming that political decisions are beyond their control, individuals also abdicate their responsibility to use their voice in the same way that they are increasingly demanding citizens in the South to use their voices to hold their governments to account. Global political action is now widely debated (Edwards and Gaventa, 2001). Jubilee 2000 is cited as an example of global action that pressurized creditor governments into change, in this case writing off developing world debt by focusing unprecedented scrutiny on official macro-economic policies (Collins et al, 2001). Through community organizations, social movements, campaigns and advocacy, citizens have influenced decisions that affect their lives (Gaventa, 2001). The increasingly intertwined global and local levels require that development practitioners understand the complexity and potential of these interrelationships. The authors argue that practitioners currently underestimate their potential to act as catalysts for change and that they have a responsibility to develop this potential.

A complex systems view of international development highlights the importance of individual agency. Individuals can change the functioning of a system by working at the local level to direct the flow of the wider system. Small and well-placed shifts can eventually lead to a radical restructuring of the system as a whole. Complex systems thinkers use the example of the fall of the Berlin Wall. The apparently sudden collapse of the wall was the result of many people and events chipping away at different parts of the system until, eventually, it came down and a completely different system resulted. To understand the whole, it is therefore important to step back, to understand the relationships that link the various actors and to view the system as a coherent whole with its own dynamism that can be influenced by individual actors.

Working with complexity

The experiences of the authors show that development practitioners are working in a complex and ever-changing environment. The new millennium has brought with it significant energy around embracing the new rhetoric and values of international development. Yet, this energy needs to be channelled more effectively if the Millennium Development Goals are to be attained. If the new rhetoric is to be translated into practice, then fundamental changes are needed in the conceptualization of aid as an inclusive system, in the organizational norms and procedures adopted, and in personal behaviour and attitudes.

The power that individuals have to influence is greater than they might suppose. It is important to be aware of the political climate, where small actions can have big effects. Minimal rules appear to allow complex and diverse behaviour to flourish (see Bunch, 2001, on the experience of the Women's Human Rights coalition). In contrast, excessive control freezes systems into patterns that are unsuited to local conditions and prevents the dynamic behaviour that enhances ownership (see Chapter 11). The moves towards new technologies are also providing new connectedness across entities within the system. With this greater communication comes the ability to make a difference even at a distance (see Derbyshire, 2003). Alliances and networks are now much more accessible to many lower in the hierarchies.

Working with a new paradigm of complexity requires a shift in thinking, and with it a corresponding shift in the focus for action. Changing the system will require a substantial political commitment and time and money. However, aid budgets have seen a significant fall in recent years (World Bank, 2001). Radically overhauling a system that has been in place for over half a century is expensive, particularly as the necessary tools and approaches for working in such a system have yet to be comprehensively developed, although some participatory methods point in the right direction. Risks and assumptions will need to take a more prominent place in assessments, planning and monitoring of progress. There is a danger, however, that attention to new approaches is falling off the policy-makers' agenda.

Development takes time; but if one accepts the significance of political influences and the need for investing in relationship-building, it is more likely that development goals are achieved in a realistic time frame. Understanding power and relations will allow practitioners to move towards a more inclusive and, consequently, more effective system of aid.

Notes

1   Although we have used the term 'donor' in its broadest sense, there is an important distinction to be made between donors and lenders since loans often put countries deeply into debt (see Chambers, 2001).
2   See McGee with Norton's (2000) review of policy formulation at the macro level.
3   See Rondinelli (1983, p2) for a discussion of planning methods 'of limited use in coping with the uncertainty and complexity of development problems'.
4   See Waldrop (1993) for a discussion of the complex systems approach compared to systems thinking discussed, for example, by Checkland (1981).
5   There is great diversity within organizations and any understanding of the nature of their behaviours and relationships requires investigation beyond the emerging patterns revealed in this diagram.
6   One significant indicator of this occurring is the move to arrangements such as silent partnerships (where countries channel resources through another bilateral donor).

7   Beth Cross is an educationalist specializing in the relevance of complexity to organizational change.

8   This two-dimensional diagram cannot depict the full complexity and fluidity of the system. To claim one 'comprehensive' version would contradict the call for a move away from a linear rationalist approach to understanding the system as a complex and dynamic web of power and relationships.

9   Civil society can offer a space for such critical thought and action (see Howell and Pearce, 2001).

10 SWAPs are the mechanism whereby donors provide sectoral funding to a common basket fund.

11 See Norton and Elson (2002) for a discussion of politics and accountability in the budget process.

12 See Nelson (2002) for a discussion of the World Bank's relationship with civil society organizations in the PRSP process and Scholte (2002), concerning civil society and the International Monetary Fund.

13 Fowler (2000) provides a comprehensive discussion of how the move towards partnerships has become a central objective of development.

14 Local community-based organizations complain of a drain of resources, previously provided by INGOs, that enabled citizen representatives to travel and participate in decision-making forums.

15 See Senge (1999) on the challenge to sustain the momentum in learning organizations.

16 Only recently have the skills and local knowledge of staff appointed in-country been fully recognized as important to giving appropriate political advice.

17 There is a pattern of reduced mobility as staff take on increased financial responsibilities, such as mortgage commitments, and geographical consideration is given to partners' or children's needs.

18 Macdonald et al (1997) note the significance of making changes in the heart of an organization as an important prerequisite for changing its gendered outcomes.

References

Bunch, C (2001) 'International Networking for Women's Human Rights', in Edwards, M and Gaventa, J (eds) *Global Citizen Action*, Earthscan, London

Chambers, R (1994) 'Participatory Rural Appraisal (PRA): Analysis of Experience', *World Development*, vol 22, pp1–16

Chambers, R (2001) 'The World Development Report: Concepts, Content and a Chapter 12', *Journal of International Development*, vol 13, pp299–306

Checkland (1981) *Systems Thinking, Systems Practice*, John Wiley and Sons, Avon

Collins, C J L, Gariyo, Z and Burdon, T (2001) 'Jubilee 2000: Citizen Action Across the North–South Divide', in Edwards, M and Gaventa, J (eds) *Global Citizen Action*, Earthscan, London

Cornwall, A (2000) 'Beneficiary, Consumer, Citizen: Perspectives on Participation for Poverty Reduction, *Sida Studies Series*, no 2, Sida, Stockholm, Sweden

Derbyshire, H (2003) *Gender Issues in the Use of Computers in Education in Africa*, DFID, London

Edwards, M and Gaventa J (eds) (2001) *Global Citizen Action*, Earthscan, London, UK

Eyben, R (2003a) 'The Rise of Rights: Rights-based Approaches to International Development', *IDS Policy Briefing*, May

Eyben, R (2003b) 'Donors as Political Actors: Fighting the Thirty Years War in Bolivia', *IDS Working Paper*, no 183, IDS, Brighton

Fowler, A (2000) 'Introduction Beyond Partnership: Getting Real about NGO Relationships in the Aid System', *IDS Bulletin*, no 31, pp1–13

Gasper, D (2000) 'Evaluating the "Logical Framework Approach": Towards Learning-oriented Development Evaluation', *Public Administration and Development*, vol 20, pp17–28

Gaventa, J (1980) *Power and Powerlessness*, University of Illinois Press, Urbana, IL, US

Gaventa, J (2001) 'Global Citizen Action: Lessons and Challenges', in Edwards, M and Gaventa, J (eds) *Global Citizen Action*, Earthscan, London

Groves, L (2001) 'A Vertical Slice: Child Labour and the International Labour Organization. A Critical Analysis of the Transformation of Vision into Policy and Practice', unpublished PhD thesis, University of Edinburgh, Edinburgh

Hewstone, M, Hopkins, N and Routh, D A (1992) 'Cognitive Models of Stereotype Change (1): Generalization and Subtyping in Young People's Views of the Police', *Journal of Experimental Social Psychology*, vol 22, pp219–234

Howell, J and Pearce, J (2001) *Civil Society and Development: A Critical Exploration*, Lynne Rienner Publishers, London

Korten, F F, Robert, J and Siy, Y (1989) *Transforming A Bureaucracy: The Experience of The Philippine National Irrigation Administration*, Kumarian Press, Connecticut

Lipsky, M (1997) 'Street-level Bureaucracy: An Introduction', in Hill, M (ed) *The Policy Process: A Reader*, Prentice Hall, London

Lukes, S (1974) *Power: A Radical View*, Macmillan, London

Macdonald, M, Sprenger, E and Dubel, I (1997) *Gender and Organizational Change: Bridging the Gap Between Policy and Practice*, KIT Press, Amsterdam

Malhi, Y, Mier, P and Brown, S (2002) 'Forests, Carbon and Global Climate', *Philosophical Transactions of the Royal Society*, vol 360, pp1567–1591

McGee, R with Norton, A (2000) *Participation in Poverty Reduction Strategies: A Synthesis of Experience with Participatory Approaches to Policy Design, Implementation and Monitoring*, IDS, Brighton

Nelson, P J (2002) *Access and Influence: Tensions and Ambiguities in the World Bank's Expanding Relationship with Civil Society Organizations*, Graduate School of Public and International Affairs, University of Pittsburgh, Pittsburgh/The North–South Institute, Ottawa, Canada

Norton, A with Bird, B, Brock, K, Kakande, M and Turk, C (2001) *A Rough Guide to Participatory Poverty Assessments, an Introduction to Theory and Practice*, Overseas Development Institute, London

Norton, A and Elson, D (2002) *What's Behind the Budget? Politics, Rights and Accountability in the Budget Process*, Overseas Development Institute, London

Population Reference Bureau (2002) *2002 World Population Data Sheet*, Population Reference Bureau, Washington, DC

Rondinelli, D (1983) *Development Projects as Policy Experiments: An Adaptive Approach to Development Administration*, Methuen, London

Scholte, J A (2002) *Civil Society and the International Monetary Fund*, Centre for the Study of Globalization and Regionalization, University of Warwick, Warwick/The North–South Institute, Ottawa, Canada

Senge, P (1999) *A Fifth Discipline – 'The Dance of Changes: The Challenges of Sustaining Momentum in Learning Organizations'*, Nicholas Brealey, London

Uphoff, N (1992) *Learning from Gal Oya: Possibilities for Participatory Development and Post-Newtonian Social Science*, Cornell University Press, Ithaca, New York

VeneKlasen, L with Miller, V (2002) *A New Weave of People, Power and Politics: The Action Guide for Advocacy and Citizen Participation*, World Neighbors, Oklahoma City

Waldrop, M (1993) *Complexity: The Emerging Science at the Edge of Order and Chaos*, Simon and Schuster, New York

Wheatley, M (1994) *Leadership and the New Science: Discovering Order in a Chaotic World*, Berrett Koehler, San Francisco

World Bank (2001) *World Development Report 2000–2001: Attacking Poverty*, World Bank and Oxford University Press, Oxford

World Development Movement (2003) *Whose Rules Rule?* Oxford University Press, Oxford

2

Changing Power Relations in the History of Aid[1]

Caroline Robb

Introduction

Aid, by its very definition, is a manifestation of inequality. Could aid then be improved by recognizing its various forms of inequality, including the unequal distribution of power? Being poor usually means being powerless; but the aid system is dominated by the interests of the powerful, as opposed to the powerless. Aid has historically been influenced by political processes, the world economic environment, commercial and political interests, as well as the success or failure of poverty reduction initiatives. But change within this system has not been linear and although trends can be identified, development agencies have reacted with a diversity of approaches and behaviours. What has emerged is a complex system of aid based on competing demands, operating within a wider, unpredictable global system. This 'big picture' matters in the politics of aid allocation and in the construction of the aid system.

Over the past few decades, the world has been restructured. These changes have influenced national identities, challenging people and the very foundations of their social structures, as well as influencing the structures of the aid system. In response to this changing world, with its shifting power relations, new aid procedures and patterns of aid agency behaviour have emerged. Today we live in a world of dramatic and accelerating change due to globalization, where more accessible communications and technology have rapidly transformed poor people's aspirations and awareness. Now, more than ever before, poor people are entering into an interconnected world, resulting in shifting village structures, customs and beliefs.

Shifts in power may occur at different levels, such as at the organizational level or at the personal level (see Chapter 13), where such shifts may gradually accumulate (see Chapter 14), to bring about significant and widespread change.

This chapter focuses on the macro level, the 'bigger picture', exploring how the aid system has been constructed through a gradual process of change influenced by historical events or accidents, as well as political processes. The following section describes the general trends in aid policy and practice during different eras: 1946 to the end of the 1960s; the 1970s, 1980s and 1990s; and the period from the late 1990s onwards. This timeline is summarized in the Appendix at the end of this volume.

1946 to the end of the 1960s: aid as technical rather than social intervention; colonialism and the rise of the nation state

During this period, patterns of aid were affected primarily by recent memories of World War II and the success of post-war reconstruction in Europe; struggles for independence; the rise of the nation state, with colonial governments handing over formal power; dominance of the theory of modernization; and the paramount influence of the Cold War and the associated divided worldviews between communism and capitalism. In many countries, power shifted dramatically with conflicts from decolonization, negotiations, transitions and constitutional arrangements. At this early stage, conditionalities of aid were minimal, due mainly to post-colonial guilt, aid agency goodwill and the power of leaders of newly independent countries. However, although early development interventions provided financial aid and technical assistance with limited conditions,[2] it was dominated by the assumed superiority of outside knowledge (Chambers, 1983). With the gradual onset of the Cold War, some bilaterals' aid began to focus on countries of strategic interest (for example, US aid to the Philippines, Thailand and South Korea).[3]

In many Southern countries, the shift from colonialism to the status of nation state led to a rise in nationalism and, as a consequence, a change in the relationship between the South and the North. By the early 1960s, governments in the South began to question the deterioration in their international terms of trade.[4] The Non-Aligned Movement and the Group of 77 (G77) were established to create a collective voice for Southern governments. As the largest developing world coalition in the United Nations (UN), the G77 continues to provide the means for Southern governments to articulate and promote their collective economic interests and enhance their joint negotiating capacity on all major international economic issues in the UN system, and to promote economic and technical cooperation among developing countries. In 1964, the United Nations Conference on Trade and Development (UNCTAD)[5] was created and became the counterweight to the Organisation for Economic Co-operation and Development (OECD).[6] Through these forums, Southern governments argued for fairer terms of trade and more liberal terms for financing development. However, the response from Northern governments was limited and they stressed that discussions on economic changes should be confined to the Bretton Woods Institutions,[7] where Northern governments held the balance of power. As a consequence, Southern governments continued to receive unfair terms of trade.

Modernization theory dominated development thinking and aid agency actions. 'Underdevelopment' was seen as an original state of backwardness, and it was argued that economic growth and investment in modern industrialized economies would transform agriculturally based societies (see Lewis, 1954, and Rostow, 1960). Economic growth was viewed as key for poverty reduction because benefits of growth would 'trickle down' to the poor. Some Southern governments, including India, however, did not focus on growth but instead focused on redistribution of income and wealth (through high marginal taxes, nationalization of banks to provide cheap credit to the masses, etc). During the late 1960s, there was dissatisfaction with distributional consequences, both within and between countries. Dependency theorists argued that the problems of developing countries were caused by European imperialism and capitalism. Many countries in Latin America, Asia and elsewhere tried to reduce dependency by protecting their industries and introducing high tariff barriers.

Throughout this period, some aid agencies used foreign aid to open up markets for domestic companies. Projects were the main vehicle for foreign aid and tended to be top-down in nature and dominated by outsiders' statistical and economic analyses, with limited consideration of the countries' context. Technology was transferred from the North and fed into large infrastructure projects. In many countries, national plans were drafted by aid agency-funded technical assistance, with the objective of promoting economic growth. Such plans were seen as a symbol of sovereignty and modernity, as well as a means of accelerating the process of economic development and preparing a sound economic basis from which the colonial territories could launch out as independent nations (Conyers and Hills, 1984). But many plans were not effectively implemented due to governments' poor administrative systems and weak capacity.

Towards the end of this period, there were two significant shifts in aid agency behaviour: first, they started lending to poorer countries; and, second, aid in general became more concessional. For example, the World Bank, established in 1944, originally lent through the International Bank for Reconstruction and Development (IBRD) at market-based interest rates. As a result, many of the poorest countries were excluded. However, in 1960, the World Bank established a concessional lending window through the International Development Association (IDA). IDA's objective was to provide long-term loans at a nominal interest to the poorest of the developing countries.

In sum, during this era, the institutional foundations and relations were laid for an aid system that focused more on Northern governments' foreign policies than reducing poverty. The Cold War produced overt and covert agendas that created an aid system that was primarily concerned with Northern governments' agendas and their national politics. In spite of the demise of colonialism and the rise of the nation state, Southern governments had limited power to control aid allocations. The ground was now set for the gradual emergence of a deep legacy of patronage and perverse self-serving aid agency practices that generated recipient government dependency.

1970s: oil crisis and focus on poverty

What emerged from the mid 1970s onwards was a proliferation of democratically elected governments around the world.[8] In the 1970s, the two main oil crises of 1973 and 1978 had a significant impact on aid, and also during the 1980s, when a new type of lending was introduced – structural adjustment (see the following section on the 1980s). As the Organization of the Petroleum Exporting Countries (OPEC) increased the price of crude oil, there was a rapid accumulation of monetary reserves in OPEC countries. Industrial countries then experienced strong inflationary pressures that were addressed by an increase in interest rates and reduction of imports. This resulted in a balance of payments deficit for many developing countries where they were paying more for oil, higher interest rates on loans from industrial countries, and finding reduced markets for their exports. High inflation from the oil crisis may have affected the poor more than the politics of aid during this decade. Many of the developing countries turned to the International Monetary Fund (IMF), the World Bank and commercial banks, where a flood of OPEC 'petrol dollars'[9] led to widespread commercial lending.[10] In response to the oil crisis, the oil-producing countries in the Middle East became significant donors of development aid. For example, in 1974, the International Fund for Agricultural Development (IFAD) was established with the support of money from OPEC countries. It was one of the first development institutions to recognize the importance of small-scale agriculture.

At the beginning of the 1970s, the possibility of promoting a stable monetary system of fixed exchange rates with the US dollar as the only international currency was collapsing under the strain of US trade and budgetary deficits. In response to this and the oil crisis, the IMF established the Oil Facility in 1974 to aid members in balance of payment difficulties by alleviating the cost of borrowing. In 1976, the IMF sold some of its gold and set up its trust fund, with low interest and limited conditionality (see Boughton, 2001a). At this early stage, bilaterals became concerned about debt relief. This was reflected in discussions at UNCTAD where bilaterals argued that giving low-interest loans to poorer countries was no longer appropriate because debt repayment was too onerous. A primary recommendation was that bilaterals should move towards grants, and this increasingly happened. For example, in 1978 the UK government introduced Retrospective Terms Adjustment (RTA), whereby over a space of years many countries that were by then receiving official aid grants from the UK had the terms of all past concessional loans amended so that the benefits of outstanding payments or repayments were retained by the country.[11]

Although the increased price of oil negatively affected many Southern governments, some G77 countries felt encouraged by a boom in the price of various developing world primary commodities (particularly oil). With increased confidence, at the UN General Assembly in 1974, Southern governments, supported by some Northern governments, demanded a New International Economic Order (NIEO). 'Trade and not Aid' became a key slogan for many developing countries. The inequality of the international economic system was criticized by the NIEO, and the West was exposed as 'exploitative'. The resolutions were influential in shaping the perceptions, judgements and approaches of developing countries and their administrative, political and commercial culture towards foreign investment. At a national level, some developing countries implemented large unsustainable projects – for example, in employment generation, subsidized credit, and free education, health and social services – without consideration of the impact on poverty or growth.

Consequent to the uncoordinated response to the oil crisis, Northern governments established the Group of Seven (G7) in 1975 at Rambouillet (France). The objective of the G7 was to increase coordination in future by having representatives of the major industrial powers meet every year to discuss the principal political and economic issues and their consequences to the international community.

Within the donor community there was a gradual realization that growth alone was not adequate to reduce poverty. This was clearly reflected in the widely influential publication *Redistribution with Growth* (Chenery et al, 1974). Chenery argued that poverty reduction should be promoted by ensuring that some of the benefits of economic growth were redistributed to the poor through taxation and public expenditure. However, government fiscal capacity for raising revenues was (and still is) low, and in many countries revenue raising is politically constrained. The balance between policies for growth and redistribution are still hotly discussed today.

During the mid to late 1970s, the basic needs approach was advocated by the United Nations Children's Fund (UNICEF) (Streeten et al, 1981). The impact on the aid system was significant, as can be seen by the switch in emphasis from economic growth to the provision of certain minimum requirements needed for an adequate lifestyle (such as food, water, shelter, housing, health and education). Some aid agencies began to support the delivery of services in rural areas with less emphasis on economic growth and industrialization that had promoted an 'urban bias' in development lending (Lipton, 1977). In Nairobi in 1973, the World Bank President Robert McNamara supported the 'basic needs' approach and declared that poverty reduction was the overarching objective of the bank. This was a significant step in shifting the aid system towards poverty reduction and was received enthusiastically by development organizations and non-governmental organizations (NGOs). The huge increase in World Bank lending to rural areas led to the rapid spread of integrated rural development projects (IRDPs). However, many of these projects were to fail due to being supply driven, difficult to manage and implemented through weak government capacity. There was also a lack of understanding of the complexities of rural development and a focus on inappropriate infrastructure.

Projects were still the main vehicle for aid agency influence. National governments continued to have limited influence within the aid system, and projects remained top-down, with limited government dialogue on project planning. They were often designed without attention to the underlying risks and assumptions and often had unclear objectives. A key procedure used by many aid agencies (for example, the World Bank and the UK Overseas

Development Administration[12] during the 1970s) was the project cycle, which viewed projects as developing through a series of defined stages, from needs assessment through to monitoring and evaluation. The manner in which project cycle management was often used resulted in a tendency to view projects as economic or technical interventions, rather than social processes.[13]

The failure of projects to reach the poorest and the lack of understanding of rural life among development professionals led to a new approach called rapid rural appraisal (RRA) (Chambers, 1993). This approach was both a philosophy and a methodology for incorporating the voices of the poor by directly consulting farmers. Not only did rapid rural appraisals provide new data, they were quicker and less costly than traditional household questionnaires. However, many organizations continued to rely on quantified household survey data that was perceived as being more 'scientific' and, thus, more credible. During this time, the World Bank employed its first ever sociologist in an attempt to introduce social analysis for better project design. Also, during the 1970s, the feminist movement began to influence aid policies. In 1975, a UN Conference on Women was convened in Mexico City, and gradually women's organizations began to cooperate more on a global level.

In conclusion, the aid system during this era saw a shift in power towards the Middle East due to the political significance of oil. Oil-producing countries became donors of considerable development aid. However, in spite of Southern governments' efforts to demand greater equality within the international economic system, Northern governments remained in control. In some cases, aid agency practices actively disempowered Southern governments. These included the dominance of the project cycle as a technical intervention, failure to listen to rural farmers and to understand rural life, supply-driven interventions, and a lack of Southern government ownership of projects.

1980s: from project to policy lending, the 'lost decade' and the emergence of debt crisis

During the 1980s, the aid system was significantly affected by the emergence of the debt crisis and recognition that structural adjustment entailed some negative impacts. The period was marked by a shift in delivery mechanisms for aid: from the project lending approach of the past to policy lending by way of a major new aid agency instrument, structural adjustment loans (SALs). Structural adjustment loans were given to governments on condition that certain reforms would be implemented. Dasekin and Powell (1999) argue that the low-income countries' debt crisis had its origins in official creditors' willingness to take risks that were unacceptable to private lenders; adverse terms-of-trade shocks; a lack of sustained macro-economic adjustment and structural reform; weak debt management practices; and political factors such as wars and social strife. The early debt crisis was recognized initially only in Latin American countries where American commercial banks were threatened. It was only later during the 1980s that the debt crisis in Africa was acknowledged. This decade also saw the emergence of the 'Washington Consensus',[14] which indicated a dramatic transformation from the last decade when many Southern governments were driven more by ideologies associated with dependency theory and neo-nationalism.

As the crisis evolved, there were calls for comprehensive adjustment measures by debtors, increased and more effective structural lending by multilateral development banks, and expanded lending by commercial banks. In 1985, US Treasury Secretary James Baker put forward the Baker Plan. Through this plan, commercial banks were encouraged to continue giving new loans to larger debtor countries to enable them to repay their debts while taking in new investments. Structural adjustment was included in the Baker Plan, where the World Bank and other institutions were encouraged to increase funding by 50 per cent. However, the Baker Plan had only limited success because it merely delayed payment of the debt, rather than reducing it.

In 1988 at the G7 summit in Toronto, major Western creditors agreed with pressure from proposals submitted by the UK and the IMF to implement a new treatment on bilateral debt for the poorest countries, called the Toronto Terms. A reduction of part of the debt of some poor countries was implemented for the first time.[15] The debt crisis caused the IMF to devise programmes for adjustment over longer periods as it was recognized that the problem was beyond the balance of payments: deep structural problems existed that inhibited growth and diversification.[16] As a result, in 1985 the IMF set up the Structural Adjustment Facility (SAF) to replace its trust fund (which only had limited resources and, therefore, limited adjustment was achieved). In 1987 the Enhanced Structural Adjustment Facility (ESAF) was established to provide even more concessional lending to low-income countries.

During the 1980s, policy reforms attached to SALs included monetary restraint, reduction of barriers to trade, liberalization of exchange rates, reduction of budget deficits and downsizing of the public sector. It is striking that these policies were so different from those supported by the aid agencies during the 1970s, where state intervention was encouraged, often leading to huge state expansion and inefficient and bloated bureaucracies. During the 1980s, aid agencies promoted policies that dramatically reduced the role of the state – the public sector was downsized, markets were freed and privatization was encouraged. Many primary health and education budgets were cut. A substantial debate developed around the consequences of SALs (see end of this section).

Boughton calls this significant shift in the role of the state a 'silent revolution' where Southern governments 'were trying to reformulate their economic policies in a way that was market friendly, brought them into the world economy, moved away from a strong development role for the state, and enabled private sectors to develop' (Boughton 2001b, p331). Many Southern governments were concerned that such policy changes were driven solely by ideological concerns of the North that promoted privatization and a reduced role for the state (as witnessed during the Reagan–Thatcher era). Although many Southern governments agreed that making the state more efficient was a priority, they argued that the state needed to remain involved, to some extent, as private sector regulation may not be effective.

Concern about the short-term negative consequences of adjustment lending becoming long term began to emerge on the development agenda (see Killick, 1999). In this regard, in 1987 UNICEF published *Adjustment with a Human Face* (Cornia et al, 1987), and the donors established the Social Dimensions of Adjustment (SDA) programme (1987–1992), where the social impacts of adjustment policies were clearly highlighted.[17] Due to the negative impacts of SALs, many aid agencies increased support to service-delivery NGOs, particularly in health and education. The political implications of the IMF-supported adjustment programmes, based principally on macro-economic measures, became more apparent during the 1980s, with violent protests erupting in some countries such as Egypt (1977), Morocco (1981), the Dominican Republic (1984) and Zambia (1986) (Boughton, 2001a). In response, some IMF-supported programmes included safety nets in addition to policies that had beneficial distributional effects. Boughton (2001a) argues that from 1975 through to the late 1980s, the IMF's focus on poverty alleviation evolved in response to internal debates, political pressure and – in some cases – riots. As the IMF started to focus more on low-income countries, its global importance increased substantially. Whereas before the IMF's main focus was on Western countries, it now became an institution with a global reach.

The continuing focus of projects on economic variables and technical issues meant that projects maintained their detachment from local reality. Yet, there was growing awareness among aid agencies of the importance of understanding other cultures and ensuring that projects and policies were culturally appropriate. This led to the publication of *Putting People First* (Cernea, 1985) that promoted a reversal in conventional project-making by stressing that development was about people, social organizations and their knowledge and institutions. Cernea also highlighted the importance of projects being designed with social goals, participation and diverse social contexts. In response to some aid interventions having a negative impact on poor people, the World Bank adopted a resettlement policy in 1980. Many governments have subsequently adopted domestic policies on resettlement. At the World Bank, this approach required the promotion of the use of sociological and anthropological knowledge (Cernea, 1996). However, the focus was still very much on project inputs and output rather than shifts in people's well-being due to the focus on increasing lending amounts as opposed to tracking impacts on poor people.

During the 1980s, RRA gained acceptance in some areas where it was recognized that it had its own principles and rigour. However, the focus on the speed of data collection led to concerns that poor people were not being included in the process (Chambers, 1997). An extractive way of working did not sit comfortably with the new debates on 'levels of participation'. Participatory RRAs were soon developed, which later became participatory rural appraisals (PRAs). PRA spread rapidly, mainly through South–South exchanges of field experiences. Furthermore, many authors began to discuss the dimensions of poverty beyond income and consumption, such as weakness, isolation, gender, vulnerability and powerlessness (see Chambers, 1983). In 1989 the United

Nations Development Programme (UNDP) introduced the *Human Development Report* that challenged the World Bank's narrow income-based definition of poverty. Due to the oil crisis of the 1970s, environmental issues began to emerge as a key development issue.

Commercial and political interests, as distinct from poverty reduction, still played a major role in defining aid agency policies (see also Chapter 5). For example, in Malaysia the Pergau Dam affair highlighted the connections between the UK government's aid programme and arms sales. UK£234 million was provided for the Malaysian project as part of a UK£1 billion deal that gave subsidies to defence exports to Malaysia from the UK firms British Aerospace and General Electic Company. The political interests of many aid agencies were also reflected in their support for Zaire (now the Democratic Republic of Congo). Aid poured into Zaire where decades of large-scale foreign assistance had made no impact on poverty. Zaire is just one of several examples where a steady flow of aid ignored, if not encouraged, incompetence, corruption and misguided policies (World Bank, 1998). US aid continued to be influenced by the Cold War and, as a result, aid was given to many countries, such as Angola, in return for their political support. On the other hand, it could also be argued that some donors gave misguided support to left-wing governments, such as the promotion by many Western governments of utopian socialism in Tanzania.

Although many large aid agencies' behaviour was still dominated by being in control of the development process, the failure of many projects to reduce poverty led to the demand for more structured project planning. In response, the logical framework (logframe) was introduced by some agencies (for example, the UK Department for International Development, DFID, and the US Agency for International Development, USAID). At one level, the logframe aimed to promote a very different view of development, where the major focus was no longer on the aid agency but on the poor. But the logframe also emerged as the ideal instrument of control (see Chapters 7, 8 and 11).

During this era, the focus on commercial and political interests led to the aid system becoming even more politicized. As a result, there was a backlash and disillusionment from aid workers and NGOs promoting participation and empowerment of poor people. Many perceived aid as being poorly monitored, leading to corruption and funds not reaching the poorest. Thus, rather than promoting growth and poverty reduction, aid flows were seen to be making countries more vulnerable by contributing towards an emerging debt crisis.

By the late 1980s there was a growing realization by aid agencies that the aid system was just not working. Many SALs had not influenced government policy, many of the policy conditions were not being met, and the quality of aid was under attack. For example, in Tanzania, aid agencies lent US$2 billion for building roads over 20 years. But the lack of maintenance meant that roads often deteriorated faster than they were built (World Bank, 1998). It was also recognized that the New International Economic Order had failed to bring about a more equal system: income poverty dramatically increased in Africa; oil prices rose; commodity prices fell; and the unintended poverty impacts of structural adjustment began to emerge. In addition, in some countries, aid performance was affected by poor administrative systems, weak implementation capacity and, in many cases, explicit corruption. As a result, the 1980s were sometimes referred to as the 'lost decade' in terms of development, and some argued that the development process was actually in reverse, especially in the case of sub-Saharan Africa (Singer, 1989). With the increased acceptance of neo-liberal ideologies and new structural adjustment policies, the 1970s' 'basic needs' strategies were very much overshadowed.

1990s: the end of the Cold War and the origins of debt relief

Three major events dominated development policy this decade: the end of the Cold War; the emergence of debt relief; and increasing political instability leading to more refugees and displaced persons than ever before. With the rise of the free market, many states lost some control over their economies and, in general, countries became particularly vulnerable to exogenous shocks, such as those associated with terms of trade. Public concern about the power of transnationals re-emerged as it had done during the 1960s and 1970s. This time there was increased concern about decisions being made at a transnational level by international finance institutions, as well as by large corporations that could affect billions of human lives.

The end of the Cold War brought about a dramatic redistribution of power with a significant increase in power in the West, mainly due to the collapse of the Soviet Union. Deeply rooted local rivalries resurfaced in a growing number of internal civil conflicts fuelled by an increasing availability of light weapons and small arms (World Bank, 1999). In the post-Cold War era, 'We have seen the criminalization of conflicts, the democratization of human suffering and deprivation, and the privatization of humanitarian protection and assistance' (Moreels, 1999, p1). Although many countries introduced multiparty democracy, others faced violent conflicts and civil war leading to huge increases in refugees and displaced persons. For example, the conflict in Rwanda led to the genocide of an estimated 800,000 to 1 million people and created 1.7 million refugees (Cernea, 1996). The collapse of the former Soviet Union and Eastern European regimes led to a revival in ethnicity and religions (Cernea, 1996). With the end of the Cold War, many aid agency governments focused on a different set of countries no longer aligned with Cold War allegiances; as a result, there was a reduction in the support for countries with weak governance. During this decade, in some countries, such as the former Soviet Union, the Philippines and Indonesia, there was a rise in 'people's power'.[18] Access to information on the web and through emails may have contributed to the increasing influence of civil society groups beyond nation states during this decade.

The decision to support debt relief shifted from being a development issue to a political one. In September 1996, the World Bank and the IMF launched the Initiative for the Heavily Indebted Poor Countries (HIPC Initiative) to provide exceptional assistance to eligible countries following sound economic policies to help them reduce their external debt burden to sustainable levels.

The HIPC Initiative was the first comprehensive debt-reduction mechanism,[19] designed to tackle commercial debt, debt owed to bilateral creditors, and debt owed to the World Bank, the IMF and the regional development banks.

Starting in 1989 and continuing throughout the 1990s, there were a series of UN-sponsored summits and conferences on topics of central interest to the development process. These included the 1992 Rio Earth Summit and others on children, human rights, women, education, population, urban development and food security. The Fourth World Conference on Women in Beijing emphasized that women were not equal to men in terms of their legal, social and economic rights. Gender equality gradually emerged as a core development issue.

A key event was the World Summit for Social Development 1995, which set an international goal for poverty reduction and partly laid the foundations for the 2015 Millennium Development Goals (MDGs). These goals (many of which were disaggregated by gender) were significant because social goals – not just economic ones – were put on the international development agenda. The outcome was the emergence of a global social development agenda where recognition was made that some social indicators had improved, although there were still problems of inequality and increasing numbers of poor people. Linked to this global social development agenda was the emergence of a global citizen movement with mass demonstrations that wanted to promote the global social agenda (for example, the Seattle demonstrations in 1999).

The 1990s saw a large rise in poor country NGOs' influence, especially in shaping national development policy. External criticisms by NGOs and public interest groups in the North increased the focus of development on poverty and social issues. In addition, after the Cold War, DFID and other donors chose to provide much of their assistance to countries in Central and Eastern Europe directly through local NGOs. At the World Bank, the *World Development Report 1990* (WDR) on poverty emphasized sharing the benefits of economic growth and providing basic social services – almost back to the basic needs approach that had been lost during the 1980s. Social development issues were increasingly incorporated within the World Bank's work. In order to do this, institutional and cultural change were required where organizational rules and procedures were modified (Cernea, 1996). With the increasing recognition of the negative impacts of adjustment loans, World Bank lending to social fund projects increased.

During the 1990s, the trend among aid agencies was to accept the need for participation in projects. But it was not until the late 1990s that a significant shift in implementation began to emerge with the use of participatory approaches at the policy level as opposed to just the project level. For example, NGOs lobbied for involvement in the World Bank's Country Assistance Strategies. They were successful due to effective lobbying, but also due to support inside the bank. This was finally endorsed, in 1996, in the IDA 11 Agreement.[20] Another example of participation at the policy level was the spread of participatory poverty assessments (PPAs)[21] that engaged the poor as key actors in situational analysis. The introduction of PPAs in some countries enabled the poor, so removed from the powerful, to influence national policy (for example, Uganda, Vietnam and The Gambia; see Robb, 2002). To date, more than 60 countries have undertaken PPAs with assistance from the World Bank; an equal number of PPAs have been conducted by other agencies, including UN agencies, bilaterals and NGOs.

In addition to highlighting the importance of participation in policy-making, PPAs also challenged the narrow definition of poverty based on income and consumption measures and health and education status derived from traditional household surveys. The poor often stressed other dimensions of poverty such as powerlessness, security, social ill-being and exclusion. PPAs highlighted the fact that people's priorities and experiences were affected by such variables as gender, social exclusion, intra-household allocation of resources, the incidence of crime and violence, geographical location, access to networks of support, and relations with those in power. A significant development was the gradual acceptance, in the field of poverty analysis, of combining PPAs and other participatory data with household surveys in order to derive a better understanding of poverty. PPAs also showed that poor people had the capacity to analyse their situations and express their priorities. It was revealing that the poor's definition of poverty and their priorities often fundamentally differed from those assumed by policy-makers.

With the failure of many isolated projects and the realization that the donor community needed to improve their collaboration, some donors (for example DFID, Sida, The Netherlands and the World Health Organization, WHO) introduced sector-wide approaches.[22] Some development organizations started to recruit a more diverse labour force (by discipline, gender, background and origin). However, many aid agencies began to cut aid back sharply[23] due mainly to aid fatigue, where domestic political support for aid in donor countries was reduced as there was a general perception that donors were ineffectual. This made the aid budget an easy target for finance ministries in donor governments looking to save money. Secondly, the 1990s was an era in which many major donors were struggling to discipline their public expenditure, either because (in Japan) recession had reduced tax revenues, or (in many European Union countries) because of the need to meet the Maastricht criteria for monetary union. Aid spending was not exempt from the general effort to tighten the belt. Those donors who were not actively cutting (such as the US and UK) were not expanding either. 1997 was a record low for official development assistance at 0.22 per cent of OECD countries' gross national products (GNPs).[24] There was a slight recovery in 1998 and 1999; but the figure sank back again to 0.22 in 2000 (World Bank, 2001).

The aid system during the 1990s was influenced by a growing dissatisfaction of both projects and policy lending to deliver poverty reduction. The influence of Southern countries remained limited, disbursements were not equated with achievement, corruption was tolerated and recipient governments and communities felt limited ownership of policies and projects. Hence, implementation of projects and reforms was resisted. In spite of this, support for aid from Northern taxpayers continued, even though aid levels declined.

Late 1990s onwards: globalization and the re-emergence of poverty on the agenda

Towards the end of the 1990s, a series of world events proved significant in influencing the aid system. Global markets for goods, services and capital became rapidly more integrated. With increasing turmoil in these global markets, a financial crisis soon emerged in East Asia and quickly spread to Russia. Many transitional economies were integrated within the international economy; but the former Soviet Union failed to make a successful transition to Western-style democracy with a regulated market economy. The end of the 1990s marked the beginning of mass demonstrations against globalization, in Seattle 1999, and increasing isolation of, and alienation towards, the US. The boom in the use of email and websites led to improved access to information and increased the ability of some local groups to organize internationally. But the lack of access to the technology in the South led to a concern about an emerging digital divide. In a post-September 11 world, it became clearer that poverty and inequality were linked to peace and stability.[25]

We now live in a world of exponential growth in global migration; escalating awareness about the spread of diseases, crime and protest across international boundaries; growing size of youth populations in developing countries; and ageing populations in Northern countries. Although there have been many health benefits over the past few decades, the recorded incidence of infectious diseases – particularly HIV/AIDS, tuberculosis and malaria – are now increasing in many developing countries. Some have argued that in spite of 40 years of aid, poor countries are still struggling. As Easterly states: 'Consider the facts and it soon becomes evident that the US$1 trillion spent on aid since the 1960s, with the efforts of advisers and foreign aid givers, the International Monetary Fund and the World Bank have failed to attain the desired results' (Easterly, 2001). But what are the desired results? It is unclear whether aid has failed outright, added to the fact that reducing poverty through aid alone is somewhat of an ambitious target.

Nevertheless, there is good news. Easterly (2001) focused on the relationship between aid and growth; but some aid has led to development measured by more than a single growth indicator (for example, poverty, equity, health, education, vulnerability and security). It is now increasingly recognized that aid effectiveness needs to be linked to the quality of country policies (see World Bank, 1998; Collier and Dollar, 1998). As a result, donors are now putting greater emphasis on governance and the tracking of poverty expenditures under the HIPC Initiative. In addition, as the case studies in this book show, aid agency patterns of behaviour are changing: aid is being untied; country offices are being decentralized; aid agencies are becoming more critical of their own programmes; local people are being given the responsibility to manage resources; and corruption and the rule of law are seen as important development issues.

However, increasingly, some aid agencies are recognizing that the impact of aid may be limited and that assessing causality in development processes is difficult due to diverse factors, including the influence of national and international politics. At the same time, aid agencies supported by taxpayers directly (bilaterals) and indirectly (multilaterals) are being asked to move to outcome-based management and, therefore, be more confident in their analysis of impacts. Furthermore, aid agencies are facing new challenges for managing relationships with governments, as influence shifts slightly from traditional rich country aid agencies and towards NGOs based in developing countries. In response to pressure from civil society groups in both the North and South, many aid agencies are increasingly using language such as empowerment, partnerships, ownership, accountability and transparency (see Cornwall, 2000). While this implies new, more open and collaborative power relationships, the necessary changes at the institutional, procedural and individual levels are likely to be achieved only progressively over time.

Within the World Bank and the IMF, some changes have been introduced. James Wolfensohn has transformed the World Bank into an internationally relevant institution where poverty reduction is the central mandate, highlighting the fact that visionary leaders can also influence the direction of the aid system. In response to the wider global context, and in recognition that the East Asia crisis had not just financial but also social impacts that negatively affected many of the poorest and most vulnerable in the region (Wolfensohn, 1998), the World Bank introduced the Comprehensive Development Framework (CDF) in 1999. The CDF focuses on a more holistic approach to development by seeking a better balance in policy-making among interdependent elements of development – social, structural, human, governance, environmental, economic and financial. The CDF also emphasizes partnerships among governments, aid agencies, civil society, the private sector and other development actors, and stresses the importance of the country being in the lead, both owning and directing the development agenda, with the World Bank and other partners each defining their support in their respective plans. Lastly, it stresses the need to focus on development results and to improve the accountability of all actors.

Another important, recent development has been the launch of the poverty reduction strategy papers (PRSPs) in September 1999. The CDF provided the conceptual basis for PRSPs to be developed by countries with the ideal of initiating consultation with civil society, including the poor. Programmes supported by the World Bank and the IMF are now based on government-driven poverty reduction strategies elaborated in the PRSPs. This initiative has, so far, been widely supported due, in part, to the fact that the two most influential aid agencies (the World Bank and the IMF) are working together to promote transparency around policy debates and decisions. This approach may have the potential to provide a framework for a radical shift in the way development agencies approach low-income countries and work in cooperation with each other, bringing together a variety of aid agency frameworks. Concerns have been expressed within donor circles, however, regarding the degree to which the poor are able to influence the PRSPs and the extent to which consultation mechanisms are being institutionalized. The emphasis on policies that reduce poverty was also behind the launch of the enhanced HIPC Initiative at the G7 Summit in Cologne in mid 1999, which made debt relief conditional upon a country's formulation of a poverty reduction framework. The introduction of the enhanced HIPC was also a result of increased pressure from civil society.

The PRSPs, therefore, provide the basis for debt relief under HIPC, as well as for all World Bank and IMF concessional lending (see Chapter 4). Although often criticized as yet another conditionality, in the short period since their introduction, the CDF and the PRSPs are beginning to change the way in which the World Bank and the IMF conduct their operations, and PRSPs have the potential to create policy space for the poor to be directly involved in the policy-making process. The PRSP approach is also helping to address another of the main failings of past aid efforts: numerous uncoordinated projects funded by different aid agencies that impose a huge burden on the countries that they are meant to help. Aid agencies are beginning to shift away from stand-alone projects towards more flexible funding at the sector or national budget level – giving more responsibility to governments.

As a result of the PRS process, the IMF-supported programmes are beginning to be based on poverty outcomes, as well as sound macro-economic frameworks. The introduction of the Poverty Reduction and Growth Facility (PRGF) to replace ESAF was based on the notion that economic growth is necessary but not sufficient for poverty reduction. The broadest and most fundamental changes to the work of the IMF arise from the fact that the targets and policies embodied in PRGF-supported programmes will emerge directly from the country's own poverty reduction strategy. This could be a major step. The PRGF-supported programmes now allow larger fiscal deficits (if financed in a non-inflationary way) to encourage pro-poor growth; focus on budget procedures – for example, tracking of poverty-related expenditures, the composition of budget expenditures and multi-year budget frameworks; encourage budgets and audited public accounts to be in the public domain; and include policies to support decreasing corruption and improving governance. Instead of a limited dialogue with the Ministry of Finance and Central Bank, some IMF mission teams are now meeting with a broad range of civil society groups in the context of the PRSP. Due to external pressure from civil society groups and internal management support, during the last seven years the IMF has changed many policies to dramatically increase its transparency.

Almost 20 years after the discussions on poverty as being multidimensional, the World Bank published the *World Development Report 2000/2001: Attacking Poverty* (WDR) 2001 that recognizes the many dimensions of poverty. The report built on the results of PPAs that emphasized a broader definition of poverty, which included not only low incomes and low consumption but also lack of education, poor nutrition and health, powerlessness, vulnerability, lack of respect and dignity, and a lack of trust in formal institutions because of corruption and irrelevance. The WDR also stressed the fundamental role of institutional and social change in strengthening development processes, and the importance of including poor people in development planning. It proposed a strategy for attacking poverty in three ways: promoting opportunity, facilitating empowerment and enhancing security. The World Bank is now focusing on how to link this strategy to its operations. The value of combining household surveys with data from PPAs to produce a more accurate policy message is now widely accepted.

Although some have called recent changes radical, power still lies in the North. Domestic politics of donor countries still influence the aid policies of countries many miles away. For example, George W Bush withdrew support for all family planning projects to placate the right wing anti-abortionists in the US. The result was a huge loss of funding for many local NGOs involved in family planning and a decrease in many poor women's freedom to choose. The risk of dying in childbirth for a woman in sub-Saharan Africa is 200 times that of her American counterpart. Yet, the voice of those thousands of women was not strong enough to reverse the trend. Too often aid allocations are still driven by donor foreign policies and domestic politics, rather than by poverty reduction.

Indeed, aid flows have not fundamentally changed even after the end of Cold War. For example, Egypt, Israel and Jordan still account for much aid from the US; French aid is primarily directed at Francophone African countries; UK aid continues to be concentrated on former British colonies; assistance from oil-rich Middle Eastern countries continues to flow only to poor Islamic countries; and Japanese aid continues to be driven by commercial interests, primarily focused on East Asian and Pacific countries. Although aid must engage with the private sector and be aware of the political system that it is inherently part of, the lack of transparency between aid, politics and commercial interests is being increasingly questioned by protesters on the street, as well as by donors. As stated by UN Secretary-General Kofi Annan: 'Aid can be much more effective today than it was 20 years ago if it is focused on building the capacity of recipient countries to run their own economies, not on tying them to the business or geopolitical interests of the donor countries' (Annan, 2002).

Contradictions still lie ahead. For example, while it is recognized that poor people's values should be respected, globalization will impact and change such values. In addition, the poor often provide cheap labour for globalized free trade; for some countries to remain competitive, labour standards are declining. Other factors such as employment and wages are also affected by globalization. As a result, some question whether it possible for large aid agencies to promote both global free trade and poverty reduction at the same time. A key ongoing concern and contradiction is the lack of trade access for developing country exports. While the US, the European Union (EU) and Japan, for example, give out aid with one hand, with the condition of open markets, they effectively take away with another by imposing trade barriers on developing countries' exports. These trade barriers support a few farms (many large corporations), undermine the agriculture and manufacturing sectors of developing countries and leave many people in poverty. Agricultural subsidies are estimated to be US$350 billion a year, six times what the rich countries provide in foreign aid to a developing world of close to 5 billion people.

There have been many successes. Over the past 40 years, life expectancy at birth in developing countries has increased by 20 years; over the past 30 years, illiteracy in the developing world has been cut nearly in half, from 47 per cent to 25 per cent of all adults; and poverty is more central to the development agenda. But many outstanding issues remain: increased global insecurity and terror; slow progress in Africa;[26] outstanding debt; donors' and governments' lack of understanding of the impacts of macro-economic reforms on poor people;

financial market liberalization that has left some countries vulnerable; agricultural trade that remains greatly distorted by irrational trade barriers;[27] the influence of narrow corporate interests and special interests that often determine policy, especially in the US; lack of success with the development of financial institutions for small and medium-sized domestic firms; 1 billion people living on less than US$1 a day and 110 million children who do not go to school; high levels of inequality and discrimination on grounds of gender, ethnicity and religion; and the disempowerment of millions of poor men and women throughout the world.

If we look back over these past decades, we can see that many initiatives to reform the aid system could have had more impact – the basic needs approach, adjustment with a human face, donor coordination, etc. Others are now gaining more ground – gender approaches, participation, sustainability, decentralization and the increased role of civil society. As described above, there are many elements that have influenced the success or failure of the aid system to deliver poverty reduction, including the world economic and political environment (colonialism, Cold War, oil crisis, debt, political instability and social fragmentation, financial crises, globalization); dominant political ideologies (increased acceptance of neo-liberal ideologies of the 1980s); domestic politics (George W Bush's withdrawal of funding for family planning or the Danish government's cutbacks under a new centre-right government); the personality of those involved in leading major organizations (the vision and commitment of James Wolfensohn to reduce poverty, leading to significant changes in the World Bank); and the increasing influence of Southern and Northern civil society (protests against debt and globalization). What remains is a fragmented aid system that continues to use many uncoordinated and inappropriate procedures; is still dominated by the domestic politics of Northern governments; often disempowers Southern governments; lacks accountability and transparency in both the North and the South; and continues to interact on the basis of asymmetric power. But sometimes it works.

Perhaps new changes will only come about through further 'big events' in history. But, as the next few chapters illustrate, power struggles exist in many forms at different levels – whether international, institutional or personal. All actors have a role to play in shifting aid procedures and policies towards improving the well-being of poor people.

Notes

1   Thanks to Anupam Basu, James Boughton and Peter Fallon (IMF), John Mitchell, Veena Siddharth and Greg Toulmin (World Bank), Robert Chambers (IDS), Alastair Robb (DFID) and Neil Thin (University of Edinburgh) for their very helpful comments.

2   However, aid agencies were able to exert some control through technical assistance, especially in Africa.

3   A World Bank report (2002) states that too often during the Cold War, aid allocations were driven by geopolitical aims rather than by poverty reduction goals.

It adds that given the diversity of motives, it is not surprising that some of this aid failed to have the direct effect of spurring growth and reducing poverty.

4   The deterioration in the terms of trade for Southern governments came about primarily because prices for their primary products were forced down. This was a result of overproduction and a declining demand due to some products (for example, jute and copper) being replaced with cheaper 'man-made' goods. At the same time, the price of manufactured goods, that many Southern governments were importing, continued to rise (see Pearson, 1969).

5   UNCTAD was established as a permanent inter-governmental body. It is the principal organ of the United Nations General Assembly, dealing with trade, investment and development issues. Its main goals are to maximize the trade, investment and development opportunities of developing countries and to assist them in their efforts to integrate into the world economy on an equitable basis.

6   The OECD is a group of 30 (mainly developed) countries. It aims to build strong economies in its member countries, improve efficiency, hone market systems, expand free trade and contribute to development in industrialized as well as developing countries. After more than four decades, the OECD is moving beyond a focus on its own countries and is setting its analytical sights on those countries that embrace the market economy.

7   The World Bank and the International Monetary Fund were created at Bretton Woods, New Hampshire, US, in 1944. Together, they are referred to as the Bretton Woods Institutions (BWIs).

8   Electoral democracies now represent 119 of the 192 existing countries. See Freedom House (2002). See also Moore and Putzel (1999) for a discussion on the differential outcomes that democracy has for the poor.

9   'Petrol dollars' refers to the supply of dollars generated by oil-producing countries from the sale of oil.

10 This commercial lending had to be bailed out during the early 1980s through official lending.

11 The RTA did not resolve all debt issues since not all countries received grant aid; a large amount of debt was export credit from export credit agencies (although, in some cases, concessional export credit loans were covered); and many countries had multilateral debt (from the World Bank, IMF and regional development banks).

12 Renamed the Department for International Development (DFID) in 1997.

13 Some aid agencies, such as the Swedish International Development Agency (Sida), did apply a less technical approach to their projects by stressing the importance of social equity from as early as the 1960s.

14 The so-called Washington Consensus has many interpretations; but Williamson, who coined the phrase, argues 'in the minds of many economists, the term has become a synonym for "neo-liberalism" or..."market fundamentalism"' (Williamson, 2000, p252). He adds that these definitions are significantly different from what he had intended.

15 By contrast with the RTA, which focused on aid debt, the Toronto Terms focused on non-aid debt.

16 See Boughton (2001a, pp637–701) for details of the IMF's role in poor countries during this decade.

17 See World Bank (1993) and Moser (1996) for an assessment of the SDA.

18 'People's power' can be defined as a mass movement of people to bring about political change. This was the case in the Philippines when Marcos was overthrown (1986) and in Eastern Europe during the collapse of the Berlin Wall (1989). In

these cases, it is significant to note that, unlike during the past, the military did not crush the protests.

19 By contrast with the RTA and the Toronto Terms, HIPC was the first initiative to aim at reducing debt to a sustainable level, rather than canceling small amounts of certain types of debt in an ad hoc manner.

20 IDA is available to countries with a per capita income of US$785 or less. Unlike IBRD, IDA is mainly funded by donor contributions. This allows the World Bank to make loans with a marginal interest rate of 0.5 per cent and a 40-year repayment period. IDA funds are replenished by an agreement among donors every three years. IDA 11 ended in June 1998. During the replenishment process, donors raise issues to do with IDA's performance and have the opportunity to influence World Bank policies (Oxfam, 1998).

21 A PPA is a method to include poor people in the analysis of poverty, with the objective of influencing policy. Findings are transmitted to policy-makers, thereby enabling the poor to influence public policy choices (see Norton et al, 2001; Robb, 2002).

22 The main features of a sector-wide approach include the following: all significant funding for the sector supports a single-sector policy and expenditure programme; government leadership; a common approach across the sector is adopted; and progress is made towards relying on government procedures to disburse and account for all funds (Brown et al, 2001).

23 In real terms, overseas development assistance (ODA) fell from US$45 billion in 1990 to US$39 billion in 2001.

24 See Development Assistance Committee (DAC) website: www.oecd.org/EN/document/0,,EN-document-59-2-no-1-2674-0,FF.html.

25 As James Wolfensohn noted recently: 'In our post-September 11 world, the need to address poverty – and its consequences in terms of despair, alienation and violence – has become not only a moral imperative (which it surely is), not only a social and economic necessity (which it also surely is), but also a central concern for everyone who strives for national and global security and peace' (Wolfensohn, 2002).

26 Sub-Saharan Africa as a region saw no increase in its per capita incomes between 1965 and 1999.

27 See the remarks by IMF Managing Director Horst Kohler at the World Bank/IMF International Conference on Poverty Reduction Strategies (Kohler, 2002).

References

Annan, K (2002) 'Trade and Aid in a Changed World', *New York Times*, 19 March

Boughton, J M (2001a) *Silent Revolution: The International Monetary Fund 1979–1989*, IMF, Washington, DC

Boughton, J M (2001b) 'History Traces IMF's Coming of Age as Participant in International Financial System', *IMF Survey*, 22 October, pp331–333

Brown, A, Foster, M, Norton, A and Naschold, F (2001) *The Status of Sector Wide Approaches*, Working Paper 142, Center for Aid and Public Expenditure, Overseas Development Institute, London

Cernea, M (1985) *Putting People First: Sociological Variables in Rural Development*, Oxford University Press, Oxford

Cernea, M (1996) *Social Organization and Development Anthropology*, Environmentally Sustainable Development Studies and Monographs Series, no 6, World Bank, Washington, DC

Chambers, R (1983) *Rural Development: Putting the Last First*, Longman, London

Chambers, R (1993) *Challenging the Professions. Frontiers for Rural Development*, Intermediate Technology Publications, London

Chambers, R (1997) *Whose Reality Counts: Putting the First Last*, Intermediate Technology Publications, London

Chenery, H, Ahluwalia, M S, Bell, C L G, Duloy, J H and Jolly, R (1974) *Redistribution with Growth*, Oxford University Press, Oxford

Collier, P and Dollar, D (1998) *Aid Allocation and Poverty Reduction*, World Bank, Washington, DC

Conyers, D, and Hills, P (1984) *An Introduction to Development Planning in the Third World*, John Wiley and Sons, Chichester

Cornia, G, Jolly, R and Stewart, F (eds) (1987) *Adjustment With a Human Face: Protecting the Vulnerable and Promoting Growth*, Clarendon Press, Oxford

Cornwall, A (2000) 'Beneficiary, Consumer, Citizen: Perspectives on Participation for Poverty Reduction', *Sida Studies,* no 2, Sida, Stockholm

Dasekin, C and Powell, R (1999) *From Toronto Terms to the HIPC Initiative: A Brief History Of Debt Relief For Low-Income Countries*, IMF Working Paper no 142, IMF, Washington, DC

Easterly, W (2001) 'The Failure of Development', *Financial Times* (London), 4 July

Freedom House (2002) 'Democracy's Century. A Survey of Global Political Change in the 20th Century', Freedom House website, www.freedomhouse.org/century.pdf

Killick, T (1999) *Making Adjustment Work for the Poor*, ODI Poverty Briefing, no 5, Overseas Development Institute, London

Kohler, H (2002) 'Opening Remarks at the International Conference on Poverty Reduction Strategies', 14–17 January, World Bank/IMF, Washington, DC

Lewis, A (1954) *The Theory of Economic Growth*, Allen and Unwin, London

Lipton, M (1977) *Why Poor People Stay Poor: Urban Bias and World Development*, Harvard University Press, Cambridge, MA, US

Moore, M and Putzel, J (1999) 'Politics And Poverty: A Background Paper for the World Development Report 2000/1', World Bank Poverty website, www.worldbank.org/poverty/wdrpoverty/dfid/synthes.pdf

Moreels, R (1999) 'No Short Cuts to Disarmament, Security and Sustainable Development', in World Bank, *Security, Poverty Reduction and Sustainable Development. Challenges for the New Millennium*, World Bank, Washington, DC

Moser, C (1996) *Confronting Crisis. A Comparative Study of Household Responses to Poverty and Vulnerability in Four Poor Urban Communities*, Environmentally Sustainable Development Series and Monographs Series, no 8, World Bank, Washington, DC

Norton, A with Bird, B, Brock, K, Kakande, M and Turk, C (2001) *A Manual for Participatory Poverty Assessments*, Department for International Development, London

Oxfam (1998) *IDA 12: A Chance to Deliver on World Bank Promises*, Oxfam International Position Paper, Oxfam International

Pearson, L (1969) *Partners in Development: Report of the Commission on International Development*, Praeger, New York

Robb, C (2002) *Can the Poor Influence Policy? Participatory Poverty Assessments in the Developing World*, second edition, World Bank/IMF, Washington, DC

Rostow, W (1960) *The Stages of Economic Growth*, Cambridge University Press, Cambridge

Singer, H (1989) 'The 1980s: A Lost Decade – Development in Reverse?' in Singer, H W and Sharma, S (eds) *Growth and External Debt Management*, Macmillan, London

Streeten, P with Burki, S J, Haq, M, Hicks, N and Stewart, F (1981) *First Things First: Meeting Basic Human Needs in the Developing Countries*, Oxford University Press, London

Williamson, J (2000) 'What Should the Bank Think About the Washington Consensus?', *World Bank Research Observer*, vol 15, no 2, p252

Wolfensohn, J W (2002) 'Opening Remarks at the International Conference on Poverty Reduction Strategies', 14–17 January 2002, Washington, DC, World Bank website, www.worldbank.org/html/extdr/extme/jdwsp011402.htm

Wolfensohn, J W (1998) 'The Other Crisis', Address to the World Bank Board of Governors, 6 October, World Bank, Washington, DC

World Bank (1993) *The Social Dimensions of Adjustment: A General Assessment*, Human Resources and Poverty Division, Technical Department, Africa Region, World Bank, Washington, DC

World Bank (1998) *Assessing Aid: What Works, What Doesn't, and Why*, Oxford University Press, New York

World Bank (1999) *Security, Poverty Reduction and Sustainable Development: Challenges for the New Millennium*, World Bank, Washington, DC

World Bank (2001) *World Development Report (WDR) 2000/2001: Attacking Poverty*, Oxford University Press, New York, www.worldbank.org/poverty/wdrpoverty

World Bank (2002) *The Role and Effectiveness of Development Assistance: Lessons from World Bank Experience*, DEC, Washington, DC

3

Reflections on Organizational Change

Jean Horstman[1]

Introduction

This chapter reflects on the role that system thinking might play in deepening understanding of the interrelationship between power, procedures and relationships. It reflects on organizations and their possibilities for deep change, beginning with a context for and caveats about change, and moves on to look at two tools for conceptualizing and understanding interconnected change. The chapter concludes with a causal-loop analysis of the logical framework (logframe) and its effectiveness as an assessment tool.

Before proceeding I must confess that, unlike the rest of the contributors to this volume, I am not experienced in international development. My role here is akin to that which I had at the workshop that spawned this book.[2] I was invited as someone with similar experience in organizational learning and change initiatives in the field of community development in the US and UK. My charge was to reflect on what insights or lessons might be of value to share, or already held in common, with those challenging organizational norms and practices in international development. Reflection was my role then, and is my role now.

I write in the voice of reflective practitioner for fellow practitioners. What follows grows out of conversation – an informal exchange of thoughts and feelings – over 20 years with both colleagues and texts. I write from a set of relationships, not a linear body of knowledge. I don't write for permanence: conversations evolve. This reflection explores organizations and change, as I understand them now. Reflections are meant to stimulate curiosity and invite further investigation. I invite you to read it as a work in progress, offered in a spirit of invitation and innovation. Bring to the text a 'what if' attitude, engage in exploration and enquiry, and remember that what is written is more in sand than in stone.

With the practitioner in mind, this reflection begins by looking at the context for change and offering some caveats about organizational change. It moves on to look at some 'tools' for conceptualizing and understanding change, and concludes with two concrete applications of those tools. The first explores their implications for planning, asking whether the logframe is still a useful tool for charting international development programmes. The second looks at implications for assessment, through a case study of a process-oriented and partnership approach to programme evaluation. I propose these tools in the context of a complex and uncertain environment and argue that in adopting a systems approach we will make visible the interconnectedness of the development system. Such tools will help us to view and understand development as an uncertain evolutionary process that is, essentially, driven by local actors within their own particular socio-political context.

Why change?

The simple answer is because all living things do. Complexity arises from understanding the relationship between change and environments. Organizations, like most of us, change when we experience pain because the way in which we are living and the environment in which we live no longer soundly support each other. Organizations, like most of us, do not make these adaptations easily or quickly, particularly if the environmental changes are evolutionary.

Charles Handy, a visiting professor at the London Business School and frequent reflector on the state of business, captures this phenomenon in a metaphor, that of the boiled frog. Put a frog in water and slowly increase the heat. The frog will allow itself to be boiled to death. Put a frog in boiling water, and it leaps out. A frog, like many of us, can't read subtle environmental shifts that have radical implications (Handy, 1989).

What are the environmental shifts that affect organizations? One way to begin to think about this topic is to take a piece of paper. At the top write '2001' and at the bottom '1991'. List the social, economic, cultural, technological, political, environmental, scientific and transportation changes that occurred over the last ten years that you *didn't* foresee in 1991 and that have seriously affected international development practice. Now get a second sheet of paper; at the top of the page write '2011' and at the bottom write '2001'. Try to imagine a similar scale of change in the same areas for the *next* ten years. The connection between boiled frogs and organizational change may start to be a little bit clearer. The current environmental factors that impact upon international development organizations reflect 'the increasing and intensifying Cs': complexity, change and uncertainty. 'The Cs' are evident in the current literature on global and societal change, organizational change and international development. They are also evident in the conversations – formal and informal – within the development world. Readers will recognize some and think of others to add. In the nature of reflections, what follows is not meant to be definitive or authoritative.

Rapid changes in technology, knowledge creation, information dissemination and information access

- The increasingly global knowledge economy and rapid changes in communications technology are symbiotic. Accessible and affordable technology makes it possible for anyone anywhere in the world to access tremendous amounts of information and knowledge. This has implications for expectations concerning transparency.

Changes in organizational roles made possible by communication and information technology

- Technology also facilitates changes in organizational roles. Relationships between donors and recipients facilitated by mail, telex, flights and expensive long-distance telephone calls were episodic rather than ongoing. Email, faxes and the internet make ongoing contact possible, as well as creating the infrastructure for working collaboratively in the rapidly changing areas of policy and advocacy.
- Major corporations such as Intel have created integrated global manufacturing processes because these technological changes enable plants in Asia, Europe and Latin America to work as one system.

Inter-generational shifts reflecting a difference in career development, expectations and possibilities

- The generation that came of age in 1968 is not the same as that which came of age in 1998. The 68ers – employed at a time of project management needs – are often the people hiring and managing the 98ers – employed at a time when partnership skills are more required.
- The hands-on international experience of the 68ers has not been an early career reality for staff hired later in the century.
- In the South, HIV/AIDS is cutting through a generation ripe for leadership.
- Increasingly, effective staff want a more hands-on relationship with recipients. Arm's length is, no longer, personally or professionally satisfying enough.

Growing decentralization and higher expectations around accountability at the local level

- There are no surprises here for the international development field, where donor agencies and Northern non-governmental organizations (NGOs) are increasingly opening offices in the South.

Results-oriented assessment

- Increasingly, organizations are asked to justify their existence by proving their impact. The tick box has become ubiquitous. Yet, how do we ever really know the impact of an action in an ever-changing environment?

- I am sure that we can all name organizations or projects in the past that everyone *knew* were making a significant impact and have since been shown to have had a devastating effect. Equally, I am sure we can all name organizations that seemed insignificant at the time and that have since been seen to be prophetic.
- Understanding impact is more than a linear, measurable process; it is also an organic, longitudinal one. In the development world, how do present models of assessment incorporate the organic nature of understanding impact?

Staff attraction and retention at a time when the international development sector is diversifying and corporations play an increasing role in social sustainability

- Diversification gives staff more employment options. As corporations learn to work outside the 'expatriate comfort zone', there will be more competition for local staff in the South.
- This competition will come at a time when business is aware of the 'global war for talent' and the role that management practices, as well as salaries, play in attracting and retaining staff. Increasingly, highly effective staff seek employment where they can make a difference and where there is real respect for people. Business knows this type of environment as 'high performance/high touch'.

Unsound relationships between organizations and their environment

- Symptoms of the unease between organizations and their operating environments include high staff turnover; increasing use of consultants; open challenges to linear approaches of planning; lack of disclosure within organizations and between organizations about what isn't working; increasing competitiveness; fear; illness; and anxiety.

How change?

There is no one set path or process by which an organization can evolve with its internal and external environments. There is no blueprint. One size *does not* fit all. No one guru holds the secret. Every organization develops its own way, informed by the external environment, internal culture, leadership and the particular mix of people who are its employees. Being successful at evolution – for example, realizing and adjusting to the water as the temperature changes – depends upon the ability of the organization, its staff and its stakeholders to *make sense* of internal and external realities; to adapt to the changing environment; and to adopt, in a timely way, new approaches to delivering the organization's mission. Timely is a key word. The above approach allows an organization to understand *dynamically* what they are seeking to achieve, the structural realities that both assist and impede their progress, and where the points of leverage are along the way.

'Structural realities', as used here, are the tacit realities that inform organizational choice. They are often intangible and invisible. In this framework, structural change is not about restructuring, downsizing or changing staff and procedures. Rather, it is a creative response to a more comprehensive understanding of how these intangibles affect organizational choice.

A possible metaphor for this shift in definition is to think about an organization as a body. The structural realities that enable a body to have movement and life are invisible on a day-to-day basis. At times of stress, they become visible in the symptoms that they generate. We completely forget about neural impulses until we suffer an accident that severs the pathways along which they travel. Bones become visible when we ache with rheumatism or have a fracture.

Tools for change: from linear to interconnected thinking

We can't solve problems by using the same kind of thinking we used when we created them (Albert Einstein).

Profound change – the type of change required to prosper in a complex and uncertain environment – requires structural change, as defined above. Systems dynamics is one approach to revealing the underlying structure of an organization and to uncovering where high-leverage change lies. A system dynamics orientation furthers understanding of the interrelated nature of the forces that exist within and outside an organization. These forces are not just the operating procedures of an organization or the political realities of accountability; they are also the attitudes, perceptions, assumptions and metaphors of the staff and management. It is these tacit aspects of structure that make profound change so challenging. In the end, they are often about change at the personal and interpersonal level.

There are many books and websites about systems dynamics and systems thinking, as well as an international professional association, the System Dynamics Society. In this chapter, I invite the reader to consider three tools for thinking systemically and to reflect on how they might contribute to deepening understanding of the challenges facing international development.

The iceberg

After *Titanic*, the dangers of icebergs are well known – what we cannot see can sink us. The bulk of the iceberg – and an organization – lies below the waterline. Organizational icebergs have three interconnected layers.

1 Events

This is the layer above the water. Events are the organizational equivalent of a newspaper story and what most people think is the organization's 'reality'. This is also the level to which crisis management responds (about one eighth of the bulk of the iceberg).

2 Patterns and behaviours

This layer sits immediately below the waterline. Patterns are observable and include the reward system, the procedures, the pattern of communication and information flow, and the explicit decision-making processes. For many of us, they are what we traditionally consider the structure of an organization. This is also where most organizational change efforts focus their attention (about one eighth of the bulk of the iceberg).

3 Systemic structure

This is the bulk of the iceberg and sits well below the waterline. It comprises the unseen forces of the organization that affect how everything operates and that only become visible when we become conscious of them. In the natural world, gravity is an example of such a force, as is a beating heart or breathing. How many of us are conscious of these forces? Yet, life as we know it wouldn't exist without them.

This is the layer where most organizational problems begin, moving up the iceberg to surface as events. At this deeper level we find the intangibles such as assumptions, ways of interpreting assumptions, emotions, attitudes and history. It is also here that the interrelationships among the key aspects of a system have their roots (about six-eighths of the bulk of the iceberg).

At the Institute of Development Studies (IDS) workshop, I asked Charles Owusu (see Chapter 8) how overseas development would be different if donors were from the South and recipients from the North. He replied, 'Accountability would be a matter of relationships and not just numbers and reports.' In our exchange, he exposed a key part of the systemic structure, the impact of the donors' culture on the basis of assessment.

During the same workshop, participants used the iceberg model to map their understanding of why in-country donor staff act as if they are powerless when they actually have a good deal of power. The concept of being a 'civil servant' was identified as a structural reality. When asked what would change if 'civil servant' was changed to 'public official', the donor agency staff spoke passionately and emotionally about why they were and *had to be* civil servants. Political realities required it. The high level of emotion around their response indicated that this was a powerful part of the systemic structure and, therefore, a possible leverage point for significant change at the deepest level. It also indicated how hard it would be to activate such a leverage point. Making it visible, however, made the discussants cognizant of the power that these two words had in the system.

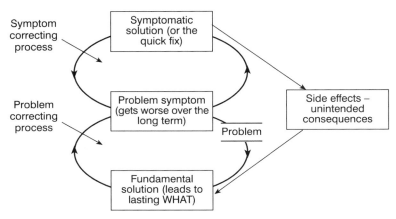

Figure 3.1 *Limits to success archetype*

Causal-loop thinking

Causal-loop thinking and the systems thinking templates associated with it are a language for moving from linear understanding to inter-linked understanding. In linear thinking, 'A' causes 'B'. In systems thinking, 'A' causes 'B' causes 'A' and both are, at the same time, interrelated with 'C', 'D', 'E' and 'F', etc. You can see how difficult it can be to capture this type of thinking in traditional noun, verb and object language. The visual language of systems thinking – causal-loop diagrams and archetypes – provides a language for complex interrelatedness.

Another important aspect of systems thinking is that it works from stories, as well as data. Stories are ways in which the systemic structure often reveals itself. Systems thinking enables us to understand more deeply how we slant our realities and, therefore, create the possibility of reframing them with fewer in-built assumptions. Systems thinking archetypes are tools for quickly understanding the governing forces in a system. The two that follow are from Senge et al (1994).

Limits to success archetype

The limits to success archetype (see Figure 3.1) helps us to think about the unintended or unexpected limiting factors that accompany any change. It can be used to understand stories of existing change processes, or it can be used to think more systemically about new ones and how to monitor their implementation.

The key aspect of this model is the *balancing-loop target* or *limit to the system*. I find that the question 'What wants to be conserved in the present situation?' is a good way of seeing what this constraint is. What wants to be conserved will come back and slap you hard if you ignore it as part of a change process. Go back to the earlier example of 'civil servant' versus 'public official'. As well as being a point of high leverage, the role of 'civil servant' is also something that will seek to be conserved. Try to change it too quickly or from the top down, and you will, most likely, trigger this constraint.

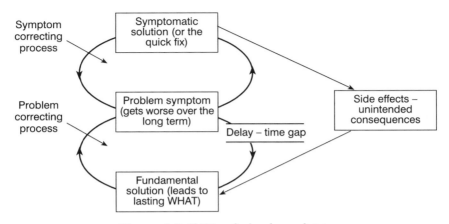

Figure 3.2 *Shifting the burden archetype*

Another important aspect is the time gap in the limiting loop. The restraints in the system will not show up immediately. Success may be apparent and then, over night, things may stall or reverse. In international development, time gaps in systems thinking raise questions about short-term two- to three-year project cycles.

This tool is particularly useful when first initiating a change process. These limiting forces have implications for the assumptions column of the logframe. Anticipating and understanding these limiting forces when they are small allows one the time to more effectively incorporate ways of addressing them in the growth loop. There will always be limits on any action; but foreseeing and understanding them can lessen their impact. This archetype is especially useful for informing the way organizations respond to calls for transparency, decentralization and greater collaboration.

Shifting the burden archetype

The shifting the burden archetype (see Figure 3.2) is useful in understanding the ways in which established procedures – if used when no longer appropriate or applied inappropriately – can impede an organization's ability to adapt in a timely way to environmental shifts.

The archetype is useful in understanding a situation where there is a *problem symptom* that prompts people to want to 'solve' it. Solutions are obvious and immediate. Symptoms get quick relief. Because quick fixes are fast, they divert attention from the *root cause* of the problem. The attention that the fundamental source of the problem should receive lessens over time. The symptomatic solution increasingly seems the only option. Fundamental solutions take longer to take effect and are undermined by the 'addiction' that the organization acquires for the quick fix. The ability to respond fundamentally is eroded over time. And, in the end, the problem symptom also continues to escalate. A possible metaphor for this system in action is taking aspirin to treat headaches associated with brain tumours. The aspirin numbs the pain and allows the cancer to grow.[3]

Applying systems thinking archetypes to the logframe

At the IDS workshop, one group used the shifting the burden archetype to understand the relationship of the logframe to power, procedures and relationships. My colleagues explained that the logframe originated as an engineering project management tool. It was designed to guarantee a deliverable outcome to a predictable timetable. However, it was not designed to anticipate the unintended negative consequences that it would create, nor could it identify factors that would constrain its effectiveness in international development.

Today, the logframe is both a planning and assessment tool, not the purpose for which it was originally conceived. Form and function are no longer aligned, and a planning tool is asked to be a *sense-making tool* in an environment of dynamic complexity, rapid change and inter-cultural collaboration. The logframe is a procedure, with its structural roots in linear thinking rather than in systems thinking.

As I understand it, the contemporary *problem symptom* (see the archetype above) that the logframe – and the many efforts to adapt it – is trying to address is how to create and measure a specific impact on a specific problem, when the *root cause* is a challenge at the systemic structural level to the international development world. Complexity and rapid change erode the applicability of specificity.

The need for profound change in how donors, NGOs and recipients interrelate defies quick fixes. At the heart of this change is the need for a different way of *being*, as well as *working*, with each other if the system is going to make sense of its environment, its actions and its unintended consequences.

Does the development field wish to continue to invest in adapting an existing planning tool to meet its need for sense-making? Lest we forget, Ptolemaic astronomy was a right mess before Copernicus tackled the root cause of the movement of heavenly bodies. The Earth is simply not the centre of it all. Is the same systemic shift happening, with the place occupied by donors?

What would happen if a team of experienced and innovative professionals from the South were asked to use new ways of thinking – in solidarity with Einstein and Copernicus – and develop alternative sense-making processes that address the contemporary environment? And to develop them within a systems thinking framework?

Why the South? One aspect of structural reality is that those at the 'edge' of the system or even 'outside' it can often see it – and the points of greatest leverage within it – most clearly. Another reason for leading this change from the South is that the power to redefine relationships in a system lies not with the 'powerful' but with the 'powerless'. It is not for the powerful to rationally direct change. As we know from our experience of our own times, the powerless will be responsible for change whether the powerful desire it or not.

Systemic sense-making in community development

The Community Development Corporation/Arts Resource Initiative (CDC/ARI)[4] was funded by the Ford Foundation and managed by the Manchester Craftsmen's Guild (MCG). It was a national programme in the US, designed to advance community revitalization through building a capacity for entrepreneurship in community development corporations (CDCs). CDCs are community-based organizations working to revitalize the economic, physical, social and human capital of low-income, urban and rural communities. They are directly accountable to the communities and constituencies whom they serve. Ten organizations participated in the programme, representing African-American, Latino, Chicano, Caribbean-American and Cambodian communities.

CDC/ARI was a four-year, US$4.5 million initiative. It partnered capacity-building with grant-making. The initiative was comprised of training, planning, implementation, and exiting phases, and was designed to build on the interdependence of economic and cultural development. Each CDC developed its own multi-year strategic plan, incorporating community stakeholders' inputs and a set of benchmarks agreed with MCG. Funding was released upon receipt of the CDC's quarterly self-assessment. At the end of the four years, eight of the ten sites had achieved the initiative's objective.

According to the terminology of international development, the *donor* equates to the Ford Foundation, the Manchester Craftsmen's Guild is the NGO and the participating CDCs are the *recipients*. MCG, like many NGOs, was accountable to a donor as well as to the communities of the participating CDCs.

Why use an example from US community development in a book about international development? This example is useful because it looks systemically at donor–NGO–recipient relationships, rather than a specific socio-economic context. As a completed intervention, it provides a longitudinal perspective on new reporting processes, such as those being adopted by ActionAid (see Chapter 8).

From its inception, CDC/ARI included an external evaluator who utilized a formative evaluation approach. In a formative evaluation, the assessor is a 'travelling companion' rather than a judge, weaving the assessment process into the operation of the programme. CDC/ARI used a 'responsive model' of formative evaluation. According to the evaluator, Bruce Jones, 'this model of evaluation is less concerned with a set of pre-established goals and more concerned with' (Jones 1996):

- How does the programme achieve its broader mission?
- *How are the concerns and issues of the participants being addressed?*
- What are the specific effects and activities of the programme and how and why did they occur?
- What are the implications for the programme of these effects?
- What does the programme look like from a variety of perspectives?

This evaluation integrated double-loop thinking into CDC/ARI. On a regular basis, it captured from the donor, the NGO and the recipients what enabled effectiveness and what hindered it.

CDC/ARI's evaluator was selected by the NGO, not the donor. He collected evaluative data through observation, interviews, surveys and archival documentation. He regularly visited each participating site. While there, he gathered data sets, but also listened to the stories being told about the initiative and how it was being experienced in the recipient community. The data sets met the sense-making needs of the donor, and the story-telling that of the recipients. The regular visits and confidential nature of the story-telling supported the growth of trustful relationships between Bruce and the recipients. These trustful relationships enabled the transparency needed to inform the initiative's effectiveness. The 'unspeakable' could be spoken.

Bruce's regular written summaries were shared with the NGO and the recipients and directly contributed to the successful evolution of CDC/ARI. Regular reporting allowed the initiative to adjust its procedures, practices and relationships to facilitate the greatest benefit for the recipients. They became the structure by which the recipients co-created the initiative. Bruce's evaluation process also developed a capacity for assessment in the recipients. Sense-making was done to meet the needs of the recipients, not just those of the donor and the NGO.

The course corrections arising from the formative evaluation were particularly important when, midway through the initiative, it was realized that the initial design needed to be adjusted so as not to impede the development of the recipients. The evaluation captured the knowledge and detailed recommendations that were required to make those adjustments in timely and effective ways.

CDC/ARI evaluation informed the implementation of its strategic operating plan. Nothing was sacred or exempt from reconsideration. The relational approach of the evaluation process enabled a significant acknowledgement to emerge in the second year. Nobody involved in the initiative – from donor to recipients – knew how to do 'it.' If anyone already knew how to do what the initiative was trying to achieve, there would be no initiative. The only way to figure out how to do 'it' was to be with each other on a regular basis in a way that respected the insights each contributed. Making sense of it all required collective thinking and mutual vulnerability.

When the CDC/ARI manager said MGC (the NGO) was not the expert but a co-learner, it gave everybody permission to be the same. The fear of disclosing a lack of ability was replaced by talking openly about what was and wasn't working, and seeking to understand rather than hide from reality.

The cost of a formative evaluation averages about 10 to 15 per cent of a programme's costs. However, it would be wrong to measure its value just in terms of its cost. The ongoing learning arising from the evaluation process enabled the success of the initiative. It is perhaps more accurate to measure its value not in what it cost, but in what it saved.

Conclusions

CDC/ARI was designed by and managed by an NGO – one that is African-American founded and led. Its systemic structure includes a deep belief that 'there is nothing wrong with poor people that good art, good food and a lot of love can't change' – and that those aren't quick fixes. A poor community takes a generation of relationships to renew itself. The CDC/ARI team believed in the power of relationships to change people and communities. Bruce Jones, also African-American, shared this belief in the power of transformative relationships.

In international development terms, CDC/ARI was designed and managed 'by the South for the South' in partnership with a Northern donor. It illustrates the enacting of the 'what if' shared with me by Charles Owusu, who observes in this volume that 'policies in themselves do not engender change' (see Chapter 8). He credits the 'collective efforts of individuals' with that. The CDC/ARI case illustrates that the *quality* of these collective interactions also contributes to effective change. CDC/ARI was effective because it honoured the donor, the NGO and the recipients as learning partners working from a basis of trust and trustworthiness.

The CDC/ARI example illustrates what happens when those without the power and money are given the freedom to design and work from their own understanding of the system. It also illustrates the constraints that arise from being funded to be an expert. The Ford Foundation's willingness to fund MCG for its ability to learn collaboratively with other organizations and communities was the structural change that enabled the success of the initiative.

Not long ago, it would have been unthinkable for a large US donor to take that kind of risk with any grant, much less one to an African-American community-based organization. It will be interesting to see how long it takes for the learning arising from initiatives such as ActionAid's Accountability, Learning and Planning System (ALPS) to create the same kind of structural shifts in international development. Is international development ready for processes and structures built on trust and forgiveness?

If development practitioners can take on board tools developed within the systems thinking framework, it will help them to gain a fuller understanding of the complex aid environment in which they work. In challenging the linear thinking of many existing development paradigms, the potential to make a significant contribution is enhanced. If aid actors are able to illuminate the assumptions about causality and universality in the way that development progresses, they may be able to embrace more fully the potential significance of indigenous modes of thinking. Adopting a systems approach will require development professionals to develop a deeper knowledge of the political and cultural landscape, and the historical context in which they seek to work. This will require organizations to rethink their incentives and structures to ensure that staff gain first-hand and ongoing exposure to the primary stakeholders. It will require greater attention to developing relationships not only within, but between, organizations. Yet, adopting a systems approach implies profound changes in the theory and practice of development. The question is, are the organizations and individuals ready to take up the challenge?

Notes

1   My thanks to Liz Goold, an organizational development consultant in international development, who helped me with this chapter and was my thinking partner. Any errors in my understanding of international development are totally mine, and any major insights grow from Liz's guidance.
2   Power, Procedure and Relationships in International Aid Workshop, Institute of Development Studies, University of Sussex, UK, May 2001.
3   For further information on systems thinking tools, and to order *Systems Archetypes* I and *System Thinking Tools* by Daniel H Kim, both in the Toolbox Reprint Series, see the Pegasus Communications website, www.pegasuscom.com.
4   The final report from CDC/ARI, 'Creating in Communities', is available from Joanna Papada, vice-president of operations, Manchester Craftsmen's Guild, 1815 Metropolitan Street, Pittsburgh, PA 15233, US; email: jpapada@mcg-btc.org; tel: +1 412 322 1773 ext 105.

References

Handy, C (1989) *The Age of Unreason*, Business Books, London
Jones, B (1996) *Community Development Corporation/Arts Resource Initiative Interim Assessment Report*, Manchester Craftsmen's Guild, Pittsburgh
Senge, P, Ross, R, Smith, B, Roberts, C and Kleiner, A (1994) *The Fifth Discipline Fieldbook: Strategies and Tools for Building a Learning Organization*, Nicholas Brealey Publishing Ltd, London

Part Two

POWER, PROCEDURES AND RELATIONSHIPS

4

Who Owns a Poverty Reduction Strategy? A Case Study of Power, Instruments and Relationships in Bolivia[1]

Rosalind Eyben

Introduction

This chapter deals with the relationships between bilateral donors and Bolivian national stakeholders in the development of a poverty reduction strategy paper (PRSP) from early 2000 to mid 2001. I wrote it at that time, when working in Bolivia as the head of the UK Department for International Development's (DFID's) country office. I explore how the preparation of a PRSP both influenced and was influenced by the structures of power and the patterns of relationships between actors in government, the international cooperation community and civil society in Bolivia. I consider the different levels and quality of influence that came into play in this relationship, concluding that – despite major challenges, over-optimism and many disappointments – the PRSP process in Bolivia did contribute to a shift in the balance of power towards poor people. It strengthened the room for manoeuvre of those in government, civil society and the international community. The process also helped some of us in the donor community reflect more on our own role, grappling seriously with concepts of 'ownership' and 'accountability'. The chapter ends with some lessons for donors with regard to playing a more useful and informed role in supporting long-term processes of policy change in favour of poor people.

The PRSP process

The origin of poverty reduction strategy papers lies in the decision to provide expanded debt relief to poor countries (the Highly Indebted Poor Countries Initiative 2, or HIPC2) in response to the highly successful civil society movement in the North. To qualify for the relief, recipients must prepare a poverty reduction strategy to be endorsed by the World Bank and International Monetary Fund (IMF) boards. Recipients know, however, that donor governments are under pressure from their own citizens to deliver the debt relief and that, ultimately, whatever the quality of the product, it is likely to be judged as adequate by the World Bank and the IMF.

Thus, the challenge is to persuade any recipient government to take the process seriously, to make a real effort to identify and 'own' its strategy for reducing poverty. This was why the participatory element of the PRSP was so important. It would provide the possibility for poor people and their representative organizations to gain a greater voice in policy processes, thus boosting their own government's will to implement the pro-poor policies endorsed in Washington.

The following sections deal with the relationships between bilateral donors and national stakeholders in the application of this new donor instrument. In this relationship, the policy choices were affected by three different kinds of influence. The first, and most comfortable one for development professionals, is that of technical judgement; this is the level at which most of us claim to be operating when seeking to influence policy decisions. The second is institutional and personal political interest, something we are less comfortable with. The third and perhaps most uncomfortable is our deeply seated attitudes and beliefs, which often come into play and unconsciously influence our behaviour and judgement.

This chapter is written from the perspective of a bilateral donor representative. I examine how the preparation of a PRSP both influenced and was influenced by the structures of power and the patterns of relationships between actors in government, the international cooperation community and civil society in Bolivia. The focus is on *bilateral* donors as agents in the process and the chapter touches only tangentially on the significant role of the three international finance institutions – namely the IMF, the World Bank and the Inter-American Development Bank. One of the reasons the bilaterals set up their own network (described on page 62), was to gain a stronger (because coordinated) voice, not only with the Bolivian government, but also with the local representatives of the international financial institutions (IFIs). This included an energetic effort to persuade them of the importance of a poverty reduction strategy that embraced the concept of pro-poor growth. Nevertheless, the detailed nature of this particular relationship is not described here. Rather, I focus on the dynamics of intra-Bolivian relationships around the PRSP process and our bilateral engagement with these.

These dynamics changed fairly dramatically during the 18-month period described in this chapter (January 2000–July 2001) and were strongly affected by broader political processes within Bolivia. Thus, it is difficult to attribute the extent to which the changing nature of these political relationships was influenced by the process surrounding the drafting of the PRSP, as distinct from the broader political events. Necessarily, my conclusions are influenced by my having been an energetic and committed actor in the process.

I conclude that the PRSP process in Bolivia did contribute to a shift in the balance of power towards poor people. It strengthened the room for manoeuvre of those in government, civil society and the international community who were seeking to focus state policies on tackling the country's fundamental and deeply entrenched problems of poverty, exclusion and failure of vertical accountability. The process also helped donors reflect more on our own role, grappling with concepts of 'ownership' and 'accountability', while – as ignorant explorers – we stumbled and groped through the idiosyncratic, dense and ancient forest of state–society relations in Bolivia.

The following section, 'Power, ownership and accountability in Bolivia', considers certain characteristics of power in Bolivia as the environment into which the PRSP was introduced. The next section, 'A poverty reduction strategy for Bolivia', explores how concepts of poverty and participation were handled in the PRSP process. Within this context, the section 'Power and relationships in the PRSP process' describes how bilateral donors were caught up in the evolving relationships between local communities and civil society, between citizens and political parties and between the centre and local government. The final section reaches tentative conclusions about the role of bilateral donors and reflects on how we may apply our donor instruments in order to play a more useful and informed role in supporting long-term processes of policy change in favour of poor people.

Power, ownership and accountability in Bolivia

It has been common for international development cooperation to ignore history. Despite a growing interest of development studies in the long-term processes of change and continuity, most development policy-makers still tend to take snapshots of the present, rather than consider what happened in the past and how this could affect the future. Like tourists, we take pains to exclude from our frame any image of unpleasant reality that does not fit our concept of how the place should be. And again, like tourists, we only stay for a short time, three years on average, generally mixing with those with whom we feel most comfortable and who may only provide us a with a partial perspective on the country's history. It is thus a challenge to understand those long-term processes that have led today to Bolivia being classified as a highly indebted poor country with equally high levels of social unrest.

The economic and political history of Bolivia since the Spanish conquest may be crudely summarized as that of a small ruling elite making a living from the exploitation and export of primary raw materials. It did this by controlling an indigenous labour force who worked in the export sector and provided the food for feeding both itself and the elite. The deep political structures of

Bolivia's history are commonly typified as clientist and patrimonial (World Bank, 2000), excluding the great majority of the population from influencing the policies that affect their lives, except in a reactive fashion and when under severe pressure. Over the centuries, sporadic indigenous uprisings were suppressed with greater or lesser violence. Arguably, independence from Spain during the early 19th century resulted in a deterioration of the economic and political status of the indigenous population, with the disappearance of a possibly more disinterested colonial civil service (Albo, 1999; Osco, 2001). The new language of fraternity, liberty and equality applied only to the elite.

In Bolivia, many – including Bolivia's only former vice-president of indigenous origin – argue that colonial rule has, indeed, never ended, that the social unrest which coincided with the PRSP process is a manifestation of 'internal colonialism, racism, discrimination' (Cardenas, 2001). The *Voices of the Poor* consultation reported that discrimination cannot be seen but can be smelt, cannot be touched but can be felt (World Bank, 1999).

While many Bolivians firmly believe that they have achieved a single but multicultural and multi-ethnic society, as expressed in the new constitution of 1994, others hotly debate the extent to which Bolivia remains a dual society. Different sources of data, for example, provide conflicting figures on the prevalence of indigenous languages; but the concept of dualism in beliefs and values is used by many on both sides of the argument to explain, for example, conflict over access to, and management of, natural resources. Shifting notions of indigenousness are being constructed as a means to obtain international support and funding (Radcliffe et al, 2001).

The first half of the last century saw the growth of a self-conscious working class and the development of a trade union movement that identified poverty as a class issue. After the 1952 revolution, the overriding public identity of the rural poor became that of *campesinos* (peasants), rather than *indigenos* (indigenous groups). Universal suffrage, nationalization of the major industries, agrarian reform and labour legislation were efforts by the state to establish a more egalitarian and less exploitative political and economic system. Despite this (and subsequent reforms during the 1990s, such as the new constitution and greater recognition of indigenous land rights), the Spanish language and the European way of doing things largely continued unchallenged. Furthermore, the impetus of the 1952 revolution rapidly disappeared; parliamentary democracy collapsed, to be followed by almost two decades of military dictatorships and repressive regimes.

James Dunkerly (1984, pxi) refers to Bolivia as a country 'with a reputation'. Its reputation was one of political instability – of military governments and peasant rebellions. Since 1982, with the re-establishment of democracy and subsequent major economic reforms, its reputation has changed. It has become an example of a developing country that wholeheartedly adopted the 'Washington Consensus' model of economic development. Bolivia was seen by the World Bank and other international agencies as a model for inclusive and participatory approaches to development. Thus, Bolivia seemed one of the prime candidates for preparing a nationally owned and high-quality PRSP that would make fast-track progress to the IMF and World Bank boards and thus to debt relief. In fact, it took an unanticipated 18 months to move from the approval of the interim PRSP to endorsement of the full PRSP and the required Bolivian legislation to distribute the debt relief in support of poverty reduction.

A poverty reduction strategy for Bolivia

The PRSP has been conceived not only as obligatory for securing access to debt relief, but also as the basis for World Bank International Development Association (IDA) credit and IMF programme support. Many bilateral donors were also prepared to realign their own aid programmes to the PRSP.

The PRSP has been seen by many in the international cooperation community as a highly significant development, linking aid to a systematic, long-term attempt by the recipient government to reduce poverty. Unlike earlier instruments and procedures, such as structural adjustment programmes, the basic principle of the PRSP is national ownership. Experience had taught that governments would only implement policies in which they believed; thus, policies for poverty reduction would not be sustainable unless locally identified. As yet unexplored is the potential reaction of the IMF and World Bank boards should a government write a PRSP that was very much locally owned, but which proposed policies distasteful to donors.[2] For Bolivia, this scenario was always unlikely. First, as a pilot for the Comprehensive Development Framework (CDF), it has been at the cutting edge of government and donors working together in a coordinated manner. Second, I would argue that the close relationship established between the local authors of the PRSP, on the one hand, and the donor community, on the other, is also due to their sharing a similar professional, racial and class background. As discussed in the following section, it all depends upon what we mean by local ownership – the capacity for a highly divided and unequal society to agree collectively on how best to reduce poverty.

The conventional wisdom of the international community assumes that broad-based ownership of the PRSP *is* possible. Following on from the successes of participatory rural appraisal (PRA), participatory poverty assessments (PPAs) and the recent highly publicized World Bank–DFID–Institute of Development Studies *Voices of the Poor* exercise, broad-based participation, particularly that of poor people, has become accepted as an essential element in designing and monitoring successful poverty reduction strategies (McGee with Norton, 2000).

In its ideal form, the PRSP would be a very sophisticated document. Tracing the links between poverty analysis, policy prescription, costing, budgeting, monitoring and consultation with poor people is a very tall order and one that has rarely been attempted by donor governments in their own countries. Many of us in the donor community knew this. We were upping the ante because earlier, more limited, instruments (projects, sector-wide approaches, structural adjustment credit) had often failed to make any impact in those countries with the biggest problems of deep-rooted poverty.

In Bolivia, the process of the design of the PRSP was characterized by three key issues: the definition of poverty reduction, the scope of the PRSP and the design of the required participatory process.

Poor and rich, Bolivians and foreigners (including donor staff) variously interpret and reshape the institutional *definition* of, and response to, poverty. Perhaps because of the very cultural complexity of Bolivian society, there may be a greater explicit appreciation of this definitional challenge than might be the case in some other aid-dependent countries. The 2000 *Human Development Report* for Bolivia (UNDP, 2000) is an interesting example of the importance attached to people's and communities' values for defining and implementing locally owned action to reduce poverty.

Poverty reduction has only become an important issue for Bolivian ruling classes during the last few years, and the Bolivian government's understanding of how to tackle poverty had evolved little during this time. In line with the *World Development Report* (WDR) 1990, poverty reduction was expected to be achieved through a twin-track unlinked approach of human capital investment and economic growth. Poor people were to be helped through enhancing their access to social services.

Some elements of civil society were not of the same opinion. Their views, supported at the start of the PRSP process by those bilateral donors who had moved beyond the Washington Consensus, led to a growing insistence on an integrated model of social and economic development that would include tackling the deep-seated problems of the political economy. The severe social unrest during September and October 2000, with protests over land and water issues, eventually brought home to the political rulers the importance that poor people attach to livelihoods, as well as access to social services.

The bilateral donor community in La Paz established a network to support the PRSP process. In a position paper, shared with government, the international finance institutions and civil society, we argued that the traditional approach to poverty reduction did not address the political and economic causes, characteristics and consequences of poverty. The final version of the PRSP reflected this new integrated approach to poverty reduction with an emphasis (although little policy prescription) on the need to tackle economic and social exclusion.

As a result, how to reduce poverty was linked to the question of the *scope* of the PRSP. It brought into play the different perspectives of the donor community, wedded to the *theory* of the PRSP – as, for example, in the DFID briefing paper on PRSPs (DFID, 2000) – and the more pragmatic, locally rooted, view of many of our Bolivian interlocutors. The latter saw the PRSP as an instrument to achieve debt relief and were not interested in a PRSP as the overarching framework for all public policies and expenditure. Too polite to tell us this directly, they were clearly sceptical as to how it could be an all-encompassing solution to Bolivia's deeply structured and complex problems of poverty, exclusion and inequality. Even in the short term, the coalition government was not sufficiently unified and visionary to be able to identify and *prioritize* medium-term pro-poor policies and actions. In these circumstances, believed our pragmatic Bolivian friends, it would surely be *more than good enough*

BOX 4.1 THE NATIONAL DIALOGUE

The National Dialogue was a government initiative, run by an independent secretariat and funded by international cooperation through the United Nations Development Programme (UNDP). It lasted from May to September 2000. Its principal conclusions were:

- 100 per cent of the HIPC2 resources would be transferred directly and automatically to the municipal governments through a special 'fight against poverty' account.
- 30 per cent of the resources would be distributed equally to all nine departments. The remaining 70 per cent would be distributed according to agreed poverty criteria, with the poorest municipalities getting a greater proportion.
- The resources would be used for economic infrastructure; support to productivity; education; health; water and sanitation; land rights; and institutional and policy issues. Concerning health and education, it was agreed that there would be a gradual and voluntary devolution of the management of these services to local government in relation to the capacity of municipalities to take on this responsibility. Access to HIPC resources would not be conditioned by, or related to, this transfer of responsibility. Those municipalities that opted for devolution could use the resources for running costs, as well as infrastructure; the remainder could only invest in infrastructure.
- Social control mechanisms would be strengthened at the local government level. At the departmental and national level, the Church would convoke civil society to agree upon the appropriate mechanism.

These elements were included in the PRSP, which was eventually approved by the World Bank and IMF boards in June 2001.

---

if the PRSP process were to result in a popular consensus on the transparent and equitable use of the funds to be made available from debt relief. In response to the international community requirement to have broad-based participation in the design of the PRSP, the Bolivians designed the National Dialogue (see Box 4.1); but they designed this around the down-to-earth question of how to spend the debt relief.

The vice-president (since August 2002, interim president) was the leader among the reformers in the government and its principal contact with donors. As such, he had overall responsibility for the commitment to design a PRSP as a participatory process. The National Dialogue was meant to start in early 2000, following the approval of the interim PRSP; but within the government there was disagreement between the young reformers and the older 'dinosaurs' as to whether it should take place at all. Those politicians who were always antagonistic to participatory processes subsequently alleged that the National Dialogue had opened up a Pandora's box in which all aggrieved interest groups felt at liberty to challenge the state and weaken democratic institutions. In fact, the government only finally agreed to launch the dialogue *following* an outbreak of severe social unrest in April, after which ministers identified the dialogue as a means to achieve constructive engagement with society at large. The next section discusses the factors influencing the design and ownership of the National Dialogue.

Despite being funded by donors, their overall influence on the National Dialogue process was probably not that significant, beyond the general point that a consultative process was required by the international community for approval of the PRSP. Despite the urging of local donor representatives, such as myself, that the dialogue should be a broad-based consultation – directly involving poor people – on the nature of poverty and how to tackle it, the focus of consultation was the use of debt relief. At the same time, while the design and implementation of the dialogue successfully maintained a consultation framework that prevented any major challenge to the Washington Consensus, there *was* sufficient room for manoeuvre for the final conclusions to include the importance of livelihoods for poverty reduction. Nevertheless, the government refused to permit discussion on the fundamental principles of the economic model despite economic liberalization discernibly not having made any improvement in poor people's livelihoods. This rejection of an informed discussion may well have contributed to the growth in popularity among poor people of the authoritarian and demagogic indigenous leaders who are challenging the Bolivian state.

Power and relationships in the PRSP process

The PRSP concept assumes certain pre-conditions for successful implementation. The challenge for donors in seeking to introduce the PRSP to Bolivia was that this instrument, conceived and designed at the international level, could not take into account the specific context of the difficult relations between state and society resulting from the Andean region's post-Conquest history.

Local ownership?

Social structures in Bolivia allow development cooperation professionals to feel rapidly included within Bolivian society, easily making a circle of friends through professional, sporting and cultural activities, with their children going to the same school. The very high levels of professional competence and education among the Bolivians with whom we usually mix makes the issues of 'ownership' and 'accountability' rather different from those countries where even the ruling elite is only one generation away from European colonial rule.[3] This may be one reason why the Comprehensive Development Framework has been a success. Perhaps the donor community in Bolivia may therefore be particularly vulnerable to this concept because the Bolivians with whom they mix most of the time do share with them a belief in the importance of the World Bank/IMF-supported reforms; there is no problem of local 'ownership'. Our pattern of social relations may also send out unintended signals concerning the extent to which we really care about political and social change in favour of poverty reduction. The Bolivian newspaper with the widest circulation in La Paz has a daily social/gossip column illustrated with photographs of the capital's elite at a round of luxurious parties and receptions who very frequently include donor representatives.

The major state policies formulated over the last 15 years with strong international support, such as privatization of state-owned industries and education sector reform, have been genuinely 'owned' by many in the Bolivian elite, but angrily rejected by those who feel politically and economically excluded. Some observers allege that even the clearly less contentious reintroduction of democracy within Bolivia, along with public policies, such as the Popular Participation Law, can be seen as attractive window dressing behind which the local elite and the international community collude to maintain the status quo (Gray-Molina, 2001).

'Ownership' thus becomes a tricky issue in which the dynamics of who in Bolivian society is supporting which kind of reform can change from day to day in relation to the political dynamic. The rest of this section considers how, in pursuit of a good PRSP, donors became caught up with four facets of this political dynamic.

Civil society and the PRSP

Important elements of civil society[4] started a consultation process on how to spend the debt relief independently of the government process. Because the government dragged its feet on the National Dialogue, a parallel event had a head start. This was the Foro 2000 (Forum 2000), set up by the Catholic Church but involving many other parts of civil society. The conclusions from this forum were integrated within the final written conclusions of the dialogue, and the Church was assigned a major leadership role in establishing the social control systems for monitoring expenditure. Many ordinary Bolivians undoubtedly have greater faith in the Church than in any state institution or in the country's democratic system. The prestige gained by the Catholic Church as a result of this process strengthened its capacity during late 2000 and the first half of 2001 to become increasingly influential as a political arbitrator. For example, it forced the quarrelling political party leaders to agree upon a solution to the problem of the legitimacy of the national election commission and took the lead in seeking to resolve the ever-more-frequent violent conflicts breaking out between the state and disaffected sections of the population.[5]

From my own visits around the country, it appears that perhaps the majority of Bolivians have never heard of, or participated in, the National Dialogue. However, many local communities, particularly in rural areas, participated in demonstrations and uprisings that have been described by one government minister as 'the other dialogue'. In April 2000, October 2000 and July 2001, under threat of widespread and prolonged disruption, the increasingly weak coalition government signed agreements with these 'anti-systemic' movements. In between these major events, the government gave way to the demands of specific interest groups, such as pensioners, co-operative miners and education workers, so that it appeared to be spending its whole time (as people remarked) 'clearing road blocks and signing agreements'. The press accused the government of 'dialogitis' and the donor community wondered how to support both state and society so that policies could be identified through informed consultation, rather than the traditional behaviour of confrontation.

Donors in Bolivia have, as yet, no relationship with the 'anti-systemic' movement. This is led by leaders of indigenous origin and the remnants of the old formal-sector trade union movement, which includes in its demands the rescinding of most of the major reforms that are either funded by, or are conditions of, foreign aid. However, we do have relations of varying closeness with those other parts of civil society who claim to represent the interests of poor people. These include the Catholic Church and Bolivian non-governmental organizations (NGOs) who have close links with international NGOs. These organizations secured funding from the donor community to help their participation in the National Dialogue. Many of the NGO leaders are from the old elite who lost their landed estates during the agrarian reform but who remain politically influential and are part of that 'society' with whom donors mingle. It is questionable whether poor people perceive these NGOs as their representatives, or themselves as their clients.

A third category of organizations lies somewhere between what government officials think of as the 'safe' and the 'unsafe' parts of civil society; they are slightly 'unsafe' because government officials have occasionally expressed concern about our supporting such organizations. It was these organizations, such as the Committee for Small Producers and the Federation of Municipal Authorities, who began to play a leading role in defining how the PRSP should be implemented and monitored, challenging the Church as the sole guardian of poor people's interests. Generally, such organizations have greater legitimacy than the NGOs because they are coalitions of representative grassroots bodies. This, and their preparedness to change the system (rather than overthrow it), gives them considerable potential power and influence, provided that they stay in touch with their constituencies. For example, by late 2001, the Committee for Small Producers had taken advantage of a more reformist administration to broaden economic development policies to respond to small as well as big business interests.[6]

Nevertheless, there are risks to donor relations with the state when supporting such organizations. First, they are more actively involved (or co-opted) within the clientelist relations of the party political system and can be accused of interfering with local politics. Second, the leadership cannot always manage the frustrations and grievances of constituent members, as for example with the Committee of Small Producers when the co-operative miners marched into La Paz and fought a running battle with the police, using sticks of dynamite from their mines as weapons.

Local communities

On the whole, donors connect to local community organizations through civil society organizations or local government leaders. These intermediaries introduce us to 'ordinary poor people' when we visit rural areas or urban slums. Both the people and their intermediaries appear to believe that the visiting donor, because of his or her control over the allocation of valuable resources, has more power and influence with the government than we, the donors, assume to be the case. At the same time, local leaders are more interested in securing direct access to our money, rather than in our influencing government, municipalities or NGOs to spend these resources on their behalf. They tend to be deeply suspicious of the capacity or willingness of those outside their local community to be genuinely committed to helping them. Thus, they express deep concern about the new donor approach of coordination around the PRSP, within which the government takes the lead in consultation with 'civil society' and where we give budgetary support rather than fund specific projects in poor communities.

The clientelistic nature of state–society relations identifies the donor as a potential 'good' patron of poor people. Today, this is a patron who abandons her responsibility and wilfully gives money, destined for poor people, to the corrupt organs of the state that have never helped poor people in the past – so why should they in the future?[7] Ironically, we are not listening to the voices of the poor themselves when, with the best of intentions, we pursue this new approach.

Party politics and the PRSP

Bolivia has a significant number of political parties, usually leading to split voting and non-majority government; in the administration of 1997–2002 three (previously five) parties made up the coalition. Government tends to be led alternately by one of three main parties (ADN, MNR, MIR). Although none of these parties has monolithic structures, or policies aligned to broad social movements, each of them has organizational structures reaching down to local level to 'mobilize' votes through the use of patronage. Parties tend to be led by charismatic leaders who are members of the economic elite and have very weak internal consultative mechanisms. Rank-and-file members of the parties belong because of the economic benefits accrued and have very little voice in the setting of policy. Many poor people, particularly indigenous women, do not possess identity cards and are not registered to vote.

Politicians, including many running sectoral ministries, initially took very little interest in the National Dialogue or in the substance of the PRSP, the latter being largely seen as the responsibility of technicians in the Ministry of Finance working to fulfil the debt relief conditions. According to the DFID briefing on the PRSP, one key element of ownership is that a wide variety of groups must be involved in this debate and priority setting, including political opposition parties. Thus, concerned by the lack of broad interest in the drafting of the document, the bilateral network undertook to engage with a wider range of actors to encourage their participation. Table 4.1 is the action matrix we developed in November 2000 to take this forward.

Despite these efforts, politicians in the parties that form part of the coalition government took little interest and, to make a short-term political point, the principal opposition party (MNR) made it clear that it had no commitment to the PRSP.

The formal PRSP process in Bolivia culminated in a National Dialogue Law. This law establishes the modalities for the distribution of the debt relief resources on the basis of poverty criteria, as well as society's right to monitor

Table 4.1 *Action matrix, November 2000*

Who	What	How
Vice-president	Cross-sectoral policy prioritization; political consensus	?
Minister of finance	Personal commitment; public expenditure priorities	Meeting with minister
Sectoral ministries	Getting into the process; identification of sector policy priorities	Taking advantage of routine project/programme meetings to discuss PRSP
Civil society	Sharing information; supporting their engagement	Meeting civil society representatives; funding relevant activities
Politicians	Commitment to PRSP as a strategic vision for Bolivia	Informal lobbying at social functions; discreet meetings
IMF/Inter-American Development Bank (IDB)/ World Bank	Engagement on policy issues, as well as on resources for PRSP	Lunch to discuss on Friday 1 December at 1 pm
National Statistical Institute	Interest in monitoring PRSP outcome	Network starts informal discussions

the state's performance in the management of these resources ('social control'). It also provides for regular dialogues to monitor the implementation of the PRSP. The law was seen both by the government and by donors as proof that the PRSP was to be more than a bit of paper. The approval of the law was held up for months by political wrangling and was eventually passed at the end of July 2001. The press alleged that the delay in approval was due to the UCS party (part of the coalition) having held up its progress through congress in an attempt to maintain party political control of the Highways Agency. This agency was one of Bolivia's biggest money spinners, and donors had insisted that it be cleaned up as a condition of further aid for road-building and maintenance. From the UCS perspective, it was giving the donors a difficult choice: a National Dialogue Law or a reformed Highways Agency. We achieved the first and then, unexpectedly, the second when the vice-president took over the presidency from the ailing President Banzer in August 2001.

The bilateral donors saw the problems with political parties' lack of interest in the PRSP and the delay in passing the law as a significant symptom of the fundamental political and institutional problems facing the country. Nevertheless, according to the previously established rules of the game, the IMF and World Bank boards were to endorse the PRSP on the *quality* and *credibility* of the document itself. They were not to make an assessment of its political viability (and the boards chose to ignore the main opposition party's public disclaimer). The Bolivian PRSP was of a high standard and written by its own nationals, compared with papers in some other HIPC countries. The bilaterals argued that the unfavourable political, institutional and social environment in which the poverty reduction strategy was to be implemented undermined its credibility; but the conventional view was that this was not a matter for the boards to take into account. It may well be that we had become victims of our own enthusiastic attachment to a genuine all-encompassing poverty reduction strategy, which we felt needed to have a real chance of being successfully implemented.

The struggle over decentralization

The National Dialogue was designed to keep alive the flame of decentralization, introduced through the Popular Participation Law under the previous administration. With the blessing of the vice-president, it was designed by *municipalistas* (those promoting a strong local government system), on loan from various donor-funded local government projects. The design assumed that local government leaders would genuinely reflect the interests and views of poor people, despite this being highly questionable (Blackburn, 2000). Furthermore, only as an afterthought was it decided to add a token woman to the municipal team of local government leaders, who were to represent the views of all the people in their municipality. The gender dimension of poverty was not significantly addressed in the National Dialogue or in the PRSP itself despite energetic efforts by the then vice-minister for gender affairs.[8] A vice-ministry was largely dependent upon donor financing for its survival; it had very little credibility with the drafting team from the Ministry of Finance and the donor voice was equally disregarded.

As mentioned earlier, most poor people living in rural areas remained unaware of the National Dialogue (although a greater number were aware of the Church's Forum 2000 event). From the perspective of previous consultative events, the dialogue was a success – and would not have occurred without donor pressure and funding. Nevertheless, it was disappointing that donors such as me, who were interested in promoting more participatory methodologies, could not persuade the secretariat to take advantage of the participatory methodology skills available within the country.[9] With hindsight, it was apparent that the *municipalistas* running the dialogue had other fish to fry – namely, a reassertion of the importance of decentralized government at a time when the current administration was doing little to strengthen local government processes.

Initially, those designing the dialogue did not wish to include civil society organizations, as distinct from municipalities, in the consultation process, seeing them as having no apparent legitimacy in terms of representing poor people's views. They gave way as a result of the decision of the donor community to establish a specific fund within the National Dialogue envelope to encourage civil society participation. Some of those civil society organizations were subsequently highly successful in taking their own agenda forward, most notably the Committee of Small Producers who pushed for a livelihoods, as well as social services, role for municipalities. Nevertheless, the short period of preparation time allowed for the dialogue, and the pre-existing patterns of relations between donors and some elements of civil society, undoubtedly privileged some over others. Furthermore, Bolivia is an example of civil society being very heavily dependent upon foreign aid when seeking to hold the state accountable (see Chapter 12).

The role of local government continued to be debated after the National Dialogue was completed. Health and education ministers declared that they wished to earmark 35 per cent of the HIPC resources for social-sector running costs' deficits. They believed that local governments would not give sufficient priority to health and education. Possibly, elements of racism and class superiority influenced their views regarding the capacity of people in remote municipalities to reach sensible decisions.

Following agreements made at the National Dialogue, municipal representatives afterwards became divided as to whether or not they wanted to take on the responsibility for managing health and education workers who are strongly unionized and frequently go on strike. There was a suspicion that the central government was trying to offload a difficult problem onto the municipalities and, in so doing, not only relieve themselves of the burden but also undermine the capacity of local government to function adequately. This suspicion was strengthened as it seemed that there would be inadequate financial resources to cover the outstanding running costs' deficit.

The donor community expressed concern that reserving 35 per cent of debt relief funds for management by the centre, rather than by local government, was breaking the spirit of the international community's HIPC2 agreement with Bolivia. The government perspective, however, was that we had been working too closely with some 'unsafe' elements of civil society. Some of us, for example, helped set up and fund the Federation of Municipal Associations, one of the major parties in this particular dispute. Ministers were concerned that we had become naive agents in someone else's agenda of political destabilization.

Influences at play in this complex issue thus included not only the long-term cross-party struggle between *municipalistas* and *centralistas* (those promoting a strong central government system), but also:

- the role of the still powerful public-sector trade unions;
- the run-up to the next elections, which made every issue (including the PRSP) vulnerable to political opportunism; and lastly
- the role of international cooperation as perceived champions of causes with which government might disagree.

Eventually, a compromise was agreed and included in the National Dialogue Law. Why the health and education running-costs problem was not discussed frankly and in detail during the dialogue reveals one of the great challenges for Bolivia in constructing a transparent and accountable state. Ministers told me that they felt their role in the dialogue was to listen to society rather than to share information with municipalities and civil society. In other words, it was not a *dialogue*, and although the process has, on balance, given ordinary (if not the poorest) people a stronger voice, a major challenge remains for the state to recognize that the right to information is a prerequisite for mature policy debate.

Conclusion

Has the PRSP in Bolivia been a useful instrument in supporting long-term processes of policy change in favour of poor people ? As a piece of paper, the lifetime of the PRSP is not likely to be very long or very influential. As a *process*, the introduction of the PRSP contributed to some significant changes in priorities and perceptions on poverty reduction.

Firstly, as a result of the National Dialogue process and the international cooperation requirement to use debt relief for poverty reduction, poverty-linked criteria have been established for the distribution of public resources, not only those from HIPC2 but also in relation to the newly consolidated social investment funds. Whereas the Popular Participation Law had assigned resources to the municipalities on a per capita basis, the new law provides for more money for more poor people.

Secondly, the PRSP process of consultation and civil society activism, with donor support, has led to a recognition of the significance of the informal economy as a major potential engine of economic growth. Enhancing the economic productivity of small producers has been established as a new responsibility for both local and central government.

Thirdly, the process has strengthened the mutual recognition between state and civil society of the right of the latter to hold the state accountable, including the need for the state to pursue anti-corruption measures in a much more energetic fashion. More broadly, there is a growing awareness of the fragility of state–society relations and the need to build on the processes of the National Dialogue so that they become more inclusive and genuinely more broad based. The current administration admits that while it seemed to them initially that the dialogue was a success, it clearly was insufficiently inclusive since it was immediately followed by major social unrest.

Whether the PRSP process has been sufficiently useful and robust to help rein in the strong negative processes of a prebendal party political system challenged by authoritarian populism is a moot question. Could the donor community have been more useful in this respect if we had been more pragmatic and less idealistic? Would it have made any difference if, from the start, we had accepted the local proposition that the PRSP was about how to use the debt relief?

The PRSP was 'approved' before the process began. This clearly affected the behaviour and tactics of all those concerned. The bilaterals insisted on institutional reform issues with mixed results. Would we have been more successful if the process had not occurred towards the end of a weak administration, nervous about the forthcoming elections? There may well have been a different outcome with a stronger leadership from the government. The interim administration established in August 2002, following the resignation of the incumbent president, has been able to demonstrate much greater energy in tackling the reform agenda.

The international community perspective on PRSPs is of an instrument that should, ideally, allow us to endorse the mainstream government policy process and to provide budget and sector-wide support. The local representatives of the donor community made energetic efforts for the PRSP process to deliver a dramatically improved policy environment where we would have sufficient confidence in that ideal model of donor–recipient relations. In reality, we find ourselves in the situation described in a DFID briefing on the PRSP:

> *Countries vary – for example, in their political structure and size; in the strength of their governance systems and policy commitments; in their vulnerability to disruption… In a weaker case, we may look for measures that increase transparency and accountability, reinforce the ability of poor people to influence the policy process, and promote more pro-poor alliances.*

Our problem was that Bolivia had been established as an example of the stronger case, and our experience with the PRSP process revealed it to illustrate the weaker. Even so, all in all, we were probably more useful than otherwise in a difficult and painful process in which Bolivians are working out their own solutions to their problems.

Bilateral donor coordination in the PRSP process in Bolivia has become noted in donor head offices as an example of 'good practice'. Nevertheless, it incurred some risks. First, we were possibly undermining the agreed Comprehensive Development Framework principle of the recipient government being in the driving seat. Our implicit message was that government-led donor coordination did not give us the scope to pursue issues that we (but possibly not the government) considered to be important. Second, our close relations with elements of civil society could also imply an undermining of government 'ownership'. Such relations could also be exclusive, with some parts of civil society having privileged access to resources and establishing a dependency relation with the bilateral community to whom, eventually, they will become accountable, rather than to the poor people they are meant to represent. Legitimizing 'social control' through the National Dialogue Law enhances this risk if social control becomes dependent upon foreign aid. An effort is underway in Bolivia to change the donor–government–citizen frame (see Chapter 12).

Some lessons for myself

Reflecting on this experience has helped me to identify a number of lessons for donor relations with recipients. As long as aid remains a phenomenon of global politics, so will donors devise instruments and procedures for controlling that aid, with all the mutual manipulative behaviour that results from this difficult and unequal relationship. We must necessarily work within the current paradox and work on changing our own organizational and personal behaviour as a stepping stone towards a longer-term vision where our rhetoric of participation and ownership begins to gain credibility (see Chapters 13 and 14). Most of the following lessons therefore concern donor behaviour in using our own instruments for a more useful and informed role in supporting long-term processes of policy change in favour of poor people. They are as follows:

- Make an effort to learn about the recipient's history and take into account how people in a recipient country act on their perceptions of their history. Outsiders can sometimes play a useful facilitating role if we give ourselves the time and space to learn, read and listen – and to use the knowledge sensitively as a contribution to a country's effort to build consensus.
- Be pragmatic in the application of the aid instrument and take heed of local advice. While, on paper, less may appear to have been achieved than if we were to be more ambitious, there is more chance of a sustainable outcome. Staff incentive systems may need to change to encourage modesty rather than (apparent) achievement (see Chapter 13).
- Be intuitive rather than conservative in supporting champions of change within government and civil society; but be aware of the risks. Being aware of the risks requires political analysis and a commitment to learning the dynamics of a society; it also means being prepared to make (frequent) errors and learn from these. Once again, it means an organizational culture that encourages *informed* risk-taking (see Chapter 13).
- Consider the power and relationship implications of our social life. At its simplest, this can be avoiding one's name from appearing in the society column. While that is easy, other aspects are much more challenging, particularly for those wanting their children to have a good education (thus, an elite school). While there are no easy answers, self-awareness is a helpful first step.
- Seek to broaden our network of contacts and learn to listen to different points of views, not just those of reformers in government and 'safe' civil society leaders.
- Avoid hiding from poor people and be prepared to face uncomfortable truths that we will often continue to ignore poor people's voices for greater strategic ends. While this seems depressing, donors can give priority to helping people realize their right to information as a contribution to diminishing relations based on dependency and patronage and replacing them with relations based on rights and responsibilities. Donors can provide resources to support a greater two-way flow of information between the state and citizens so that words such as *dialogue* can begin to acquire a real meaning.
- Continue to use conditionality when it can help unblock non-representative political resistance to needed reform, as illustrated with the reform of the Highways Agency.
- Coordination between donors is a powerful means to exert conditionality; but there is a high risk of establishing 'hollow institutions' within the state, which exist only to service donors' demands and, ultimately, are disregarded by those in charge, such as the Vice-Ministry of Gender.
- Seek to support the strengthening of state–society relations without distorting the lines of accountability (see Chapter 12). This may require donors, individually or collectively, giving up 'cosy' relations with particular elements of civil society and apparently losing direct political influence. Ideally, it might mean becoming invisible and, therefore, from a head office perspective, not making any impact!

Notes

1   This chapter was written in late 2001, based primarily on the author's own notes and journal, kept sporadically from March 2000 to August 2001. An earlier draft of the chapter was shown to my colleague, Oscar Antezana, for fact-checking and for feedback on my analysis of events. While I am very grateful for his perspective and comments, the conclusions remain the author's responsibility, and I accept that the commentary on the PRSP process has been overtaken by the events of the 2002 elections and the major political crisis in October 2003. The views presented here are my own and do not represent in any way official DFID policy.

2   Oxfam's comment: 'The IMF and the World Bank note that their boards will "endorse" a country PRSP. This endorsement amounts to a veto on national approaches to development.' Quoted in *The Reality of Aid* (Randel and German, 2001).

3   See Chapter 14, concerning the influence of our own personal attitudes and behaviour in transforming the power–procedures–relationship dynamic.

4   By 'civil society' I mean people organized through social movements, NGOs, churches, trade unions, chambers of commerce, etc, as distinct from 'society', which is a broader concept, including territorially based communities and family networks. The Bolivian government includes elected local government representatives as part of civil society.

5   However, the legitimacy of the Church was challenged by the followers of the Aymara separatist leader Felipe Quispe during the events of July 2001 when a peace-making bishop was beaten up.

6   My threefold categorization is, of course, a simplification. Leading individuals and their networks may move from one category to another, as did the committee's coordinator, who had previously run an NGO umbrella organization. From an elitist background and used to dealing with donors, he was much more 'user friendly' than the working-class men (only one woman) who made up the committee.

7   The history of aid has contributed to reproducing clientelistic relations and created deeply rooted stereotypes and expectations of dependency that also makes this relationship with donors hard to alter at central government level, as much as in villages. Bolivia is one of the world's most aid-dependent countries.

8   Representing DFID, I was one of the funders of the National Dialogue who worried about the inadequate handling of gender concerns; but I failed to persuade the secretariat to change its approach. To no great surprise, it has since emerged that many of these women had been chosen simply because they were the wives or relatives of the mayor.

9   As a consequence of failing to persuade the National Dialogue organizers to change their methodology, DFID separately funded Bolivia's National Working Group on Participatory Methodologies (which had undertaken the World Bank 'Consultations with the Poor' study in 1999) to work simultaneously in a number of selected municipalities. The aim was to illustrate the value of directly involving poor people in poverty diagnosis and policy identification.

References

Albo, X (1999) 'Diversidad Etnica, Cultural y Linguistica', in Toranzo, C et al (eds) *Bolivia en el Siglo XX*, Harvard Club de Bolivia, La Paz

Blackburn, J (2000) *Popular Participation in a Prebendal Society: A Case Study of Participatory Municipal Planning in Sucre, Bolivia*, unpublished PhD thesis, IDS, Brighton, UK

Cardenas, V-H (2001) 'CSUTCB: crisis del liderazgo autoritario y ethnicista', *La Razon (Tiempo Politica)*, La Paz, 19 July

DFID (2000) 'Poverty Reduction Strategies', *Background Briefing*, Department for International Development, London

Dunkerley, J (1984) *Rebellion in the Veins*, Verso, London

Gray-Molina, G (2001) 'Exclusion, participation and state-building', in Crabtree, J and Whitehead, L L (eds) *Towards Democratic Viability*, Palgrave Publishers, St Anthony's, Oxford

McGee, R with Norton, A (2000) *Participation in Poverty Reduction Strategies: A Synthesis of Experience with Participatory Approaches to Policy, Design, Implementation and Monitoring*, Working Paper 109, IDS, Brighton, UK

Osco, M F (2001) 'La Ley de Ayllu: justicia de acuerdos', *Tinkazos*, vol 4, no 9

Radcliffe, S, Laurie, N and Andolina, R (2001) *Transnationalism, Indigenous People and Development in Ecuador and Bolivia*, ESRC Research Briefing on Transnational Communities, no 6

Randel, J and German, T (eds) (2001) *The Reality of Aid: Poverty, Inequality and Aid: Rhetoric and Reality*, Earthscan, London

UNDP (2000) *Informe de Desarrollo Humano en Bolivia 2000*, United Nations Development Programme, La Paz

World Bank (1999) *Consultando con los Pobres*, Reporte Nacional Bolivia

World Bank (2000) *Bolivia from Patronage to a Professional State*, Institutional and Governance Review, World Bank, Washington, DC

5

Questioning, Learning and 'Cutting Edge' Agendas: Some Thoughts from Tanzania

Leslie Groves

Introduction

This chapter provides three case studies from Tanzania that question current approaches to learning and the regular introduction of 'new' 'cutting edge' agendas in development. The author argues that if development initiatives are to truly support the needs of poor people, then there must be more of an emphasis on continuity of process, consistency in approaches and commitment to working with people and relationship-building. In this way, a more inclusive system of aid can be achieved and development practitioners may be able to move away from a system based on organizational imperatives and a constant need to regenerate itself, to a system that has a genuine means to listen to the beneficiaries and thus achieve their goals.

The case studies

I have recently been working in Tanzania, a country that has seen its position on the Human Development Index worsening since 1992,[1] despite the huge presence of donors in the country. Both donors and the government have found themselves in a mutually dependent and yet mutually frustrating relationship, with all the best declared intentions, ideas and funding apparently incapable of lifting the country out of poverty. Tanzania has been a testing ground for many new development initiatives and has one of the highest proportions of overseas development assistance (ODA) to gross national product (GNP) of any developing country.[2] During the last two decades alone, a wide array of 'new' 'cutting edge' ideas have been tested in the country from 'structural adjustment policies',[3] 'process not blueprint projects',[4] 'basket funding' and 'sector-wide approaches'[5] to the most recent initiative of all, the World Bank poverty reduction strategy papers (PRSPs). These strategies have shifted the emphasis away from empowering local communities to empowering national governments to design and implement their own national anti-poverty strategies.[6]

Tanzania was one of the first countries to wholeheartedly embrace the poverty reduction strategy (PRS) process, and donors rushed to be at the cutting edge of this new development framework. The consequences of this rush have been significant and potentially detrimental for poor people, particularly when the organizational realities of donors and government departments have been ignored. While the PRS is based on notions of 'partnership' and 'participation',[7] it is in danger of being unable to deliver either, due largely to the failure of those involved to learn adequately from the lessons of their organizational pasts.

Two short stories from my own experiences in Tanzania are illustrative of the negative consequences of jumping onto the latest development bandwagon without sufficient questioning or learning from past and current experiences. Each story teaches us lessons of its own; but there are also generic issues that arise from both that will be considered later in the chapter.

One story involves a mining community in northern Tanzania. An influential donor, committed to child labour elimination, approached the International Labour Organization (ILO) and indicated its desire to fund a child labour reduction programme in Tanzania. The donor proceeded to set in place a number of procedural hurdles that the ILO would have to jump over before funding could be granted. At the time, the development fashion was that baseline surveys should be carried out to gain a better understanding of where aid could most usefully be granted and to provide a line by which progress could be measured. Furthermore, local communities should be empowered to participate in the design of project proposals and should engage in capacity-building to ensure that they would be able to become active participants in project activities. The aim was that local people would take ownership of the process, ensuring its long-term sustainability. Over a period of three years, during which both organizations expended a great deal of staff time and energy, not to mention financial resources,[8] the ILO commissioned a baseline survey and hired consultants to 'empower' and 'capacity-build' local community members to participate in the design of logical frameworks (logframes) and project proposals. I was also seconded by the donor to the ILO and was therefore actively involved in the 'empowerment' and 'capacity-building' process. The process was needlessly drawn out due to the most common of organizational constraints within and between the two organizations: staff changes; conflicts of personalities and ideologies; unnecessary bureaucratic delays and miscommunications; and unclear and conflicting leadership. All of these issues can be addressed by development agencies; and, yet, a refusal to recognize such organizational realities meant that the process became painful and frustrating for those community members wanting to start direct action to help the project beneficiaries.

While the process in itself was problematic, the situation was made worse by the fact that a decision was made not to follow it through. By the time that all the bureaucratic requirements had been carried out, projects were no longer considered to be 'cutting edge' and, even more astonishingly, were declared by many donor staff to be 'failures', justified by the phrase 'projects don't work', despite evidence of a number of highly successful process projects in Tanzania. Budgetary support on the basis of the PRSP was declared to be 'the only way' to gain national ownership, and in what seemed to be an extremely short space of time the donor decided to 'close its books'– that is, stop funding projects altogether to make way for the PRS. Community members involved in project design and capacity-building workshops felt that they had completed their end of the bargain – they had attended workshops, hosted donors and donated land, time and resources to the project. Despite this, the result was that they were left with nothing but shattered expectations. The start-up funds needed for the project never arrived.[9]

The central lesson from this story is the failure of the donor organizations to sustain an ethical commitment either to a particular community or to a defined process. The delays in setting up the project were caused by internal organizational constraints within both organizations and not by those in the community committed to setting up the project. Yet, despite this, the project was discarded at precisely the moment when it had the most chance of becoming sustainable: after the necessary research, 'participation', 'empowerment' and 'capacity-building' had been carried out. What will happen when another development fashion comes into being? Will those communities of poor people who have given time and resources to the process be left, once again, with nothing? This is not to say that development activities that have proved to be unsuccessful in reducing poverty should be continued purely out of an ethical commitment to individual groups of people, but that initiatives which are positive should be developed and learned from – not merely dropped due to new fashion or avoidable bureaucratic failures. Development takes time.

The second story involves an established project in Rujewa, southern Tanzania: the Sustainable Management of the Usangu Wetland and Its Catchment (SMUWC) project. The project aimed to develop local capacity to manage the Usangu wetland and its catchment for the benefit of all stakeholders, particularly the poor. I was part of a multi-disciplinary donor team brought in to conduct an Output to Purpose Review (a procedural tool based on the logframe), similar to a mid-term evaluation. The first phase of the project was nearing completion and the project team was looking for renewed donor funding for the second phase. The evaluation team made a unanimous recommendation that second-phase funding should be given on the basis that the project had been extremely successful in meeting its targets. Furthermore, it had succeeded in influencing national policy from the bottom up, as seen in the development of the new National Water Policy.[10]

The project had successfully taken an innovative approach to project design, focusing on community empowerment, capacity-building and participatory poverty research. The aim was that the voices of poor people should remain at the forefront of project design and implementation. A process approach was adopted to ensure that capacity was built at a local level, which in turn would help to ensure local ownership. Procedures were used flexibly and in a participatory way. Local staff were trained in using the procedures as required by international donors. The behaviours and attitudes of international staff were very much ones of facilitation, rather than of preaching or teaching. The key strength of the project was that it invested considerably in developing a participatory approach to design, as well as to research. Local opinions were sought and incorporated that had positive implications for the long-term sustainability of the management plan.

Benefits flowed to a diverse range of stakeholders in the local communities. For example, village environment committees have been set up and provided with training in environmental management and planning. The committees bring together different resource users to resolve existing conflicts over resources and attempt to develop village land plans. Through these committees the villagers of two villages got together to build bricks for the construction of their dispensary and primary school; another village raised funds to build community wells; and conflicts between livestock herders and cultivators in another village have been resolved through the village land plans. Throughout phase 1, responsibility was gradually handed over to local government, and qualified and experienced local staff were used not only for research but also for management – key to local acceptance and ownership of the process.

However, due to the rapid change in donor policy – from one of supporting projects that empowered local communities to one of empowering national governments, as described above – phase 2 was not given funding. The decision not to give funding took almost one year, which meant that project staff were forced to spend the limited time remaining in their phase 1 contracts in a state of confusion, not sure whether they should be winding down the project, developing further plans for phase 2 or seeking alternative funding. Fortunately, project staff were committed enough to develop strategies for all three options. This, however, was a needless waste of limited energy and resources. The donor should have been clearer regarding its intentions to 'close its books'. The primary issue here was internal to the donor agency. Different staff had different ideas about the speed with which projects should be closed down after the introduction of the PRSPs. While many staff felt that this project should be extended, management wanted the books to be closed as fast as possible. This internal organizational conflict meant that mixed messages were sent to the project stakeholders. Again, the poor paid the highest price.

This story highlights, once again, the issue of ethical commitment to declared intentions. If donors are to engage with a population, this commitment must be long term, particularly if funded projects are seen as successful by all stakeholders. The reality of aid, however, is that while the overall agenda is long term and geared to more abstract, ideological goals, such as 'elimination of poverty', the objectives of particular organizations are short term and results oriented. Projects and strategies tend to have a two- to five-year life span. Staff remain in particular appointments for around three years and then move on. Their successors may not be as keen to focus on the same issues for a number of reasons. New staff may have new ideas about 'what works'. If an approach is not seen as successful within a few years, it may be abandoned and a new one adopted. Furthermore, it must not be forgotten that the ultimate accountability of most donor organizations is to their taxpayers or sponsors at home, rather than to poor people themselves. This means that results must be tangible within a short time frame, such as an electoral term or a financial year. Greater honesty in recognizing this is important if development practitioners[11] are to learn from mistakes, as well as learn from the positive experiences of projects such as the one just described. This lesson is important in the PRSP process: although the stick has now, in theory, been handed over to national government, donor funds are still going to be used by local government at the local level. As a result, there needs to be an ethical commitment to ensuring that funds are available in the long term or that there is, at least, a commitment to ensure an adequate winding-down phase.

A third story from Tanzania highlights the value of persisting with one agenda, of learning from mistakes, and of moving forward along one path instead of consistently jumping from one rock to the next in a haphazard fashion. The Rural Integrated Project Support Programme (RIPS) was initiated in 1988 by the Finnish Department for International Cooperation (Finnaid) and the Tanzanian government. This programme provides a contrast to the two previous Tanzanian examples, and reveals the positive consequences that can result when a donor and a national government learn lessons from unsatisfactory outcomes and choose to continue with a particular programme, while modifying its direction as an outcome of learning. As a result, the programme has achieved a great deal in terms of improving the lives of poor people in two regions in Tanzania.

Finnaid started to support a water programme in Lindi and Mtwara regions almost two decades ago. The primary focus was the construction of boreholes and dams. The first phase ended in 1993 and the evaluation report indicated that project implementation was not adequately reaching poor people or responding to their needs. In fact, water sources had been abandoned, were eroded or were simply not working. Rather than drop the programme, the Finnish and Tanzanian governments took the courageous decision to continue with funding and to learn from the mistakes of the first phase in order to design a better second phase, which would take a comprehensive approach to assisting poor people in their efforts to achieve sustainable livelihoods. Consequently, phase 2 was designed through a participatory and community-based planning process. The earlier top-down implementation framework was dropped and replaced with a process approach, which aimed at facilitating local communities and government authorities in identifying priorities, available resources and opportunities for local action. The Finnish ambassador recognized that while investing in human resources in terms of changing attitudes, developing skills and mobilizing action was not easily quantifiable, it was an important goal that should continue to be pursued (RIPS, 1998, p9). The results of this flexible approach have been extremely positive. There has been significant progress in changing both attitudes and behaviours of government, as well as community members. People have learned to identify and promote their own priorities, as well as to demand accountability from those receiving funds in their name. Local institutions have been strengthened and a number of highly successful income generation projects have been initiated.

Forty-five per cent of the project budget (co-funded by Finnaid and the Tanzanian government) was spent on local government capacity-building. Local leaders and government staff, among others, were trained in local government reform programmes and participatory rural appraisal (PRA) work. Forty five per cent was spent on agriculture and natural resources – for example, strengthening agricultural extension; developing processing capacities; pest control; irrigation technology; community-based forest management; land tenure programmes; and fish farming. The remaining budget was spent on developing vocational training, primary schools, environmental health programmes, improving transport, and communications and micro-credit programmes.

At a programme level, key achievements are the creation of a replicable and alternative model for development, which has been developed and tested in 850 villages and 120 projects. New institutions, such as non-governmental organizations (NGOs), credit committees and other community-based organizations have been set up. Grassroots planning has been integrated into top-down government bureaucratic systems. There has also been a significant influence on government and donor policies, primarily in developing a more participatory work culture. Most importantly, there has been a noted shift in attitudes, roles and responsibilities. Increasing self-reflection and debate have led to a greater confidence among rural communities and government staff. This has been accompanied by a shift from dependency towards greater self-reliance. Government officials have also come to recognize the value of participatory approaches and the strength of community capacity. This has led to more collaborative work (RIPS, 1998; Widagri Consultants, 1998) and to the sharing of experiences outside the immediate vicinity of the programme. For example, a two-day retreat of permanent secretaries was held in Tarangire, supported by RIPS, entitled 'Whose Priorities in Policy-Making?' The retreat was the first opportunity for such senior government officials to come together to discuss approaches to promote participation in community development (see Ministry of Regional Administration and Local Government, Tanzania, 1999).[12]

While this is an impressive list of activities and achievements, it is important to move from the descriptive plane and attempt to pull out the factors underlying the success of the programme. What can be learned from the experience of RIPS and how does this help to move towards a more inclusive system of aid? The two concepts underlying the development of the programme are continuity and commitment. Both factors were missing in the first two stories. Yet, these two factors are central to any system of aid that aims to be inclusive.

The commitment to learning and innovation in the field meant that officials, whether government or donor staff, came to value the importance of shedding their role of 'professionals' and 'planners' to 'facilitators' and 'negotiators'. Building personal and participatory relationships was seen to be essential to developing sustainable development, which worked in collaboration with local villagers: 'Personal commitments to a coalition of people proved much more important than scientifically adequate project logics, but required a totally different approach to project planning' (L Johansson, cited in Chambers, 1997, p224). There was commitment and continuity on both the donor and Tanzanian sides, including, notably, the two regional commissioners, Colonel Nsa-Kaisi and Colonel Anatoly Tarimo.[13] RIPS staff and consultants, both national and international, also provided long-term commitment to the initiative, both in Tanzania and in Finland. Development professionals from Finland spent periods in Lindi and Mtwara, returning regularly, gaining long-term understanding of the programme and local dynamics, building relationships with key stakeholders and championing the approach in Finland. This continuity and commitment were essential to the success of the programme and to ensuring continued funding by the donor.

RIPS has now been active for over 14 years, a rare occurrence in the short-term framework of most development initiatives. During this time, it has explored and developed new approaches, which have truly sought to empower poor people and to bring them into a more effective dialogue with government. While the process has not always been easy, it has revealed that development – based on a long-term and continuous approach to facilitation and the use of local resources, as well as a long-term ethical commitment to a process and a community – can produce concrete and sustainable results that increase the livelihoods of poor people.

These three stories have revealed that the focus on the new development vision, on 'partnership' with national government and on 'budgetary support' has very real consequences for poor people. While the focus on government poverty-reduction policy is necessary, these stories highlight that important questions need to be asked before discarding all that went before this latest in a long line of development frameworks. Continuity and commitment are key to the development of a more inclusive system of aid and must underlie current moves towards budgetary support and influencing national governments.

One important question arises, however: commitment and continuity to whom? While it is necessary to build relationships with national government, development practitioners should not ignore their commitment to poor people. The development of relationships with civil society will become increasingly crucial if citizens are to hold government to account and ensure that demand is made for effective service provision. Good governance and human rights are thus important considerations in the current policy shift (see Chapter 12). They are particularly important in countries where good governance is not to be taken for granted. What happens to those local groups who have little access to national government and who live in societies where lobbying is conducted by groups with money and power, and not by people who do not have the *pesa kwa chai* or tea money to pay the gatekeepers?[14]

In terms of human rights, there are also a number of questions relating to the current aid framework that need to be considered. For example, in Ethiopia and Rwanda, donors are pressing ahead with budgetary support, despite proven human rights abuses and governance issues. What happens when a donor government has internally conflicting policy? Whose interests come first: those of the donor agency or those of its national business interests? The controversy over the sale of the UK military air traffic control system to the Tanzanian government illustrates the hypocrisy of a donor government that, on the one hand, gives UK£65 million of budgetary support to a national government on the basis that it is spent on poverty eradication, while, on the other, selling them an inappropriate and overpriced military defence system at the cost of UK£28 million. This military system was worth almost half of the 2001 aid allocation by the UK. Tanzanian civil society groups criticized the Tanzanian government for a lack of transparency on the sale and the UK government for issuing the licence for a system that is 'inconsistent with their international aid, debt relief and sustainable development policies' (see IRIN, 2001). Surely this goes entirely against the PRSP push for encouraging poverty-focused, transparent policy-making?

In an environment that prides itself upon open debate, it is worrying that such questions are so rarely asked within donor circles. If there are voices, these voices are muted to whispers over coffee or at a dinner party and are rarely voiced aloud, for fear, perhaps, of being branded as unable to engage in 'cutting edge thinking'. Yet, the questions need to be asked.

The issue of incentive systems within donor agencies is pertinent in answering some of these questions. In the current environment, rewards seem to be given to those at the 'cutting edge'. The 'cutting edge' of what, however? It would seem that the term applies to those who argue for bureaucratic change, and who rush headlong to implement the latest thinking from above, which – while seemingly dramatic – is only peripheral in terms of improving the lives of poor people. We are only taken to the edge, yet refuse to look into the mirrored abyss where we see that effective development involves dramatic change from within – not just skirting around the edges with so-called organizational restructuring, but transforming the fundamental ways in which we, as development agents, relate to our 'beneficiaries'.

Donors are happy to hand over power to governments on the basis of PRSPs; but this power is granted on donors' terms to discuss issues that donors feel to be of priority: education, health, etc. These sectors still require funds from the gift-givers, from donors, and therefore may not give governments or civil society autonomy to make their own decisions, to cut the umbilical cord, to take responsibility for their own mistakes, to develop their own fund-raising strategies. Reward is given to those instigating the next big policy shift, not to those who advocate the need to look at the context – at the history – or to learn from our own development successes, as well as mistakes. As the first story revealed, in Tanzania closure of projects to make way for PRSPs happened in a haphazard manner. In a relatively short space of time, it was decided that 'projects don't work', regardless of the fact that among the so-called 'failed' projects there were a number of extremely successful ones to be learned from in relation to future development initiatives. Moreover, the relationships that had been established within these projects are vital for an active civil society in the 'new world' where government has to be held to account.

Yet, instead of building on the lessons from our past, once again a new approach has been rushed in with negative consequences for those local people whom development agencies claim to be so desperately trying to help. Expectations were raised that financial assistance would be forthcoming once 'capacity' had been built and people had been sufficiently 'empowered'. At the end of the day, however, the long-term financial assistance did not arrive and was, instead, diverted to PRSP-related initiatives.

Of course, we all want to see a new way and a tangible reduction in poverty; but there needs to be pause for breath and time for reflection. One moment, civil society in many countries in the North as well as in the South was celebrating its success in getting debt relief onto the global agenda, the next there was a new solution: debt repayment would be conditional on the development of certain poverty strategies. While laudable, the fact that this is still a condition is hardly mentioned; nor is the fact that poverty strategies supposedly developed with the full participation of civil society have seen key issues suggested by civil society dropped at the last minute in a more than hushed-up fashion. Furthermore, power relations remain the same as under previous initiatives in that Southern governments are forced to second guess what the World Bank and other donors want to see in the document, rather than producing a national plan that truly reflects the needs and aspirations of their people. In times of despair, any rescue line is grabbed at; but surely we need to learn from the lessons of structural adjustment policies and their predecessors? Time for reflection is essential.

Structural adjustment policies forced national governments to cut back on spending on social sectors, which led to donors funding local-level projects to ensure that basic levels of health and education could be met. Donors are now cutting their funds to these local communities and giving them back to national governments to spend on the very same social sectors that, not so long ago, they had told the same governments to cut back on. Will the next swing of the fickle development pendulum be a return to local-level projects in ten years' time when PRSPs are deemed to be a failure and poverty has continued to increase? Perhaps the inherently pessimistic nature of the development agenda needs to be turned on its head: from a focus on failure, which historically leads to a rush to the next 'new' 'cutting edge' initiative, to looking at those successful experiences that have had a positive impact on communities, such as the three cases described here.

Through learning from the positive as well as the negative experiences, development practitioners may be able to move away from a system based on organizational imperatives and a constant need to regenerate itself, to a system that has a genuine means to listen to the beneficiaries and thus achieve their goals, as highlighted in the RIPS case. There needs to be a continuity of process, a consistency in approaches and a commitment to working with people and relationship-building. In this way, a more inclusive system of aid can be possible and will avoid the situations illustrated by the first two cases, where local communities jump over the hurdles set by the donors only to be let down when support is most needed.

The overarching lesson from the three stories is, therefore, one of ethical commitment to the communities with which we work. It is one of breaking down the power relations between 'us' and 'them'. It is one of recognizing that we are all humans, and although we may make mistakes, we have the responsibility to learn from these and not just continue to repeat the same ones again and again. If we continue with our fickle, pessimistic and short-term development practices, we will never reach our optimistic and long-term goal of poverty elimination.

Notes

1   From 126th in 1992 to 150th by 1998 (UNDP, 2000, p30), and to 156th in 1999 (UNDP, 2000, p1). Although this had risen to 140th in the *Human Development Report 2001* (UNDP, 2001), this was still well below the figure of 1992 and earlier years.

2   Between 30 to 50 per cent throughout the 1990s. For a useful perspective on aid dependence in Tanzania, see Catterson and Lindhael (1999).

3   Countries requiring International Monetary Fund or World Bank loans had to adhere to structural adjustment policies that prioritized debt repayment with a condition that countries should devalue their currency and cut back on government expenditures. The tragic consequences of this policy were cutbacks to vital health and education provision. See Hilary (2002).

4   In a 'blueprint' project, objectives were fixed, time frames were predetermined and costs had to be set. The 'process' approach is designed to cater for changes in the project environment, offering more flexibility in developing objectives and methods. Participation of project stakeholders is encouraged, with an emphasis on learning and capacity-building.

5   Through this framework government funds were pooled with non-earmarked donor funds into a 'basket' funding system for implementation of approved plans. These plans and funds were allocated to particular sectors as opposed to individual projects – for example, health or education – hence the term sector-wide approach.

6   The theoretical strength of these strategies is that they are designed by national governments (rather than according to donor priorities) through a participatory process, involving civil society and development partners. In this way, all actors should be united behind a common strategy, increasing the chances of wider and more sustained impact. For a more detailed explanation of poverty reduction strategies, see Chapter 2 and www.worldbank.org/poverty/strategies.

7   Words such as 'participation', 'empowerment' and 'ownership' are placed in inverted commas to highlight that they are contested terms. Often donors use the terms without ensuring that there is genuine 'participation', 'ownership' or 'empowerment'. See Chapter 2 and Cornwall (2000).

8   The direct costs were over US$140,000, not including the staff time of employees on permanent contracts.

9   At the time of publication, more than three years after the decision not to fund the project was made and almost six years after original discussions, leftover funds from previous activities were found to support project implementation. While this is a relief for those involved in the work, the granting of funding was due to good fortune and leftover funding, rather than to the recognition of the need to continue with the process. On a positive note, there are currently signs that the ILO is aiming to support the community through its new Time Bound Programme.

10   See SMUWC (2001) for a detailed report of the project.

11   This includes those from the North and South or working for government, NGOs or other donors. While the group is clearly extremely diverse in terms of agendas and approaches, I would argue that the issues raised are worth consideration by all.

12   A year later when the regional administrative secretaries had a retreat at Lobo, the first day was devoted to participation (at the initiative of the permanent secretary who had been at Tarangire), with inputs from RIPS staff.

13 Another knock-on effect of RIPS is that when Colonel Tarimo was posted to another region, he introduced participatory approaches and methods very effectively there, with some donor support (pers comm).

14 A review by McGee et al (2002) of participation in the development of PRSPs revealed that civil society in many countries, including Tanzania, found it very difficult to engage with the process at all, and this was reflected in their failure to significantly influence PRSP content.

References

Catterson, J and Lindhael, K (1999) 'The Sustainability Enigma: Aid Dependency and the Phasing out of Projects. The Case of Swedish Aid to Tanzania', *Expert Group on Development Issues*, Almqvist and Wiksell International, Stockholm

Chambers, R (1997) *Whose Reality Counts: Putting the First Last*, Intermediate Technology Publications, London

Cornwall, A (2000) *Beneficiary, Consumer, Citizen: Perspectives on Participation for Poverty Reduction*, Sida Studies no 2, Gothenburg, Sida

Hilary, J (2002) 'Structural Adjustment Policies', OneWorld Guides, OneWorld.Net website, www.oneworld.net/guides/sap/, accessed 3 July 2002

IRIN (2001) 'Tanzania: Critics Decry Purchase of Air Traffic Control System', News, IRIN website, www.irinnews.org/report.asp?ReportID=20848, accessed 4 July 2002

McGee, R with Levene, J and Hughes, A (2002) *Assessing Participation in Poverty Reduction Strategy Papers: A Desk Based Synthesis of Experience in Sub-Saharan Africa*, IDS Research Report no 52, IDS, Brighton, UK

Ministry of Regional Administration and Local Government, Tanzania (1999) 'Whose Priorities in Policy Making? Reflections from the Permanent Secretaries', Retreat on Participation in Tanzania', February

RIPS (1998) *Paths for Change: Experiences in Participation and Democratization in Lindi and Mtwara Regions, Tanzania. Rural Integrated Project Support (RIPS) Programme Phase 2*, Oy Finnagro Ab, Vantaa, Finland

SMUWC (2001) 'Towards a Future for Usangu', Usangu website, www.usangu.org, accessed 4 July 2002

UNDP (2000) *Human Development Report 2000: Human Rights and Human Development*, United Nations Development Programme/Oxford University Press, New York

UNDP (2001) *Human Development Report 2001: Making New Technologies Work for Human Development*, United Nations Development Programme/Oxford University Press, New York

Widagri Consultants (1998) *The Rural Integrated Project Support Programme, Phase Two: Programme Evaluation*, evaluation report by Widagri Consultants Ltd for the Government of Finland and the Government of the Republic of Tanzania

6

The Donor–Government–Citizen Frame as Seen by a Government Participant

Margaret Kakande[1]

Introduction

The lack of collaboration between different donors has serious consequences for national government's capacity to define and implement its own development agenda. This chapter explores the effects of donor harmonization in Uganda and highlights the impacts of recent moves towards greater collaboration. In recent years, there has been a move towards local ownership, with improved 'partnerships' between donors, national governments and civil society organizations. This is exemplified by the determination of Uganda to maintain its own development plan (the Poverty Eradication Action Plan or PEAP) when poverty reduction strategy papers (PRSPs) were introduced. The PEAP has exposed the difficulties of collaboration with civil society and raises the challenges that lie ahead.

Over the decades, many developing countries have experienced 'disjointed' development efforts between national governments, donors and civil society organizations. Despite the fact that all parties were supposedly working for the good of citizens in poor countries, there has, until recently, been no coordination of effort, little transparency and a lot of mistrust. It is no wonder that little impact has been made on the lives of the poor, although billions of dollars have been spent.

The reluctance to move towards coordinated aid is often due to an underlying inertia. The status quo often serves the individual interests of both the donors and the recipient government. Donors have bigger political agendas to work towards that supersede national interests. Individuals within government departments are often reluctant to lose the control they may have through relationships with individual donors and the resultant programme funds that can be generated. There is a perceived, and potentially real, risk that centralizing efforts may mean that fewer government staff are involved in decision-making (see Chapter 4 on the experience in Bolivia and Chapter 5 on Tanzania).

The apparent failure of most development approaches has resulted in stakeholders calling for sustainable 'partnerships'. The demand is being made at every stage in the development process to jointly undertake analytical work, appraisals, programme design, implementation, monitoring and evaluation. All stakeholders are required to have a shared vision and work towards its effective attainment.

It is now widely recognized that donors add to the burden of national governments through their failure to work together effectively. In Uganda, for example, there are many donors working with each of the key ministries. Harmonization of procedures can significantly reduce the transaction costs for government, preventing the need for multiple reporting and budgeting. In 2001, the Development Assistance Committee (DAC) of the Organisation for Economic Co-operation and Development (OECD) set up a committee to examine ways of improving the coherence of donor work with policies of recipient governments in order to enhance effectiveness and improve consistency over time.

Uganda is often cited as a success story in terms of a national government taking control of its own development process and working in partnership with donors and civil society. However, the process of developing partnerships has not been a smooth one and a number of lessons have been drawn. This chapter explores the implications and challenges of implementing such partnerships as viewed by a representative of the Ugandan government who works in the Ministry of Finance, Planning and Economic Development.

What types of collaboration should we envisage?

The new partnerships call for collaborative arrangements between stakeholders, built on a strong foundation of transparency, accountability, respect and trust. Nevertheless, this gives rise to the question of how equitable relationships can develop when stakeholders are starting from very unequal power relations. A number of issues are raised below on the form that the collaboration should take.

In Uganda, there are over 1000 registered charities and many faith-based organizations, a number of trade unions and numerous private-sector organizations. All over the world, a movement towards collaboration between governments and other public, private and non-profit actors is taking place (Atkinson and Coleman, 1996). Networks and partnering are becoming common in the public sector and there is now a wide variety of such arrangements (OECD, 1999). Uganda is no exception and this helps the process of consultation, with civil society demanding a more collaborative national planning process.

In many countries, new public management reforms have emerged, linked to decentralization and changes in governance structures. These reforms are designed to enhance citizen participation and, hence, the quality of service delivery, and have led to growing use of network-type arrangements (Peters, 1996). The use of the terms 'network', 'partnership' and 'partnering arrangement' to describe collaborative arrangements between government and non-government entities may refer to a wide range of circumstances, and the meanings are often blurred. It may be useful to examine the characteristics of these networking and partnering arrangements, which may be formal or informal.

A network is made up of organizations and individuals engaged in reciprocal, preferential and mutually supportive actions. For example, in Uganda the networks that form the basis for joint government/donor-sector working groups are in sectors such as health and education. The key feature of networks is the way in which cooperation and trust are formed and sustained (Thompson, 1991). Network coordination depends upon a mixture of factors, including the nature of horizontal and vertical linkages and the development of partnering arrangements. In the sectors of health and education, government and donors operate in line with a memorandum of understanding that contains rules governing the behaviour of parties, while recognizing that the senior management in the respective ministries has responsibility for taking key policy decisions. Thus, through these networks, the partners have found ways of coordinating the network effectively –for example, good communication and procedures to resolve differences (Metcalfe, 1994).

Many commentators believe that the most critical characteristics of a strong partnership are mutual respect and trust. A complementary view is that networks are created because they are economically efficient and effective. Establishing trust and confidence among organizations depends upon organizational capacities; a belief that other organizations have useful skills and resources; and commitment and good faith in making and implementing agreements (Metcalfe, 1994). Trust is something that, in the end, depends upon relationships; it is nurtured between people (Coleman and Skogstad, 1990). Common values and motivations facilitate the emergence of trust, often demonstrated by reference to a track record or a good reputation. Trust ties are very commonly facilitated through social connections between individuals. The significance of these are commonly underestimated and poorly understood by outsiders. They may be based on shared professional training and norms, geographical proximity or cultural or ethnic ties. Few staff within the donor community have the cultural and social knowledge to understand the way in which these social factors operate – hence, leaving them without the necessary knowledge of how power is transmitted and replicated within the local aid community.

The networks of trust ties between government officials in Uganda and their counterparts in the donor community largely explain why, in the recent past, the Ugandan government has been able to steer the development process. Uganda funds about 48 per cent of its total public expenditure out of donor assistance. This indicates the fact that Uganda is a typical low-income country with very low levels of domestic revenue since subsistence agriculture continues to provide a very significant share of production and cannot be taxed. Money often equates to power; but the fact that a national government is poor and largely dependent upon foreign resources should not be an issue in forging partnerships of 'equals'. Fortunately, Uganda has been successful in attracting significant inflows of donor assistance because of the strong reputation it has built over the last 15 years of sound economic management and commitment to poverty reduction. What is critical is that poor governments know what they want and are able to articulate their demands.

Despite Uganda's high level of financial dependency, the government of Uganda takes the lead in guiding the participation of the development partners. The government coordinates the sector-wide approaches in all sectors, and ensures that planning involves the relevant donors and civil society members who help to determine the priority areas for public expenditure, which are financed through the Medium-Term Expenditure Framework (MTEF).

With so many donor partners in a national planning process, there is the risk of poorly defined arrangements limiting the chances for success and the risk of partners not meeting commitments to the common cause. In Uganda, in order to ensure that the partnerships operate effectively on the ground, areas that foster mistrust were identified and guiding principles agreed upon for improvement. These principles were based on the shared commitment that donor support would only be sought for programmes that are in the PEAP. Even if networks as trust ties are established, there will be a question about how partnerships are operationalized. Are we going to see loose alliances of government agencies, international organizations, corporations and civil society organizations joining hands to achieve what none of these can accomplish on their own, or more formal networks represented by written agreements clearly spelling out roles and responsibilities? In Uganda there are formal networks operating in some of the more established sectors (such as education and health, and the Plan for the Modernization of Agriculture); whereas in other areas, working arrangements are much more ad hoc. This is a critical area of concern as the type of alliance determines the level of commitment, voice and accountability of the stakeholders.

The role of government in partnerships

In the current policy development environment, where participation is high on the agenda, the role of the government is somewhat similar to that of a movie director making multiple realities combine. Whatever happens in development paradigms, a government, whether poor or rich, will always be a government – a powerhouse – and policy-making processes will always be political. It is the government's role to share power, work, support and/or information with others for the achievement of joint goals. The implication is that there is a cooperative investment of resources (time, funding, material, human resources, etc) and, therefore, joint risk-taking, sharing of authority and benefits for all partners.

Recipient governments in poor countries must have the capacity to take the front seat. The Ugandan government had an independent initiative in developing the PEAP in 1996 as a national planning framework for eradicating poverty. In 1998, a participatory poverty assessment (PPA) was carried out that brought to the fore the priority concerns of the poor themselves. The PPA process was instrumental in bringing the voices of previously marginalized stakeholders into dialogue with government. The findings of the PPA necessitated the revision of the PEAP in 2000. In parallel to this revision, the World Bank was also introducing PRSPs as a basis for debt relief allocation. The Ugandan government was in a strong position to argue that the PEAP should be used as the planning document or PRSP. The World Bank accepted the case for a truly nationally owned plan.

It is interesting to reflect on how significant the in-country PPA was in providing strong evidence that the PEAP was based on sound country analysis and poor people's needs. This shows how self-mobilization is a prerequisite for poor recipient countries to stand up as equal partners with donors. Our governments must be innovative and remain a step ahead of the think tanks of the powerful donor organizations – as was the case in Uganda. This is not to deny that involvement of all partners in the initiatives is desirable; but the lead must come from government.

The capacity of governments to be equipped to stand up to Western donor demands cannot be assumed. In order that this may happen, there must be adequate time for governments to build this capacity for self-mobilization. In Uganda the process took three years (1997 to 2000). During this time, government built the knowledge base, networks and analytical skills to confidently take the lead role, despite the high dependency on foreign funds. At this stage, government was able to contact other development partners for resources and technical advice, where appropriate, but retained control (to a large extent) of how resources were used.

The Ugandan government's guiding principles demanded a shared commitment from all donors. The principles laid down both government and donor responsibilities (outlined on page 93). In addition government will:

- Continue with increased focus on poverty eradication (at a minimum, programmes funded by the Poverty Action Fund will remain constant as a share of total budget).
- Continue with increased tax revenue effort.
- Assume full leadership in donor coordination process (at central, sectoral and district levels).
- Decline any offers of stand-alone donor projects.
- Strengthen monitoring and accountability (including value-for-money evaluations).
- Continue to improve transparency and combat corruption.
- Continue to strengthen district capacity.
- Develop comprehensive, costed and prioritized sector-wide programmes eventually covering the whole budget.

- Further develop participation and coordination of all stakeholders, including parliamentarians.
- Strengthen capacity to coordinate across government so that it speaks with one voice.

Is it realistic to anticipate joint risk-taking among partners with different constituencies? Many national governments are elected and are, therefore, very risk averse. One can then ask: 'To whom are civil society organizations accountable in order to justify joint risk-taking and sharing of authority with governments?' The bottom line is that the level of risk determines how much power governments are willing to share. This depends upon the political system in a given country. In many multiparty political systems, with their inherent power struggles, most governments view civil society organizations as channels for opposition. In such situations, the proposed partnerships may not flourish, as has been the case in Uganda, which professes a political system that embraces all.

Challenges for implementing partnerships

Given the history of collaborative arrangements between institutions, the implementation of the proposed partnerships is bound to meet a number of challenges. The formulation of effective structures of partnering arrangements will depend upon the mix of partner organizations and the pattern of interactions. In countries with hundreds of civil society organizations, for instance, which ones should be selected as partners? As noted already, it is people within the institutions that close deals who trust each other and are willing to work towards joint accountability. The way in which people communicate within networks and exchange information and rewards are important factors in explaining and predicting the performance of a partnership. Already, there is evidence that informal relationships and networks exist between individuals within organizations. With the move to open up, the challenge is how to break the glass ceilings perpetuated by people who wish to reduce interactions for certain groups within society in line with the 'old boys' network'. It is common knowledge that officials in many finance ministries, and their counterparts in the International Monetary Fund (IMF) and the World Bank have developed a common language that must be internalized by civil society organizations before new proposals are put forward or opportunities are provided for them to become part of the inner circle.

'Equality' of partners

Any true partnership depends upon reciprocity, preferential and/or mutually supportive actions. When resources mean that partners are inherently unequal, the power imbalance is important to understand and should not be brushed under the carpet. The availability and command over financial, human and physical resources among partners will always be critical for managing and controlling partnerships. In the absence of management for equality, there is a relationship of unequal partners that makes it difficult to establish a common belief system, code of conduct and established pattern of behaviour. Although the Ugandan government, poor as it is, appears to have made headway in establishing true partnerships with the donors, its experience may not readily be replicable in other countries. This is because of the unique political system of the movement,[2] which, in principle, embraces all and allows for a wide range of voices to be heard in public debates. In addition, the fact that Uganda has been used as an example of success for structural adjustment programmes gives them a level of confidence in leading partnerships. Uganda was determined enough to ensure that donors signed up to the following guiding principles:

- Jointly undertake all analytical work, appraisals and reviews.
- Jointly set output/outcome indicators.
- Develop uniform disbursement rules.
- Develop uniform and stronger accountability rules.
- Ensure that all support is fully integrated within sector-wide programmes and is fully consistent with each sector programme's priorities.
- Continue to increase the level of untied sectoral budget support.
- Increase the level of delegation to the country office.
- Abolish topping-up of individual project staff salaries.
- End individual, parallel country programmes and stand-alone projects.
- Progressively reduce tying of procurement.

Accountability

The key to a successful partnership is having a good flow of information, as this enhances accountability and, therefore, increases levels of trust. With increased transparency and participation, many development partners are taking blame or praise for the failure or success of Uganda's poverty reduction actions. During 1999 to 2000, many sectors did not meet their performance targets as listed in the PEAP. World Bank staff were so concerned that they worked with the relevant sectoral ministries to set more realistic targets for the near future, as non-achievement seemed to indicate a failure on their part, too. This type of reflection and ensuring that lessons are fed back into policy is often low on stakeholders' agendas.

Stability of partnerships

Countries enter partnerships for very different reasons. The arrangements may be pursued for ideological reasons, or because of the desire to follow a trend. One issue to ponder over is the source of the initiative for partnerships. Some countries view this as another imposition from the donor community following the Poverty Reduction Strategy Papers. In this case, the stability of the partnership arrangements may depend to a large extent upon the conditions prevailing in the external environments.

In Uganda, key government personnel became involved in the donor-led 'partnership' debate very early on. They saw the advantages of adopting the concept of partnership for the success of their own relationships with donors. However, the partnership is subject to policy shifts, both on the side of the donors (multilaterals, but possibly more for bilaterals) and on the side of the partner government. If partners on either side shift in a direction that is not respected by the other, the potential arises for the partnership to break down.

The extent to which partnership arrangements stand up to changing external pressures may depend upon the current level of transparency among partners and, therefore, upon a degree of predictability of possible future trends. Are *all* the cards on the table?

Feasibility of new procedures

Current practice has been for donors to have their own procedures, which recipient countries must follow. This has left many government officials with the task of internalizing and using a multitude of procedures from the many donors. With the new partnerships and with recipient governments in the driver's seat, governments are able to establish uniform country procedures (for disbursement, procurement, etc) that have to be adopted by the many donors.

This implies that for donors operating in more than one developing country, they will have to re-orient their staff and their systems at all levels to the different countries' procedures that may be defined under the partnership arrangements. The feasibility of this is questionable! This implies that the technical expertise requested by governments to implement the PRSP may differ from the current staffing priorities of the donors. Governments may also prefer the particular expertise of a specific donor country if they feel that personnel are well trained and possess the most appropriate skills. The potential consequences of this are dramatic. It remains to be seen whether donors would be truly prepared to reduce their power and modify their staffing according to national government demands.

Consideration of public concerns

Although it is desirable to have policy networks that share uniform visions and programmes, there is a danger of 'everybody' getting into the 'business' and therefore leaving no whistle-blowers. In a number of cases where donors are deeply involved in country programmes, criticizing such programmes may be tantamount to criticizing all partners. This may not bode well with some officials in different institutions; careers must continue to be developed.

Will effective accountability be achieved?

Since the current mechanisms to ensure public and citizens' rights are often not present, attention should be paid to the protection of the public interest and related accountability concerns. The key question, of course, is accountability to whom for the different partners? The donors have their home citizenry, as do the governments. On the other hand, civil society organizations are torn between the international public and/or donors and, to a limited extent, the local citizenry. The ideal is to be accountable to the citizenry in both local and international communities. However, we know that local communities have a limited capacity to hold both governments and civil society accountable to them. In many poor countries, the majority of the citizens are illiterate, coupled with poor information flows from policy-makers and implementers. Without major strides in literacy achievements and improvements in communications, it is unlikely that the status quo will change in many countries.

One can also envisage a situation where policies in donor countries are in conflict with those of the recipient governments; therefore, the choice of whom to be accountable to depends upon the powers that the citizens in the different locations wield. The classic example is the current move towards global free trade as proposed by the development donors, although some citizens in the developing world (particularly Uganda) are in favour of reintroducing the co-operative movement and greater price protection for farmers. These are very different policy positions that put governments in the precarious situation of choosing between their people and the donors.

Another issue of concern in the area of accountability is how to ensure that all partners stay committed to the internationally agreed upon goals and programmes. The withdrawal of the US from the Kyoto Protocol on climate change is an example of a powerful player just opting out.

Conclusions

Yes, we can have true partnerships that must follow an evolution within our governments – moving from the passenger to the driving seat; giving time to national processes to ensure capacity-building; fostering effective communication channels; and encouraging donors to learn to listen and take the passenger seat, while assisting the drivers in avoiding 'accidents,' as everybody may suffer injuries.

The 1998 PPA clearly illustrated the need to consult widely to ensure the design of relevant and effective development policies. The challenge is how to define the scope for participation. Most donors still suffer from the 'visibility syndrome' (the desire to attribute achievements in a country to their own efforts). The government now encourages wide participation of donors and civil society in budget formulation processes and monitoring activities. This makes attribution more difficult, and some donors have expressed a view that too large a number of participants hampers meaningful exchange.

On the other hand, participation of civil society was, in itself, exclusive as it hinged upon organizations' capacity to conceptualize technical issues and discussions in the jargon of economists. Many such organizations have conducted economic literacy programmes for their members to ensure effective participation. On its side, government has worked with civil society to produce 'popular' versions of technical documents, such as the budget.

Uganda has made great strides in attempting to establish partnership principles, which define the roles, responsibilities and behaviours of the various partners involved in their development process. Progress has been made; but there are many challenges that lie ahead.

Notes

1 The author would like to thank Bella Bird in Uganda for her useful inputs on earlier drafts of this chapter.
2 The movement is a political system in which election to public office is based on individual merit.

References

Atkinson, M and Coleman, W (1996) 'Policy Networks, Policy Communities and the Problems of Governance', in Dobuzinski, L (ed) *Policy Studies in Canada: The State of the Art*, University of Toronto Press, Toronto

Coleman, W and Skogstad, G (1990) 'Policy Communities and Policy Networks: A Structural Approach', in Coleman, W and Skogstad, G (eds) *Policy Communities and Public Policy in Canada*, Copp Clark Pitman, Toronto

Metcalfe, L (1994) 'The Weakest Links: Building Organizational Networks for Multilevel Regulation', in OECD, *Regulatory Cooperation for an Interdependent World*, Organisation for Economic Co-operation and Development, Paris

OECD (1999) 'Lessons from Performance Contracting Case Studies: A Framework for Public Sector Performance Contracting', PUMA/PAC (99)2, Organisation for Economic Co-operation and Development, Paris

Peters, G (1996) *The Future of Governing: Four Emerging Models*, Kansas University Press, Kansas

Thompson, G (1991) *Markers, Hierarchies and Networks: The Coordination of Social Life*, Sage, London

7

Exploring Power and Relationships: A Perspective from Nepal

Ruth Marsden

Introduction

Drawing upon diary excerpts and informal conversations, this chapter presents a glimpse of the relationships behind one programme in Nepal from the perspective of a part inside, part outside observer. It illustrates two sets of relationships – between donors and non-governmental organizations (NGOs), and between international and local NGOs – and considers how these impact more widely upon critical relations with communities and local government. Two key aspects of relationships are highlighted: organizational and personal. These two aspects are shown to interrelate in the process of creating or hindering positive relationships. The case studies illustrate how aid systems can exclude those whom they aim to embrace. However, through good organizational systems and strong personal commitments, relationships that enable positive change can be built.[1]

The case studies

In this chapter, I present two cases that highlight different relationships and dynamics of power. The first is an interaction between donors and a local NGO, which reflects upon how one particular bureaucratic procedure, the logical framework (logframe), plays a role in framing and structuring the relationships between different actors. It illustrates how procedures can reinforce existing patterns of exclusion. The second is a series of scenes that examine partnership relations between local NGOs and an international NGO, and the impact of these upon relationships with the community and local government. These cases illuminate two key dimensions of relationships: *personal* and *organizational*. Both dimensions are critical in building positive relationships to empower people, but they weave together in a complex way that can either enhance or create obstacles in these relationships.

To understand the programme environment, it is important to outline some basic issues of communication in which the relationships were embedded. The programme brought together a wide array of participants who interrelated in different places and contexts. It was funded by the UK Department for International Development or DFID (a large bilateral donor), was managed through ActionAid (an international NGO) and was implemented in partnership with Creation of Creative Society and Udaya Himalaya Network (two local NGOs working in two quite different rural communities). It also sought to create links with both local and national government. Across the programme, there was no commonly understood 'language'. Basic features in the style of communication and in the procedures used within the aid organizations were derived from Western ways of working. These do not readily give space for styles of communication that are more dominant in other contexts in Nepal.

One particular procedure, the logframe (a complex planning tool popular with donors) had a strong impact on organizational procedures and relationships between groups and the programme (see Gasper, 1997, for a full critique). NGOs have been pressured to adopt it in order to secure project funds. The training available locally presents the tool in its most inflexible form as a magic key demanded by donors. The rigid way in which it is used has become widespread throughout the country. Its matrix form demands a very particular style of linear communication and analysis that embodies a cultural logic and mindset that is neat and boxed. It often differs radically both from Nepali experience of an unpredictable world and from other less bounded, more metaphorical and fluid communication processes, such as stories. As a dominant communication media in the programme, power and control are held by those with the skills to use logframes, and those without these particular communication skills easily become voiceless. As with other examples in this book, the use of this tool does not create the environment for inclusive aid, in which all stakeholders can participate. This chapter shows how stakeholders are often excluded in the current system by virtue of language, knowledge of bureaucratically imposed procedures and geographical location.

The widespread use of English as the 'international language' of development immediately set the boundaries of inclusion around a select few and created hierarchies of competence within the programme (see Crewe, 1997, for a more detailed analysis of language as a specialized domain in development, and the powerful, reiterative role that it has in creating 'insiders' and 'outsiders'). Hierarchies of competence in the programme were extended through donor preferences for written over oral communication. Yet, NGO staff, as well as local people, presented information and reflected upon it much more freely and fully in oral rather than written forums. Often informal conversations and spontaneous occurrences lucidly articulate insights; but they are seldom recorded and rarely reach the pages of formal reports. Thus, the learning articulated in these media is not shared and the consequent improvements to programmes often fail to occur. I try to draw on some of these informal discussions here as a lens through which to view areas of conflict in relationships and some of the ways in which people chose to address these struggles.

The perspective given in this chapter is my own, based on my observations and experiences as a British female trainee. This position was particularly revealing in that, although I was a junior participant, I was present during scenes that spanned a wide range of settings, interacting with local NGOs, the international NGO and the donor over the course of one year (another four months living with one project community the following year gave additional insight). My movement across settings, between a wide range of actors and beyond the boundaries of this one stage has enabled me to become a narrator of the story here.

Language, hierarchy and logframes in the far western hills: reflecting on donor–local NGO relationships

Two advisers from the donor organization came from Kathmandu to visit the local NGO in the far west of Nepal for an evaluation visit (an 'output-to-purpose' review in logframe terminology). Their visit demonstrated how differences in *organizational contexts* and framing communication on the logframe affected how relationships were built. Differences in the *personal interaction* of the two advisers with the staff of the local NGO highlighted how language choice not only determines effectiveness of communication, but can also influence perceptions of the hierarchical power invested in donors. The donors arrived late one night:

> *We had been waiting in the office all day. From the office gate you could look out across the steep slopes of the surrounding terraced hills and see most of the villages that belonged to this village development committee area and trace the path on which the visitors would arrive. The staff of the local NGO had been called to the head office, walking in from field offices spread out over the programme area, the furthest six hours' walk away. The nearest road head was a good half day's walk away and the rough paths winding up and over the steep hills were not amenable to bikes, so all travel was on foot.*
>
> *A large meal had been prepared to welcome the guests. Much care and effort had gone into preparing the special meal, as is the tradition amongst people in the far western hills who bestow generous hospitality on honoured guests. The hosts had managed to find fish and Dinesh,[2] one of the office staff, had walked up to the orchard on the top of the hill to bring back oranges and lemons. The oranges were already finished but the lemons were still in the trees and the old orchard owner had called his daughter-in-law to come and climb the trees.*
>
> *At 10 pm the advisers from the donor organization finally arrived, with the team from the international NGO office. They were tired from their long journey and a full day of programme observations, but were happy to have made it. They*

had stopped to observe an evening literacy class, which was why they had arrived so late. The meal was served and spoons were found in case the guests did not want to eat with their hands. Informal chatting began but the conversation was slow.

Plans for transport back to Kathmandu were discussed immediately. Andrew was concerned about getting back for an urgent meeting in Kathmandu. Flight tickets had not been available. Instead, it looked like they might also have to return by foot and then the long arduous road, which would mean leaving the next day at noon.

Life and work in the far western hills were dictated by very different rhythms from those in the donor's large office in the capital city. Tight time schedules driven by bureaucratically determined deadlines and an organizational work culture of urgency and efficiency contrasted with the realities of a pace of work that was largely determined by the environment – by the remoteness of its geographical location and sometimes by the weather.[3] This was the first time since the programme began over two years earlier that donor representatives had been able to visit, the long distance and difficult accessibility from Kathmandu presenting significant obstacles. Very few of the Kathmandu-based international NGO staff had visited this programme area either. It was staff who were based in the international NGO's western regional office who provided the link in relations, frequently travelling across the country. Direct contact of donors with the communities and field staff in the local NGO was, therefore, rare, presenting an immediate limitation for building relationships.

The donors were regarded as *thulo manche* (big people), the benefactors of the programme. Honouring the guests with a special meal and waiting patiently were very much part of this. The expectation that the *thulo manche* speaks and others listen is widely characteristic of this type of relationship. To a certain extent, these characteristics and features of the *thulo manche* relationship were evident in the hierarchies of seniority within the local NGO and between them and the international NGO. Burghart (1993) presented a fascinating account of this type of relationship in a development research programme, and astutely highlighted the space for differing interpretations of relations to coexist. In this programme, the *thulo manche* relationship was challenged personally by individuals in different contexts and also organizationally in the promotion of participation, as will now be explored further.

As the next day unfolded, two meetings were held that were significantly different in style. The first was centred 'inside the boxes' of the logframe and very few people could contribute; but the second opened out into a more inclusive discussion that focused on the programme across these boundaries:

In the morning, a meeting was held to talk through the programme's logframe outputs. The advisers from the donor organization led the conversation, giving various observations and suggestions as they worked through the different boxes. The conversation was in English and was very much 'logframe speak'. This was the lingua franca *of development professionals and, yet, remained incomprehensible to most of the front-line staff. Nothing was translated – and the advisers did not openly enquire, nor did the local managers notify them that this was needed. Consequently, only a minority of the local NGO staff clearly understood what was being said. A short discussion followed; but, as well as language, communication barriers were evident both in the framework of the discussion and at a deeper cultural level.*

The advisers were representatives of the donor organization who fund the programme and thus sustain the organization. They were also senior and respected guests to be listened to politely. There was uneasiness amongst the local staff when asked questions, and one colleague asked me in the break, 'What is the "right" answer?' A question came up that had been discussed amongst the local NGO staff in a previous conversation about the role of businesses and NGOs in Nepal's development. The opinion that Muresh had given in our earlier conversation was the exact opposite from that which he offered in this context. Preconceptions of what people in the local NGO thought that the donors wanted to hear were very strong.

During lunchtime, arrangements changed again, as they are prone to. Tickets were secured for the return advisers' flight. They could stay until morning and the discussions were able to continue into the afternoon. This became an opportunity for talking 'outside the boxes' of the logframe and discussions flowed more easily, although they were still very much led by the advisers.

One of the advisers, Rebecca, decided to speak in Nepali. This radically changed the dynamics. The silence of hierarchy was broken and competence was suddenly reversed as the adviser sought help and clarification as she tried to express herself in Nepali. This reversal of competence gave local staff the confidence to speak more and participate fully in the discussion. Andrew (without the language skills) remained silent for most of this discussion.

The shift in language was significant in increasing mutual understanding between the donor advisers and the local staff and in disturbing the hierarchies of competence. This altered the dynamics of the relationship in an enabling way. Andrew was an older man who had worked for many years with the large bilateral donor, but had only recently come to Nepal. He was not able to speak Nepali and so spoke in English. Despite being in the hills of far western Nepal, he did not appear to adjust his speech style in any way and spoke as if in a policy meeting, using vocabulary that even those who understood some English could not understand. Rebecca had been in Nepal for over a year and had built up good relationships with people in the organizations. Her manner of interaction was markedly different as she purposefully tried to overcome the hierarchies of relationships between herself as a donor representative and the staff in the local NGO. She challenged the conventions of the *thulo manche* relationship in the afternoon meeting by asking for responses rather than simply presenting her own views. Her status as a younger woman rather than as an older man may well have made this easier, as gender and age hierarchies were juxtaposed, instead of aligned with the seniority of her donor status.

Her approach was also attuned to the underlying ethos of participation as an organizational tool that should be valued within the programme. While having the power to radically challenge the hierarchy of relationships (see

Chambers, 1983), it is quite possible for the promotion of a participatory ethos to coexist with hierarchical relationships (as outlined in Mosse, forthcoming). Personal and organizational aspects of relationships interact in a complex way, which is not always immediately apparent. Speaking with colleagues in the local organization much later, it was remarkable what different impressions the two advisers had made. They had found it easier to relate to Rebecca than Andrew and, consequently, shared more with her about the programme. However, despite the apparent insensitivities in relating to the local staff, Andrew, in fact, remained more clearly within the expectations of the *thulo manche* relationship. The senior authoritative voice that he commanded personally was important in formal contexts, particularly with the government, where he would have the opportunity to represent the local citizens' case.

As a central organizational procedure around which the programme revolved, the logframe had considerable impact upon shaping relationships. During the early stages, due to the manner in which it had been introduced, the logframe had enabled clear and strategic decisions to be made about planning, and had encouraged team-building with the new partner organizations. As the programme developed, the procedure of reporting back against the logframe was less positive, solidifying hierarchical power relations and presenting a barrier to more holistic communication. Local NGO staff felt strongly that to understand the logframe required special training, so those without training did not feel confident in using the tool. Alienation of local staff from the logframe was enhanced because often it was senior staff in an office far away from the programme area who completed the details of the final reporting logframe. A Nepali translation had been made at some stage; but it was partial and was left almost forgotten on a back shelf. The logframe is used a little more by the senior staff who recognize that it is useful for planning; but they also struggle with it. It remains surrounded by a certain degree of mystery and perpetuates a hierarchy of different levels of comprehension. Mastery of the procedure becomes a significant achievement. The director of another partner organization stated that successfully reviving and submitting the logframe was a major achievement of the programme over the last year and, personally, one of his major highlights. The impact of the activities within it had seemingly taken second place!

Perceptions of the logframe also had an impact upon how programme activities were communicated in reports. Once planned activities had been written into the logframe, there was much hesitation and reluctance to add or alter anything. The possibility for flexibility and encompassing change in the logframe, although encouraged by donors, was not evident in its use at field level. The perception that the logframe couldn't be altered was widespread and firmly held. As a consequence, the flow of activities was lost as they were fitted into very different sections. The integrated philosophy of the project was hidden by the logframe format. The rounded context of the programme and changes were masked by the 'tick-off-against-plan'-style reporting. Important details and explanations that had emerged in discussions were left out as we filled in the boxes.

Frustrations with the logframe were embedded in the wider context of pressure from donors' reporting demands. The local NGOs often worked with more than one donor organization at a time and were required to report back to each in the donor's own specifically favoured format, and to accommodate their different financial systems and cycles. Although, at government level, there has been a positive response to collaboration among bilateral donors, this has not been taken on by all donors and has not altered the demands for different styles of reports requested by local NGOs.

The following section moves on from the discussion of relations between donors and NGOs to focus on the partnership relationships between international NGOs and local NGOs.

Changing community relations and demands for government transparency: reflecting on international NGO–local NGO relationships

Many international NGOs have shifted their policy and approach from direct implementation of projects to partnerships with local NGOs (see Chapter 2). This has been in response to recognizing the value of assumed strong relationships between local organizations and communities. The close links at village level help to ensure successful implementation of projects. The role of international NGOs has become more managerial and focused on the capacity-building of local NGOs. In this context, the relationships between international and local NGOs have become critical to the impacts of development programmes.

In the programme, the procedures and structures of the international NGO played a major role in shaping its relations with the local partner NGOs. They also had practical implications – both positive and negative – for relationships with communities. They brought both the wider networks and support for greater advocacy work, but also more extensive time demands. Personal commitments were, again, critical in building positive relationships with communities and local government, and these wove together with organizational procedures in ways that this section will now trace.

Ironically, opportunities given to the local NGOs for growth and expansion through partnerships with the international NGO seemed to have the possibility to detract from the positive relationships with communities. New organizational demands quite literally decreased the time for personal interaction of local NGO staff with communities and, hence, reduced community members' ability to influence programmes:

> *The director of one local NGO involved in the programme explained how his relationship with project communities had changed as his organization had grown and built relationships with international NGOs. He spoke with enthusiasm about all the time and energy that the small group of staff had put in as they established their organization. Long periods were spent travelling around different villages, encouraging people to get involved in programme activities. He regretted the fact that, as the organization and programme had expanded and taken on*

more projects, there had been less chance for him to spend time with communities; he now rarely had the opportunity to leave the office to visit the villages. Nowadays, he would be much more likely to travel up to the regional or national office of an international partner NGO.

This pattern was echoed by other local partner organizations. Too often, partnership demands meant that focus shifted away from the communities to the offices of the international NGO. The project coordinator in one programme area estimated that he spent only six months of his time at the project office and the rest of his time away at meetings and training sessions. This was an issue that the international NGO had noticed and planned to address; but it was complexly embedded in styles of training programmes and management procedures. Despite attempts at decentralization, these procedures still tended to draw people away from the project communities for meetings, workshops and training.[4] An underlying hierarchy in the relationships between international and local NGOs is emphasized in this pattern of international NGOs calling local NGO staff to the cities for training. This hierarchy may then extend to local NGO staff relations with communities because both training and travel enhance status for local NGO staff and emphasize a difference between them and the communities with whom they work.[5]

Relationships between the local partner NGOs and the international NGO were generally positive; but the local NGOs did not feel in a position to speak with the international NGO openly about the problems of frequently being called away from the field or to challenge their decisions. They often felt that the quality of the work did not justify the time and money invested. The case of a market research survey, proposed originally in a donor evaluation report, illustrated this well:

A market research survey had been commissioned by the international NGO, following a recommendation from an evaluation study. It was carried out by consultants who were competent in producing a good written English report, but were less concerned with actual research in the local areas. The agricultural adviser was not prepared to study the soil and get his hands dirty. Subsequently, the report gave little useful information to the partner organizations that they did not already know and, in fact, merely repeated back to them the knowledge that they had given the 'researchers' – but this time with the language and authority of consultants.

Here, the hierarchical relationships between the international and local NGOs are reflected in the hierarchical relationship between the outside expert researcher and the local NGO: the knowledge of the local NGOs and communities is subsumed within written expertise. Improved relations between international NGOs and local NGOs hold the key to accessing and working with the wealth of knowledge and skills that different players bring.

A large campaign for the rights of bonded labourers in Nepal illustrates well how international and local NGOs who work together complement each others' skills and bring about positive change. The international NGO brought inspiration and support to the local NGOs to challenge local attitudes about bonded labour. A network of international and local NGOs was built up. The central-level lobbying of the government by international NGOs was mirrored by the power of local voices at local government level and brought about considerable success in policy changes. These organizational support structures for the bonded labourers' campaign were woven through with strong personal commitments. When taking a stand for the bonded labourers, the director of one local NGO described how he had argued with his father against their family taking on bonded labourers (which was one of the traditional agricultural labour systems in the area). He had angered some of his extended family by his position of advocating for the bonded labourers and had experienced conflict with some of his board (many of whom were also high-caste, relatively wealthy landowners). Decisions that he took in the programme affected his personal relationships directly; but his personal commitment to the bonded labourers' campaign from his position as a local leader was powerful in bringing about change.

Relationships between local NGOs and international NGOs also affect relationships with government, as well as communities. The local NGO was given support in making demands for greater transparency from local government. Personal commitment to making a stand on this issue from the director of the local NGO was equally critical. He described the relationship he built up with the district development committee (DDC):

> We entered the DDC council for the first time, while we were working with ISDP [the Integrated Social Development Programme.]. There wasn't a culture to have NGOs present, and many questions were being raised. Being a local and a voter of those politicians, I said: 'We think as voters that we have the right to be here and we are also working for development here.' All NGOs must be at the DDC meetings and be asked to present their programmes and budgets in front of 300 people. In front of 300 people there must be answers. Nowadays, the DDC allocates two days just for NGOs and INGOs [international non-governmental organizations].

Although the relationships between this organization and the DDC were not always smooth, through taking this stand the local NGO played a very significant role in instigating change towards greater transparency among the government and district NGOs. Once again, the organizational support and encouragement from the international NGO combined with personal commitment to change this relationship with the local government. Through the energy and insight of a few individuals, a precedent was set in place for a new degree of inclusive aid and openness between local NGOs and local government.

Concluding reflections

These cases have presented a behind-the-scenes glimpse of the relationships between key characters on the stage of a development programme: a bilateral donor, an international NGO, partner organizations, communities and government. They have illuminated areas of struggle and the power hierarchies that prevail, as well as steps that different actors are taking to respond to these. Specific organizational procedures such as the use of the logframe have often worked to reinforce stereotypical hierarchies of language, educational status and time priorities. These procedures have resulted in the focus being drawn away from project communities to address the perceived demands of international NGO partners and donors. Far from being mechanisms for embracing the voices of the poor, they have used a form of communication that has excluded the very people whom they claim to serve. Cautions about how relationships with communities can change as an organization expands have also been noted. On the other hand, the bonded labourers' campaign and the network of organizations that built up around it illustrates the potential for bringing about effective change through positive relationships. These cases have illustrated how critical personal commitment is to building positive relationships and inclusive aid. Personal commitment weaves powerfully with the possibilities that organizational procedures create for building relationships. It also has the potential to overcome barriers created by organizational structures and hierarchies. Ultimately, it has been shown that reflective organizational procedures that facilitate openness and effective communication, along with positive personal commitment, provide great possibilities for enabling more inclusive relationships on the stage of development.

Notes

1   The author is very grateful to ActionAid Nepal for the opportunity to work with them and their partner organizations.
2   All names have been changed.
3   Freak floods a few months later during the monsoon washed away a truckload of programme materials.
4   The international NGO is now in the process of a radical refocusing of procedures to enable both its own staff and local NGO staff to spend more time with project communities (see Chapter 8).
5   In the far west of Nepal there is a strong perception of a hierarchy of different types of work – working in an office is of higher status than working the land.

References

Burghart, R (1993) 'His Lordship at the Cobblers' Well', in Hobart, M (ed) *An Anthropological Critique of Development: The Growth of Ignorance*, Routledge, London, reprinted in Burghart, R (1996) *The Conditions of Listening: Essays on Religion, History and Politics in South Asia*, Fuller, C J and Spencer, J (eds), Oxford University Press, Delhi

Chambers, R (1983) *Rural Development: Putting the Last First*, Longman, Harlow

Crewe, E (1997) 'The Silent Traditions of Developing Cooks', in Grillo R D and Stirrat, R L (eds) *Discourses of Development: Anthropological Perspectives*, Berg, Oxford

Gasper, D (1997) *'Logical Frameworks': A Critical Assessment – Managerial Theory, Pluralistic Practice*, Working Paper Series no 264, Institute of Social Studies, The Hague

Mosse, D (forthcoming) 'The Making and Marketing of Participatory Development', in Quarles van Ufford, P and Giri, A K (eds) *A Moral Critique of Development: In Search of Global Responsibilities*, Routledge EIDOS series, London and New York

8

An International NGO's Staff Reflections on Power, Procedures and Relationships

Charles Owusu[1]

The horns cannot be too heavy for the head that must carry them (African proverb on being true to mutually agreed responsibilities).

Introduction

This chapter is based on the initial findings of pilot action research conducted by ActionAid[2] in Ethiopia, The Gambia, India and Kenya. It examines the practical implications of ActionAid's new Accountability, Learning and Planning System (ALPS). The chapter examines the issues of power, participation, learning and downward accountability to local people and partners. The study shows that it is possible, with the necessary commitment and management support, to effectively remove the fears, uncertainty and suspicions that often characterize relationships between international non-governmental organizations (INGOs), local-level people and partners. Despite modest progress, the practical challenges and tensions of ALPS are just beginning to be understood. As expected, there are still big gaps in terms of poor people's representation, unequal power relations, and well-meaning but constraining processes, procedures and attitudes. The experience does show clearly, however, that change must begin from within development organizations themselves and must go beyond just restructuring when things appear not to be working. Often development organizations are quick to embark on restructuring in the belief that adjusting organizational structures is enough to solve underlying problems. But new structures do not, in themselves, herald new dawns. Rather, it is the attitudes, behaviours, values and commitment that underlie these structures that hold in them the seeds of success or failure.

ActionAid's global strategy and accountability framework

A decade ago, poverty was conceptualized and analysed differently. Our understanding of its causes has broadened beyond the narrow view of people's lack of basic services, material possessions or income. The current literature captures the complexity of poverty. It is no longer defined as merely a lack of resources, but examines issues of access to resources; information; opportunities; mobility; voice and participation; marginalization; powerlessness; increasing deprivation; vulnerability; and exclusion (UNDP, 1997). Amartya Sen's (1999) entitlements and capabilities approach illustrates a clear conceptual link between poverty and human rights. Sen argues that development or the lack of it is best judged by the extent to which a nation's citizens enjoy certain basic freedoms: freedom from hunger, diseases and illiteracy. If poverty is the absence or inadequate realization of certain freedoms and rights, then respect for the international human rights framework, including its principal features of accountability, non-discrimination, equality and participation, become central to poverty eradication efforts. ActionAid's global strategy subscribes to this view.

Fighting Poverty Together (1999 to 2003) is ActionAid's new global strategy (ActionAid, 1999). The strategy represents a major shift from ActionAid's previous focus and reflects the changing nature of our understandings of poverty. *Fighting Poverty Together* seeks to contribute to poverty eradication by promoting a rights-based approach to development. The strategy focuses on empowering poor people to secure their basic human rights. It aims to do this through advocating and promoting public accountability and good governance, strengthening anti-poverty movements and strengthening North–South linkages. In order to mitigate the international constraints to poverty eradication, the new strategy aims to influence official donors and multilateral institutions to promote responsible private investment.

Fighting Poverty Together represents a significant and unprecedented shift in management style, both in strategic and operational terms. In operational terms, ActionAid has moved away from being directly operational – implementing sector-specific and discrete projects or programmes – to supporting local people and partners to take responsibility for implementing their own development programmes. Challenges identified with this shift include the apparent loss of direct experiential learning resulting from the lack of direct contact with local people as we work increasingly through intermediaries who represent local people. Another challenge relates to the operational and conceptual tensions regarding how we strike a balance between meeting the immediate needs of poor and marginalized communities with whom we work, and addressing the underlying causes of their poverty.

Many practical initiatives and steps have been taken to address the internal challenges demanded by the new framework. For instance, management has been decentralized to lower levels; decision-making has been devolved; institutional incentives such as ALPS (see the following section) have secured full management backing and support; a shared learning unit has been established; our governance structure has been internationalized; income sources have been diversified; reliance on child sponsorship has been reduced and communication with sponsors and supporters has intensified; and links and alliances are being established.

ActionAid's Accountability, Learning and Planning System (ALPS)

ALPS is the accountability system designed to support *Fighting Poverty Together*. The Impact Assessment Unit (IAU) in London where I work as an impact assessment facilitator was charged with the responsibility of piloting ALPS to help us understand some of the practical implications of the strategy. My position in ActionAid is of someone who has worked in the field, later managing ActionAid's Bawku West programme in Ghana and now working on the piloting of ALPS in the policy division in London. These different roles within the organization have meant that I have had the privilege to experience, first hand, the nature and type of challenges and conflicting demands a system such as ALPS poses at various levels within the organization – at operational, management and strategic levels.

ALPS replaced the old *ActionAid Planning and Reporting System* in September 2000. The old system was thought to be out of sync with the spirit of the new agenda. Staff thought it to be too upward focused, too bureaucratic in its orientation and disproportionately centred on ActionAid's internal information needs, as well as those of donors. It hardly engendered learning from poor people, themselves. Nor did it focus on their information needs. Furthermore, the onerous procedures for accountability and reporting consumed large amounts of valuable staff time. One estimate was that staff were spending three months each year writing and rewriting reports (see also Chapter 7). For many of them, English was their second or third language, but it was the medium of reporting. They spent much time and effort polishing the prose on which they felt they would be judged. On top of this, many reports were of little use and were little used.

For several years, attempts to reform and simplify the system were largely unsuccessful. Participatory processes to devise new procedures ended up making similar levels of demands on the people at country level. Finally, in frustration, six international staff were given a week to come up with a solution. This resulted in the leaner, simpler and more radical system of ALPS. Paradoxically for an organization that prided itself on participatory approaches, the ALPS system was then endorsed centrally and disseminated in a centre-outwards manner to ActionAid teams in some 30 countries. Central authority was used to change procedures and requirements and to even out and reverse power relations between all levels (Scott-Villiers, 2002).

It is important to note that although the dissemination of ALPS bore central authority, its intention was to empower. Teams were to interpret the intentions but were encouraged to explore and devise, with their partners, their own processes. Country programmes were no longer required to write formal annual reports but had to conduct participatory review and reflections processes (PRRPs)[3] at least once annually with multiple stakeholders, involving poor people, communities, partner organizations, ActionAid staff and ActionAid's donors. PRRPs aim to increase our accountability to poor people, learn from our successes and failures and, more importantly, endeavour to improve the quality of our work. Reporting could be in new formats – by video, in local or national languages or in other forms. Downward accountability was stressed, with transparency of budgets between all levels. Significantly, no single formula was laid down. Diversity was encouraged as an efficient way of learning, with exchanges of experience within and between countries. Users were encouraged to use the approach in a flexible manner.

In order to simply illustrate the differences between new emerging procedures, such as that of ALPS and more established procedures for planning and monitoring, such as logical framework (logframe) analysis (see Chapter 11), Table 8.1 characterizes some of the contrasts between the two approaches.

Table 8.1 *Established and emergent procedures*

	Established	Emergent
Origins	1950s and 1960s engineering and management, including management by objectives	Prolonged frustration with failures to reduce laborious reporting; search for means of downward accountability
Goals	Set	Evolving
Form and structure	Fixed	Flexible
Procedure/process	Formal, predetermined sequence, standardized	Informal, invented, improvised, interactive, diverse
Dominant activities	Planning, monitoring, evaluation	Reflecting, sharing, learning
Quality assurance and characteristic monitoring process	Objectively verifiable indicators Output-to-purpose review	Sharing and judgement in 360 degree annual review and reflection meetings
Main language	Dominant external language	Local language
Accountability stressed	Upwards to donor	Downwards at each level, as well as upwards
Reporting medium and direction	Written, upwards	Various – verbal, video, theatre, etc, 360 degree
Ownership (theory) (practice)	All stakeholders Donors	All stakeholders Spread out
Transparency	Upwards	360 degree
Relationships	Donor dominated, recipients often resent	Recipient led, intended to empower, with donor avoiding dominance
Intelligibility to local participants	Lower	Higher
Controls	Imposed from above	Minimal? Mixed?

Source: devised by Robert Chambers and Jethro Pettit

ALPS is an example of an emergent approach that has a flexible and informal structure, based on an interactive process of sharing critical lessons with the aim of improving the overall performance of programmes. It is, thus, primarily a tool that prioritizes downwards accountability while still providing essential data on progress to donors. It is a set of working principles intended to guide how ActionAid as an organization relates to poor people and partner organizations in all aspects of our work. ALPS places considerable emphasis on the importance of building good working relationships; having the right attitudes and behaviour; ensuring gender sensitivity in programming; promoting accountability to poor and marginalized people; ensuring that participation goes beyond mere consultation; engendering genuine openness and transparency; and permitting more inclusiveness and mutual learning.

The approach proposed by ALPS is clearly a radical one. In the first year after these pilot studies started, ActionAid's global report had this to say:

> *The organizational analysis of change has significantly benefited from the recent introduction of ALPS. As an organization, we are still exploring issues of accountability, transparency and greater honesty. However, progress has been made. The annual PRRP processes during 2001 represent a real change in the way that we assess the value of our work. The involvement of local people, partners and other stakeholders in the rich discussions of progress has been fascinating. A wealth of reports, videos and analysis has been generated which detail ActionAid's failures, progress and strengths. This year, reports are more honest, more self-critical and – most importantly – many of them include the perspectives of our major stakeholders – poor people* (ActionAid, 2001a, p2).

In 2001, ActionAid and the Institute of Development Studies (IDS) conducted pilot studies on ALPS in Brazil, Kenya, India and Ethiopia. The studies are still in their initial stages; but lessons shared indicate quite exciting and encouraging breakthroughs, although there are also daunting challenges. This chapter attempts to share some of our early learning.

In my experience, most of the challenges we identified are by no means new to social development. What is, perhaps, new and interesting is the way in which ActionAid is acknowledging, responding and trying to break down some of the traditional challenges to effective action. These challenges are summarized in this chapter as reversing the accountability flow; recognizing and transforming the power imbalances between different actors; a view of participation that recognizes the needs of local people and partners; and improving learning and sharing internally and externally.

Accountability

Improved accountability is an important element in ensuring that the aid system is more inclusive (see also Chapter 12). Governments have to face elections and must account for their stewardship to the people through parliament. Business concerns must demonstrate their viability to their stakeholders in the form of profits and have to account and seek consensus at general assembly meetings.

Development organizations, on the other hand, have stayed behind the screens of values and altruism and largely remain unaccountable – particularly to poor people on whose behalf they raise funds – except when they have to provide donor reports or conduct an evaluation. In my opinion, these do not constitute and should not be equated with accountability. Fowler (1997, p181) argues that a:

> ...*critical issue is the ability of different stakeholders to exert accountability in terms of information, reporting, appraisal and sanctions. Poor people's ability to exert these forms of accountability is often severely constrained. Such accountability rests in the hands of professionals within the aid system.*

Accountability and legitimacy are one of ActionAid's key concerns in its new agenda. INGOs are increasingly being accused of lacking transparency, accountability and legitimacy (Edwards, 2000). Claims about representing poor people have been called into question since those we claim to represent are unable to demand accountability from us. For ActionAid, many of these concerns are real and the criticisms are often justifiable. We also realize the grave responsibility that *Fighting Poverty Together* places on us with regard to these concerns. Crucially, too, we recognize that we have a moral obligation to live by the values and principles espoused in ALPS. To do this we need to show by example that the principles of ALPS are, indeed, achievable. We cannot afford any semblance of rhetoric if we are to succeed with *Fighting Poverty Together*. Otherwise, we seriously devalue what we stand for.

One of the key lessons from ALPS has been the increasing accountability of ActionAid to its stakeholders. Indeed, the process is not only opening the organization up to challenge from partners, it is beginning to make partners more open and accountable to the people and communities whom they claim to represent. The PRRP is improving personal and institutional relationships with stakeholders, promoting positive action at the local level, and forcing us to look at our own behaviours and attitudes. The obvious question is what is causing these changes and how does the PRRP differ from earlier review processes?

The answer to the first part of the question can be traced to the strong support for ALPS at all levels within the agency, including, in particular, management and people in key leadership roles. This has resulted in a more genuine and committed effort on the part of staff to apply the principles of ALPS. Field-level staff, local partners and community groups alike are more forthcoming and much more open about failures, difficulties and challenges, hitherto concealed from general knowledge. The second part of the question echoes the first. It relates to acknowledging power relations within the organization and between the organization and its local partners (see the section on 'Power').

Disclosing relevant information is an important step in ensuring greater accountability, as well as more effective participation and the breaking down of power relations. ActionAid has realized that a key step in this direction is the disclosure of financial information. In Kenya, after plans and budgets had been explained to community partners, we discussed the justification for each project and how much the projects cost to implement. One of the key lessons to emerge from this process was the importance of providing unrestricted access to relevant financial information to assessing, or reflecting upon, progress or the lack of it.

What is worthy of note is that it was only after staff in Kenya shared detailed budgets and financial grants that were invested in the work of the local community-based organization (CBO) partner with the community (in visual form and using Swahili) that local people were able to ask relevant and informed questions about why certain decisions were reached. Local people and partners openly expressed their frustrations regarding certain items of expenditure that were perceived as not addressing their priority needs. They complained about the lack of clarity about child sponsorship and how money was allocated to specific projects. They had concerns about inadequate involvement in deciding project priorities and even less involvement in deciding how finances are allocated and used. While these concerns primarily relate to ActionAid partners (ActionAid is not directly operational in Kenya), it clearly shows the need for development organizations to be a little more generous in sharing relevant financial information.

We were also subjected to some hard questions by communities: 'Why did you have to spend so much on capacity-building?' 'Is it necessary to go so far [to Nairobi] for exposure visits?' 'What happens to unspent funds still with ActionAid?' 'Why does the community have to provide free labour for some projects?'

In the above example, two interesting things happened. First, the community members insisted that Genesis, ActionAid's local NGO-implementing partner, must declare its budget, too. Second, they challenged the choice of projects and expenditure categories, especially the purchase of a four-wheel drive saloon car instead of a pick-up truck, which would have carried both people and goods.

The community in Kwale went further. According to the director of Genesis, 'They refused to participate in any review process until they had formed their own committee to review the previous year's work on the basis of financial information made available to them.' Genesis took up the challenge at the local level and even went a step further. It provided financial information about its work to government officials, a move that won it praise from government as 'one of the most transparent and honest CBOs' in Kenya.

The extent to which this rather commendable and practical example of downward accountability will influence other partners and communities in Kenya is yet to be seen. But, at the very least, it is a welcome change, described by Genesis staff as 'the small beginnings of a revolution in Kenya'.

Country offices such as ActionAid Kenya are now using *Jadili*, a senior management forum, to address management issues that arise from the PRRPs. But the above discussions highlight the need for more formal mechanisms of enforced accountability to the constituency that INGOs, non-governmental organizations (NGOs) and CBOs claim to represent. Consultation or involvement in planning, in their current form, while important, do not adequately resolve and provide space for negotiating priorities, resource allocation and receiving and acting on feedback.

Power

The resources and status of any large NGO bring a certain level of power imbalance to any relationship with local partners and poor people. If we deny or fail to recognize our power over local people and partners, we would also fail to take steps to transform our power positively in terms of constructing equitable human relationships in our work. If we do not show willingness to challenge and be challenged by poor people, partners and each other, how can we possibly talk about promoting a rights-based approach that, in essence, involves reminding and challenging government and international institutions to live up to their responsibilities to poor people? What if we were as much part of the problem as we are part of the solution in terms of our own management styles, operational procedures and structures?

ActionAid has been trying to build two-way open and transparent relationships with the communities over whom they are perceived to have 'power'. However, this attempt at levelling out power relations has been a challenge, particularly in terms of financial accountability. In Brazil, our identity as both a 'donor' and a 'partner' raised questions about ownership and ultimate accountability. Ownership implies leadership and control. When donors give up ownership there is an implication that they are also ceding control. Yet, donors – local, national or international – do have legitimate concerns about the extent to which the objectives for which they commit their funds are being achieved. Donors also have to demonstrate to the original source of their funds – whether individuals, government or corporations – that they are making a difference in the lives of poor people. Financial disclosure policies, now being developed in ActionAid, highlight the potential to compel all parties in funding relationships to demonstrate to their representative constituency that they are performing – although these do not guarantee changes in how key decisions about finances are reached at the local level.

While efforts to level out power relations with communities and partners may be genuine, it is clear that this aim would require a drastic rethink of procedures. The traditional approaches used for tackling planning and budgeting processes; strategic and operational decision-making; financial resource generation and allocation; expenditure and performance control; and even community involvement in audit processes are inherently disempowering to local people and partners. All of these are seen as key to improving the quality of relationships.

A practical example is illustrative of the ways in which current procedural requirements may be inappropriate. Managers rightly charged field staff and local people with the responsibility of supervising, monitoring and reporting on the construction of a surface dam in the Kwale community in Kenya. Yet, neither ActionAid staff in Kwale district nor local people were signatories to the contractual agreement for the dam construction. The privilege of approving and signing the contract fell to the contractor and headquarters staff – primarily senior programmes and finance staff. Against expectation, the work was shoddy and its implementation seriously delayed. With headquarters staff miles away, it was extremely difficult for field staff and local people to put continuous pressure on the contractor to keep to the agreed schedule of work. The former tried their best; but, without any real authority, they were unable to bring the contractor to order. Two years later, the contractor is still playing hide and seek. Yet, in practical terms, the simple act of allowing local partners or staff to sign a piece of paper could have given tangible meaning to the concept of delegation and, perhaps, empowered local partners to carry out their responsibility.

Such delegation of authority could have ensured proper supervision and a speedy and scheduled completion of the project. More importantly, it would have increased the sense of ownership of local-level staff and community members. This illustrates two points: delegation by management went ahead without granting the accompanying authority to enforce responsibility; and the inflexible application of financial procedures and rules ended up being disempowering to local staff and people as they felt that their efforts were not leading to concrete outcomes.

To put this Kenyan example in context, we need to explain why this happened. To ensure judicious use of donor funds and to prevent fraud, authorization levels have been established for relevant categories of staff. Staff or partners cannot approve expenditures above their established authorization level. In this case, however, the well-intentioned policy had a negative effect. It wasted vital resources in the form of funds and time. Since those responsible were not made parties to contractual agreement, decentralization lost its practical meaning and decision-making at the local level was severely constrained.

Such cases have led to the recognition of the need for granting greater power to 'front-line' or field staff and the leadership of our community partners. Crucially, field staff and community partners must be encouraged to be more challenging, assertive, informed, skilled and supportive of poor people. As shown above, front-line staff (particularly during the recent past) have all too often been at the receiving end of instructions, with little of their own perspectives taken into account in terms of management decision-making, or only as an exception rather than the norm. This is changing with ALPS.

For instance, to help partners and front-line staff respond quickly to changing priorities, Kenya is reviewing current financial reporting and regulations. More radical measures have been suggested in Ethiopia, where the programme is considering giving grants directly to poor people's organizations directly, rather than through intermediaries such as ActionAid NGO partners. The Gambia has gone ahead with what is considered by them to be a 'radical but risky' venture in which CBOs manage their own budgets and accounts.

Another source of disempowerment is language. Over the years, our language forms have tended to relate to or imply good relationships. We very liberally use words such as 'empowerment', 'partnership', 'participation', 'ownership', 'transparency' and 'accountability' (IDS, 2001); but there is often little consensus regarding what these words mean for local people. Neither has their continued popularity in usage helped to achieve the ideals that they espouse. In fact, there is no overriding evidence that NGOs and donors themselves exhibit these tenets in their own relationships.

Rather than relish this conceptual maze, we need to integrate a range of languages and appropriate media within our own institutional work. We need locally appropriate and effective forms of communication – drama, stories, proverbs, role plays, video, radio – that permit local-level analysis and understanding if we are to be culturally sensitive and truly listen to the voices of the poor. We need to build a common set of mutually binding values and principles that give practical meaning to these ideals.

This means that we do need to challenge the institutional dependency on the English language as the primary form of communicating, documenting, sharing and learning. Furthermore, the use of non-literary-based tools and approaches will not only improve communication, learning and involvement in decision-making, but also local-level analysis and – in a limited sense – representation.

For example, the use of participatory communication through video, drama and role plays that is currently being piloted in Malawi has proved important in attempting to level the power imbalance caused by the inability to communicate through the 'correct' language as used by those in power – that is, written text, generally in English. For instance, in one year alone, seven children drowned trying to cross a river on their way to school. Parents in affected communities formed alliances to take action to prevent further deaths. By enacting and recording a play of these sad incidents, they succeeded in bringing this tragedy to the attention of district authorities in Malawi. The potential to raise funds for a bridge seems good. Of course, they cannot write a project proposal; but the direct anecdotal evidence provided in the video forced officials to listen, even if they have not yet acted.

Participation

The third key question that ALPS attempts to tackle asks is it possible, with the necessary commitment and adjustments, to achieve direct representation of poor people in key decision-making processes? From our initial lessons, this is one of the most daunting challenges of downward accountability at the moment, considering the fact that time is a very scarce resource for poor people. Already there are complaints about unrealistic demands placed on poor people's time; in fact, it may not be in their interest to give too much of their time away for free.

In Ethiopia and Kenya, for example, there were suggestions that we should examine from the perspective of communities whether or not it is justifiable for development practitioners to request or even coerce poor people, most of whom can hardly support their own families, to invest inordinate amounts of their time in community development processes for free, while INGO and NGO staff and development professionals remain salaried. Another important concern was raised regarding token participation. For example, to what extent would the opinions of those consulted be taken on board? As staff and partners in Ethiopia asked: 'Who sets the development agenda and whose agenda carries the day?'

Faced with conditions of severe deprivation and concerned primarily with day-to-day survival, poor people are very careful about suggestions that may upset the status quo, unless there are clear guarantees that they will not suffer from any negative consequences that may arise from their involvement. When we asked communities in Kenya about how they would rank local CBOs in terms of integrity, we often got the answer: 'We can only respond honestly to this question if you can promise that you will not victimize us by cancelling our community projects' (ActionAid, 2001c, p5). This response raises questions about the extent to which local people trust development agencies, generally.

I suggest that it is realistic to expect the participation of poor people, but in ways that guarantee that their perspectives and priorities are captured through CBO or community representatives. In this process, it is important that poor people are made aware that they can exercise their inalienable right to withdraw their stamp of legitimacy if strategies, expenditure choices, actions and development objectives come into conflict with their expressed expectations. Similarly, if consultation, feedback or joint decision-making fail to guarantee a legitimate and accountable intermediation on their behalf, poor people must be able to withdraw their consensus or mandate. I believe that development NGOs have, to a large extent, denied poor people this right.

The PRRPs raised a number of issues that must be considered if the participation of poor people is to guarantee their rights to equitable participation.

The first is to critically review the range of relationships and agree context-specific principles to guide relationships. For instance, ActionAid's work revolves around a complex set of human relationships with poor and excluded people; partner organizations; allies in coalitions and alliances; people in powerful institutions, governments or donor organizations; people who are sponsors or supporters; and with each other as colleagues. These relationships generate dynamic power relations, and we cannot promote or hope to achieve true representation of poor people if we are not sensitive to these.

The second is the importance of providing space and time for reflection and analysis of power relationships. Of course, given the range of stakeholders in any one particular context, we also need to ask ourselves: 'Whom do we represent?' If, as expected, we represent poor people, then we have to realign systems and procedures to meet their information needs.

Third, we need to provide space for, as well as encourage and support, the emergence of strong networks of partners (NGOs, CBOs, community groups and poor and marginalized people) who are sufficiently empowered to exert mutual accountability. This will require clear mechanisms for accountability supported by unambiguous, transparent and mutually agreed principles of engagement. It is noted that the ALPS principles provide the normative framework that recognizes one's rights and scope of responsibility in a given relationship. They represent ownership and provide a yardstick for judging compliance to agreed commitments.

It is clear, then, that active and informed participation of poor people in formulation, implementation and monitoring of development programmes requires specific mechanisms for accessing information and detailed arrangements for making the right to participation real. Inclusive participatory and review processes have a key role in this, but should consciously promote critical sharing and reflection on mistakes and 'worst practice'. This self-critical process needs to be internalized and actively supported by management.

Learning

Lessons from a participatory communication project in Malawi indicate that appropriate communication, documentation, reporting and a good understanding of contextual issues are all key to building trust and good working relationships. Similarly, work in India shows that a good understanding of the socio-economic, political and cultural context is relevant to our own understanding. As we begin to comprehend the challenges we face, we offer ourselves the opportunity to improve and promote policies and adapt institutional frameworks, which build on relationships, promote trust and openness, and develop new forms of partnership and cooperation with poor people and other development practitioners.

There are currently many new initiatives in India that intend to increase learning, both organizationally and externally. These initiatives range from people planning and budget hearings to supporting lower-caste groups to leverage funds from government, or even employing people with disabilities to work with ActionAid. In contrast to the past, and in response to concerns raised by partners, institutional frameworks are now being made sufficiently flexible, particularly at the local and national levels, to cope with the different interests, priorities and perspectives of different stakeholders.

One encouraging learning is that when the right frame of analysis is highlighted and provided, the necessary supporting conditions created and the needed space and relevant information provided, poor people willingly raise and discuss development concerns and act. For example, minority groups in Ethiopia, using drama, discussed how some of their rights are being violated. Women, in particular, voiced their concerns in areas such as female genital mutilation, early marriages and abductions. In Kenya, children staged a mock debate to generate discussion on gender roles, gender discrimination and inequality at the household level.

Now, more than ever, development NGOs and their partners have a role in helping poor people to understand how these age-old norms and oppressive structures work to conspire against poor and powerless people. This can be done by galvanizing support at all levels, but will require more practical forms of collaboration, cooperation and joint effort on the part of development organizations. We can no longer afford insularity if we are to tear down oppressive structures. The growing importance and role of civil society nationally and internationally is an added advantage, although this role is not necessarily unproblematic. The literature suggests that such collaboration is one of the more viable options for INGOS in the current context. As Michael Edwards (2000, p24) points out, there is an urgent need for greater 'emphasis on horizontal working relationship among equals; stronger links between local, national and global action; and more democratic ways of deciding on strategy and messages'. The literature suggests that the time has come for networking coalitions and alliance-building. This will require that work is organized in quite different ways and it will not be easy. Rather, it will be both difficult and challenging (Ndegwa, 1996). It can even generate tensions and conflict conceptually and practically (Lewis, 2001; Salamon and Anheier, 1999). Indeed, 'many NGOs are somewhat territorial and are not willing or eager to work with others in conjunction with the coordination of projects, cooperation and information-sharing' (McRae, 2002, p15).

The other area of learning that needs strengthening is advocacy-based research and documentation to support the new development agenda. Command-and-control-type behaviour is being contested by ALPS and is actively discouraged in ActionAid. Changes in strategies and policies are important for organizational change; but our experience shows that policies in themselves do not bring about change:

> *While ALPS should release staff time and give greater priority to reflection with key stakeholders, many of the underlying problems are seen to be behavioural, particularly from people in leadership positions. There are still many factors that make staff feel disempowered, particularly staff at the front line or those not in positions that traditionally hold power inside ActionAid* (ActionAid, 2001b, p15).

Conclusions

The challenges posed by development practice, in terms of accountability, participation, learning and power relations, indicate the need for far-reaching changes in how we engage in dialogue, how we give and receive information and feedback, our management styles and our behaviour and attitudes. ActionAid started with the premise that change must begin from within the organization itself. In other words we decided to act exactly in the same way as we expect others to act. This called for practical action, appropriate and relevant to each level, to translate ideals into practical steps and actions. Next, the practical steps and actions, appropriately communicated, needed to be negotiated, agreed and acted upon by all key stakeholders. Such change requires ongoing support, understanding and encouragement as the basis for mutual learning.

This chapter has highlighted the challenges of developing downward accountability and breaking down unequal power relations. I have attempted to explain how processes (planning, budgeting, reporting), procedures (financial systems, internal controls, working arrangements) and power (funding, information, knowledge, attitudes and behaviour, management styles) reinforce existing stereotypes. In spite of the rhetoric of change, fears, uncertainty and mutual suspicion remain.

This chapter has also presented a number of valuable lessons for development organizations and donors. It has shown that we need to consciously look for and tackle institutional systems, structures and procedures that often inadvertently undermine or weaken relationships. It is vital that new means are developed to assist partners and local people to recognize their right to accountability and how this can be brought about. As donors, we must acknowledge our responsibility for the power that we hold and manage it in ways that promote the interests of poor people. This requires shedding the 'expert' image that has gradually built up over the years and acknowledging that we do not have all of the answers. Internal learning, self-critique and honesty need to be promoted. We also need to be more proactive in responding promptly to local-level concerns, and in promoting more dialogue and locally appropriate forms of communication. We have embarked on the beginning of a long and difficult but worthwhile journey. We hope that those who believe that poverty is a phenomenon of human creation will come along with us.

Notes

1   Many thanks to my working partner Patta Scott-Villiers for all of the development debates we had in the field while working together in Ethiopia and Kenya. These debates informed this chapter. My thanks to Salil Shetty, whose honest presentation at the 'Power, Procedures and Relationships' workshop in IDS gave me the courage to write this chapter. While in Malawi for a separate assignment, Su Braden gave me valuable comments on my draft. I owe her thanks. My thanks go to my colleagues in the Impact Assessment Unit, Antonella Mancini and Ros David, for encouraging me to take on the work on ALPS. My thanks are also due to Robert Chambers, at whose insistence I attended the 'Power, Procedures and Relationships' workshop in IDS – the product of this work. Thank you also to Robert and Jethro Pettit for allowing me to use their table comparing logframe analysis with ALPS and to Rosemary McGee for reviewing the chapter and providing extremely useful comments. Finally, and most importantly, very many thanks to Leslie and Rachel for editing this piece. Without their help this contribution would hardly have seen the light of day.
2   ActionAid is one of the UK's largest development agencies, working in over 30 countries. Its mission is to work with poor and marginalized people to eradicate poverty by overcoming the injustice and inequity that cause it.
3   A process of capturing the aspirations, priorities and perspectives of poor people and partners on progress, or the lack of it.

References

ActionAid (1999) *Fighting Poverty Together: ActionAid Strategy 1999–2003*, ActionAid, London
ActionAid (2001a) *Global Progress Report*, unpublished draft, ActionAid, London
Actionaid (2001b) 'Transforming Power', proceedings of a workshop in Dhaka, Bangladesh
ActionAid (2001c) 'Impact Assessment Exchanges', September, Actionaid, London
Edwards, M (2000) *NGO Rights and Responsibilities: A New Deal for Global Governance*, Foreign Policy Centre, London
Fowler, A (1997) *Striking a Balance: A Guide to Enhancing NGO Effectiveness in International Development*, Earthscan, London
IDS (2001) *The New Dynamics of Aid: Power, Procedures and Relationships*, IDS Policy Briefing no 15, Institute of Development Studies, Brighton, UK

Lewis, D (2001) *The Management of Non Governmental Development Organizations*, Routledge, London

McRae, H (2002) *Development in the Third World and Emerging Countries: A Sensible and Successful Approach*, McRae Foundation, US

Ndegwa, S N (1996) *The Two Faces of Civil Society: NGOs and Politics in Africa*, Kumarian Press, Bloomfield, US

Salamon, L M and Anheier, H K (1999) 'The Third Sector in the Third World', in Lewis, D (ed) *International Perspectives on Voluntary Action: Reshaping the Third Sector*, Earthscan, London

Scott-Villiers, P (2002) 'How the ActionAid Accountability, Learning and Planning System Emerged: The Struggle for an Organizational Change', *Development in Practice*, vol 12, no 3, August, pp424–435

Sen, A (1999) *Development as Freedom*, Alfred A Knopf, New York

UNDP (1997) *Human Development Report*, Oxford University Press, New York

9

'If It Doesn't Fit on the Blue Square It's Out!' An Open Letter to My Donor Friend

Everjoice Win

Introduction

This chapter, written from the perspective of a Zimbabwean activist, uses a letter format to explore the changing dynamics and power relations between herself and a foreign aid worker, 'Christine'. The imposition of donor reporting procedures is critiqued as being based on donor, as opposed to local, needs. In this way, learning is defined by, and developed for, donors rather than for local usage. The consequence of the failure of donors to harmonize their procedures is made clear. The author argues that when development is reduced to simplifying difficult contextual realities into, for example, logical framework formats, more problems may be created than solved. While donors need certain forms of information in a format that is easy to manage, local aid workers have their own needs and requirements. The activist returns to question the individual motivations of her Western colleague. She calls on Christine to 'meet half way'. She suggests that donors listen to the language used by local activists and understand their visions and, consequently, that they adapt some of their procedures to locally defined ways of doing things.

'Dear Christine'

Dear Christine:
I have resorted to writing you a letter because I feel this may be the only way you will understand. I have tried to explain things in my annual reports, verbally and at conferences. But I do not seem to be able to get through to you.

We first met when you came to my country as a young university graduate. They called you a 'volunteer', coming to us to learn about 'Africa', and to 'help us' where possible. You were a lovely person then – full of enthusiasm, reading books, asking questions. You even took to eating *sadza*, our local staple. When we went to workshops you put on long skirts and head scarves (even though I tried to tell you the latter was not necessary – I guess you wanted to behave according to your perception of a proper Zimbabwean woman?). You spent a year with us and went back to finish your Masters.

The next time we met was at the Beijing conference in 1995. You had just joined a small organization in the US as a volunteer intern. I remember you darting from workshop to workshop in Huairou, still as enthusiastic as ever: 'Oh EJ, these women are incredible! I want to see everyone. I want to hear everything!' you enthused breathlessly. The joys of youth.

In your next incarnation you became a donor! We met again when I came to the US for a workshop. I could have fallen off my chair as you introduced yourself thus: 'My name is Christine. I am a gender expert, specializing in southern Africa'. This was now 1997. I wondered how in such a short time you had become 'an expert'? As for specializing in southern Africa, eh my dear? When you lived in Zimbabwe you had gone on a Christmas jaunt to Mozambique, Botswana and Zambia, all in three weeks. Does this make one an expert on southern Africa? I have lived in this country for a good 34 years and have never acquired the gumption to call myself an expert on Zimbabwe. Maybe I should not be so surprised. You were just imitating what I have heard many people from your part of the world say. Up there it appears a requirement to puff oneself up, whereas down here we are taught to be modest. The only time I have heard people waxing lyrical on credentials is at a funeral, not while you are still walking this Earth. We joked about your introduction at tea. But I digress.

In your new incarnation, you are now responsible for the southern Africa desk in your organization. Gender is your speciality. My organization had been getting money from your foundation for two years when you came on board. We now report to you, via your office in Harare. I was happy to learn that you were at the other end of the accounting chain. At least here is someone who understands us. So we thought. Alas, our relationship has now changed. You are now Christine the big donor, not Christine my old (dare I say 'little'?) friend. Every nine months you come down here and I cannot help but notice the new you. Gone is the enthusiastic, learning and 'with the women' Christine. You are the donor. You know almost everything. You no longer ask questions; you have the answers. You are critical of what we are trying to do and point out what we should have done. For example, you wondered why we did not mobilize women to go on a street march when we failed to get all the clauses passed on inheritance rights. I tried to explain to you how the groups we work with feel about mass action of that kind. I explained the need for time to work more with women until they are at a point when they feel that they can engage in such a 'risky' activity – by the women's and our definition! 'But in South Africa they demonstrate all the time. In Latin America, too!' Your frustration was obvious and so was your verdict: we are not doing enough.

The blue square!

You recently came to show us your new proposal and reporting format – all boxes and 'fill in the blank spaces'. Do you remember that workshop you and I attended in Nyanga when you volunteered with us? The one facilitated by a German donor for all their 'partners' in Zimbabwe? The donor was teaching – yes, teaching us – how the ZOPP (objective-oriented project planning, '*Ziel-Orientierte Projekt Planung*'.) format worked.[1] Remember how we laughed all night about the absurdity of the framework? 'No, no, no, Everrrzhois and Kristiiin, not like so! No, no, no! If it doesn't fit on the blue square, I am sorry, it is out!' Karl had exploded. We spent three days trying to fit visions, objectives, strategies and our way of seeing the world into the differently shaped blue, green and yellow cards. It was really not funny, though. It was painful. Nobody understood this method and the logic behind it. It did not make sense for many of us who are Ndebele- or Shona-speaking. In our languages we express ourselves in paragraphs, not in short phrases or sentences. We are an oral people. We don't think in boxes either.

Now you have gone and developed your own 'template'. Template. It reminds me of the oral learner driver's licence test that you were made to take in Zimbabwe. After our Vehicle Inspection Department had refused your American licence, you were forced to take local tests and learn how to drive all over again. You had to take the oral test, which is done in fifteen minutes flat. Because there will be some 100 or so people, the multiple-choice test is marked using a plastic template. The marking takes another 15 minutes flat. I remember that you were so incensed. That is exactly how I feel; that is why I am giving you an example that I think you can relate to. We have to fit our visions, our way of thinking into your template. Gone are our free expression, our long paragraphs and our way of seeing and interpreting our reality. We are now forced to express ourselves in a way that you understand and want.

Words, words, words

My language has also changed. Gone are the various words I used to use to describe women's reality in this part of the world. I now play what I call the word game. Accountability, transparency, civil society, good governance, poverty alleviation, engaging the state, critical, cutting edge, stakeholders, participation, advocacy. I could go on and on. These are the words we now use. Yes, we do believe in these concepts. We do work around them. But it is almost as though if we don't use these words, we fail the test. Remember that report we wrote in 1999? How you sent it back with lots of questions and comments because you said you 'couldn't follow' what it is we were trying to say. Well, the simple solution was to use all of the big favourite words. It worked like magic. You stopped complaining. Your foundation has consistently refused to fund one very good organization that I know. Not because they don't do good work, but because they are not, as you put it, 'cutting edge'. Loosely translated, that means they don't speak your language and they don't use the 'flavour of the month' expressions. I stand to be corrected on that.

Different strokes for different folks

Remember how shocked you were to realize just how much time we spent writing reports and proposals to donors? 'Why don't you just write one report and one proposal for everyone. When do you ever get to do any real work? This is terrible!' So you once asked in an understandable rage. But now you have your template, and so do the other six donors we deal with. Added to this is the whole nightmare of the different languages you all use. We have to constantly try and remember what a goal, purpose, objective or output means to each one of you. We have learned painfully that all of these terms don't mean the same to everyone. The whole thing has been reduced to a farce. We laugh in workshops when you Northerners aren't there. 'Is that a goal? No, maybe it's an output!' Depending upon whether you were trained by Canadians, Danes or Swiss, you call the same thing something else. But we have to follow procedures.

'Procedure': it reminds me of another game that you and I used to play. Remember how we used to go visit my friend Sofie at the Department of Foreign Affairs? Procedure required that we fill in little slips of paper before they would let us into the building. We had to fill them out, indicating who we were, who we were visiting and why. That procedure made me angry, initially, until I turned it into a game. When I realized that none of the men at the desk ever read those pieces of paper, and neither did they really care what you wrote, I decided to have some fun. I remember 'teaching' you – I love that word – how to play the game. So, on some days we were 'Mrs Mugabe of State House, Harare' or 'Mrs Thatcher of 10 Downing Street', coming to see the president. On other days, we were Mata Hari, Eva Braun or Mother Theresa. It was great fun. All you had to do was follow the writing procedure and they let you in. Totally inflexible. I play the same game with you. As long as I follow the template, say the right words and do what you ask, then you will 'let me through' – as in: through to getting funding.

For you or for us?

Instead of writing reports or documenting experiences in ways that help us to learn, we spend a great deal of time trying to please you and doing what you want. Think of any NGO that you have funded during the last five years. If you were to ask them right now to give you something that provides enough depth and critical reflection to contribute to learning, would they have it? They would certainly have their annual reports and reports written for their other donors, but not much that is deeply reflective. We have little time, energy and resources to commit to such time-consuming processes. That is why our story has often been written by Northern academics, visitors, journalists or anybody else passing through – but not by us. Your reporting 'format' – or shall we call it 'template' – is all about you and what you want to know. It is not about us and what we want to learn.

I, too, have changed. I no longer feel relaxed, sharing information with you. I now 'report' to you. I tell you what I think you want to hear. I focus on the projects you are funding. What else is there to talk about? I am too scared to talk too much, just in case I say the wrong things. I withhold information that might damage my organization. I spend time trying to understand the language that you speak and how to fit my organization into the relevant templates. We have to move with the times, keep up with the latest lingo. I suppose that is why we are regarded as 'cutting edge'? But, in truth, we are still talking about the same group of women whom you knew way back then. Little has changed, including, perhaps, the language that we use to describe their world and our interventions.

Let's meet half way

Development is not about words and procedures. It is about changing the reality of people's lives. We need procedures, concepts and methods, but only as tools to help us do the work that needs to be done. When development is reduced to fitting things on blue squares, then we create more problems than we claim to solve. When these tools begin to imprison and consume all of our energies, where will we get the extra energy to do real work?

We need to find ways of relating to each other that are not based on templates and inflexible procedures. Indeed, we do need to have systems that will help you get the information that you require and that are easy enough to manage. But, at the same time, we too need to do more than satisfy your requirements. All we are asking of you is to develop ways of listening to our language and our visions, and adapt some of your procedures to our way of doing things. You and I are only part of the story of development. The bigger story has probably not yet been told. That is the story of the ordinary woman and man out there, and that story certainly does not fit on a blue square.

Note

1   ZOPP is an early version of logical framework (logframe) analysis (see Chapter 11). It was designed and implemented by Deutsche Gesellschaft für Technische Zusammenarbeit (GTZ), the German development agency.

10

The Bureaucrat

Katja Jassey

Introduction

This chapter explores some observations about bureaucrats and bureaucracy from experiences that the author has had during her work with Sida, the Swedish International Development Agency. The author argues for the importance of delivering aid through more flexible mechanisms, which reduce power imbalances and improve accountability and transparency. In conjunction with this procedural flexibility, organizational incentives are required to address staff motivation. If bureaucrats are to be effective agents of change, then processes that engage, animate and activate the commitment to public service need to be introduced. Bureaucrats need to become participants, rather than the objects or instruments of other people's change strategies. Finally, the author calls for initiatives that rekindle the kind of passions – about inequality, about fairness, about improving the lot of poor and excluded people – that were the initial motivating factors for public-service employment.

Bureaucrats and bureaucracy

With a job title like 'socio-cultural adviser' and being placed at the Division for Policy and Socio-Economic Analysis, it certainly sounds as if I have an extremely interesting and intellectually stimulating job. And I do. Sometimes. But most of my time is devoted to attending to administrative matters. In fact, I spend very little time dishing out clever socio-cultural advice and quite a lot of time drawing up consultancy contracts, deciphering agreements and harassing people to hand in their financial reports. This world, the world of bureaucracy, may be far distant from the worlds of the poor people whose lives development agencies seek to improve and about which socio-cultural advisers are supposed to be giving advice. But it has its own socio-cultural dimensions and is, in its own way, something with which I have become fascinated. In this section I share some of my observations and reflections about bureaucrats and bureaucracy, gleaned during the five years that I have spent at Sida.

It seems as if bureaucracy has been under fire for as long as we have known it – a subject of complaints and stories of many great novelists such as Frantz Kafka and August Strindberg. As de Gay (2000, pp1–2) points out in his *In Praise of Bureaucracy*:

> *...popular anti-bureaucratic sentiment trades on two dramatic, but rather contradictory, representations of the 'typical bureaucrat'. One has this creature endlessly drafting diabolic regulations, cunningly contriving new controls over the private citizen, while extending its own malign influence. The other has bureaucrats positioned as idle loafers.*

I will focus on the former representation of bureaucrats as the people who keep on inventing new control mechanisms and procedures, since the focus and aggravation of many of the other actors whom we deal with is directed towards these procedures.

It is not just the public at large for whom images of the bureaucrat are so negative. The development scene is characterized by typecasting. Those who work in it are given a category, a label and a set of presumed characteristics to go with them. And what we say and do is often interpreted according to preconceptions about our motivations and interests as members of these categories. To be cast as 'the donor from the bilateral agency of an Organisation for Economic Co-operation and Development (OECD) country' certainly carries with it a series of striking stereotypes. At a recent Sida workshop on popular participation, we were asked to consider how we thought others saw us – not donors in general, but Sida, specifically. Words such as *naive, democratic, less hierarchical, in the vanguard in relation to other donors, but also 'big and clumsy and walking around with dollars falling out of our pockets'* in relation to partners in the South came to our minds (IDS, 2001). These were, of course, nothing but our own reflections on how we felt (and possibly wished) we might be perceived. And it remains unknown if our self-perceived identity was the outcome of real lived experiences or merely the representation of those endless discussions we have about our role and place in the development world.

The ideas partly represent to us, the 'donor', our identity. And to be walking around with dollars falling out of your pocket is certainly not a picture you would want to cultivate if the aim of your work is poverty reduction. The image becomes even less flattering if one adds to this the dimension of *bureaucracy* and the fact that we are bureaucrats. Think, for example, about Weber and how he feared that bureaucracy would, in the end, lead to the destruction of all social diversity, cultural variety and political pluralism (Nisbet, 1976). Here is what he said about us, the bureaucrats:

> *It is horrible to think that the world could one day be filled with nothing but those little cogs, little men clinging to little jobs and striving towards bigger ones... This*

passion for bureaucracy...is enough to drive one to despair (Max Weber, quoted in Mayer, 1943, pp127–128).

I think one can safely say that to become a civil servant or bureaucrat was not what most of us dreamt of when growing up. It sounds rather boring and safe. And who wants to be boring? It was more likely the drive to change the world that brought most of my colleagues to Sida. Personally, I had nourished a romantic dream ever since my childhood that I would, one day, fight the inequalities of this world. Growing up in the countryside of Sweden, I studied Spanish so that I could become a guerrilla soldier in Central America. I didn't know much about the outside world, but I did know that it was unjust. I now work for an organization where values such as democracy and solidarity have had a core place in most of its documents and discussions over the past four decades. So, what is stopping myself and my colleagues from bringing about the change that so many are asking for? The change towards handing over power, more flexible procedures, more accountability and transparency? After all, the red-tape mentality – the demand that certain procedures should be followed even if it takes time – is nothing that anyone derives pleasure from and is, indeed, challenged by many from the inside.

The challenge from bureaucracy's critics

The call for our transformation as development organizations comes from all quarters. The quest for the modernization of state bureaux in OECD countries can be summarized in ten points, a broth made up primarily by ingredients from public choice theory and contemporary managerialism (de Gay, 2000). I believe that most of us who work in the development field will recognize these demands; they are strikingly similar to what we preach to our counterparts:

- competition between service providers;
- empowering citizens through pushing control out of bureaucracies and into communities;
- focusing on outcomes rather than inputs;
- organizations and persons driven by missions and visions, not by rules and regulations;
- redefining citizens as customers;
- preventing problems before they emerge, rather than simply treating them once they have arisen;
- earning money, not just spending it;
- decentralizing authority and encouraging participatory management;
- using market-type mechanisms rather than bureaucratic techniques and practices;
- catalysing partnerships between public, private and voluntary sectors (de Gay, 2000, pp82–83).

According to de Gay, one of the problems with this type of entrepreneurial governance is that it takes so much of its inspiration from commercial enterprise. And the two sectors or arenas do not necessarily share the same ethos. A commercial enterprise wants to maximize the profits of its own business. It can take risks in its pursuit of this goal, as one loss can hopefully be regained later. It's a game. A state bureau cannot calculate losses against profits. The task we are set to do is not to maximize our own profit and welfare, but the welfare of others. If a state bureau is working with development, it is not only 'gambling' with the taxpayers' money, but also meddling with other countries' and people's development and welfare. In that sense, we have to be doubly sure that our decisions are the best possible, even if it takes time and is cumbersome.

It should also be noted that, as much as one may hate the workings of a bureaucracy, we also get equally agitated if we discover that somebody else is given preferential treatment. And unlike the competitive ethos of the private sector, we do not believe in 'the survival of the fittest', if that means 'best connected' or 'most manipulative' or 'most powerful'. After all – and in particular for those of us working in development – striving for justice and *equality in treatment of all people* is one of our guiding stars. Hence, the argument for some standardized form of procedures is strong. The hope is that procedures should prevent preferential treatment based on personal contacts (such as the giving of funds to people to whom you are related, even when the proposals are poor); preference for your own group (in terms of ethnicity, caste, sex, etc); or bowing to power rather than to merit (for example, overlooking the misuse of funds because the non-governmental organization (NGO) chairperson is the president's nephew).

So there we are – the clumsy bureaucratic donor from the North. A briefcase filled with procedures and protocols. Although there are good reasons for having standardized procedures, there is an urgent need to think about how they are implemented and whose procedures should be prioritized and applied. Most of us realize that we shouldn't use specific rigid procedures any longer. An ideal that is slowly emerging is that we should take our starting point as the problem – the situation – and identify with whom we can collaborate. We shouldn't merely look to our own organization as we used to do in the past. Ongoing work at Sida around the revision of our working procedures focuses more on the need for flexibility, dialogue and mutual learning than planning, outputs and results. There is growing consensus that overburdening collaborating partners is detrimental to our common objective: fighting poverty. This is one of the reasons why donor coordination has become so popular (something that is also occasionally interpreted as a sign of donors ganging up). We simply cannot demand that one organization or ministry should make ten different presentations and account in ten different ways to its different donors. Thus, we need to move towards prioritizing partners' own frameworks, rather than starting with our own bilateral bureaucracy and procedures. For example, the much-debated logical framework (logframe) should not remain a necessary requirement; for some, its matrix acts more like a straitjacket than a useful development tool.

The passionate bureaucrat

However, as these clumsy donors and bureaucrats are also passionate people who can be as eager at networking, making friends and promoting change as the next person, we need to have at least some regulations in place. Otherwise the power that we hold as keepers and administrators of the Swedish taxpayers' money would be transformed into personal and individual power. And just as much as Weber hated bureaucracy, he also saw it as a necessary ingredient for the democratic development of a society (by which he meant a transition from a traditional society characterized by *Gemeinschaft*[1] and charismatic powerful leaders to a society based on individual contracts and rational centralized leadership and decision-making). So, one could say that the rules are there to help us ensure equality in treatment, and also to minimize the risk we take with other people's money. On the other hand, many bureaucrats find all of the different rules frustrating to the point that they sometimes feel that the only way to deal with them is to bend them. We do so in order 'to get things done'.

Nothing is black and white, something that is certainly true for development. There is, at present, a balance between procedures and personal judgement of donor bureaucrats. The recipients learn to use the networks to their advantage, and they often seek out a supportive champion as their donor contact. They complain when there is a 'change of face' in the donor agency as they fear that the new person will not provide the necessary support. While procedures and regulations may function as safeguards of the principle of equality in treatment, the exact process of social and economic change can never, however, be predicted – nor what it will lead to. However, the very basic foundation of almost all governments, bureaucracies and development organizations is that development *can* be planned. Maybe the passionate bureaucrat has to believe in social engineering in order to survive – if only we could do our planning better, include more poor people and have a more sophisticated economic analysis, we would be able to eradicate poverty. This is a philosophy that underpins not only the World Bank-endorsed poverty reduction strategies, but also a philosophy to which many donor agencies ascribe. It follows that our work naturally centres on making project plans, writing the perfect document and following up these documents – more so than engaging with real life, which reacts so strangely to our actions. In all honesty, development is about taking risks; yet, today our systems discourage risk-taking. They work with the principles of social engineering and corresponding upward financial accountability. We must report to the National Audit Office of Sweden with details of how our accounts are kept. As a result, the top priority becomes the financial management of funds.

Rules of the game and moves for change

Context matters – it has been said before and needs to be said again (it is as important to the ways in which bureaucracies work as it is to projects and programmes in the field). If we want to reform procedures of development aid, we must understand the context that produces and shapes these procedures. When talking about a bilateral donor agency, we need to understand not only what is said, but also the strategies and policies that guide its development work. We also need to make sense of how it functions, the kinds of unspoken rules of the game that underpin its administration. At Sida, there is often talk about a tacit 'Sida knowledge' – a knowledge that you can't gain from reading manuals or even talking to others, only through years and years of actual work. This is experiential knowledge in its finest form. And a lot of this knowledge is about how to bend the rules. Maybe more importantly, though, part of 'being in the know' is to know how and when the real decisions are made. It is a knowledge that makes it possible for a Sida desk officer to create the flexibility and risk-taking that is required in development work. And, quite possibly, our whole system would come to a standstill if that knowledge didn't exist.

If we are committed to the values of solidarity and democracy, why are we not able to deliver changes such as moving to more flexible arrangements, handing over power and improving accountability and transparency? Moving to flexible arrangements shouldn't mean losing a commitment to fair treatment or taking irresponsible risks; individual judgement does not have to result in unchecked individual power over public funds. These are legitimate concerns; but this should not prevent the necessary reform of procedures, rewriting policies and making vision statements of intent. However, support is required to enable such processes of change, change that challenges the tacit and established ways of doing things within organizations. Yet, these kinds of moves are not sufficient to make a difference in themselves. Making bureaucrats work as agents of change requires more than this. It calls for processes that engage, animate and activate the commitment to public service that many of those seemingly dull and boring bureaucrats do share. It calls for ways of working in which we are participants, rather than the objects or instruments of other people's change strategies. And above all, it calls for initiatives that rekindle the kind of passions – about inequality, about fairness, about improving the lot of poor and excluded people – that for many of us were the reasons for getting into these jobs in the first place.

Note

1   *Gemeinschaft* refers to social relationships characterized by relative smallness, cohesion, long duration and emotional intensity. It is believed to be followed by *Gesellschaft* – large-scale, impersonal relationships that depend upon a higher degree of formality.

References

de Gay, P (2000) *In Praise of Bureaucracy: Weber, Organization, Ethics*, Sage, London
IDS (2001) *Meeting the Challenges of Participation for Poverty Reduction – Making It Real: The Challenges and Opportunities for Sida*, Report from workshop held at the Institute of Development Studies, University of Sussex, Brighton, 18–20 September
Mayer, J (1943) *Max Weber and German Politics*, Faber and Faber, London
Nisbet, R (1976) *The Social Philosophers: Community and Conflict in Western Thought*, Paladin, London

Part Three

THE WAY FORWARD

11

Shifting Power to Make a Difference[1]

Robert Chambers and Jethro Pettit

Introduction

During recent years, the wind of development rhetoric has changed. The new words – partnership, empowerment, ownership, participation, accountability and transparency – imply changes in power and relationships, but have not been matched in practice. Viewing aid as a complex system, power and relationships can be identified as governing dynamics that prevent the inclusion of weaker actors and voices in decision-making. Organizational norms and procedures, combined with personal behaviour, attitudes and beliefs, serve to reinforce these existing power relations.

Four action domains present vantage points for effecting systemic change. The first is to use methods of critical reflection and analysis that can make the governing dynamics of power more visible and transparent, and expose avenues for action. The second is about using language itself, reclaiming meanings and applying the new words to induce changes in awareness and action. The third is about identifying rules and procedures that can help to balance relationships of power and open up space for greater inclusion and diversity, and recognizing when existing procedures have had their day. The fourth is focused on transforming aid organizations through approaches to learning and change that involve critical internal reflection.

In all four domains, personal agency is decisive. In making or not making a difference, personal choices, actions and non-actions are central. Champions have shown what some have been able to do through their character, imagination, commitment and leadership. For others, understandings of our increasingly interconnected world suggest that the scope for personal agency and making a difference is not only expanding, but is increasingly dispersed and democratic. Agency brings with it obligations and responsibility. The concept and ideal of responsible well-being demands efforts to be aware of the effects of one's actions and non-actions. It can apply to all actors, but especially, and in a liberating way, to those with more power. In inclusive aid, all actors can see good things to do, do them and gain from making a difference for the better.

Recent years have seen a dramatic shift in the policies of most international aid agencies. Promising new directions are suggested by the rhetoric of development. Poverty reduction is stated as the primary goal of aid, and a broader and more meaningful involvement of citizens and institutions is invited, even required, in efforts to achieve this goal. A global language speaks of partnership, empowerment, ownership, participation, accountability and transparency, and now, increasingly, of good governance, citizenship and rights. These fine ideals stand in contrast to a development landscape littered by failure, corruption, secrecy, greed, blueprint-thinking and contradictory motives. The language of this new consensus does, however, invite the hope of a more just and inclusive path towards human development and well-being.

Yet, as noted throughout this volume, there remains a huge gap between words and practice. Like many development trends to date, the very use of new terms dilutes their potential meanings and increases the chances of their becoming little more than fashionable labels attached to the same underlying systems. While new ways of thinking and speaking can be effective tools for change – and we think they can – they are also easily abused to conceal and advance business as usual. This, we suggest, is because beneath the shifting sands of rhetoric are complex systems governed by enduring relations of power and control that serve to exclude the less powerful. Established organizational norms, procedures and professionalism intertwine with personal behaviour, attitudes and beliefs to reinforce these power dynamics and resist change. For this reason, technical and procedural fixes will often have limited effect. Applied as neutral tools, without sufficient understanding of power and relationships, they tend to address symptoms rather than causes.

Power and relationships as governing dynamics

Viewed as a complex system, international aid can be understood as governed by the dynamics of power and relationships within and among key actors: governments, donor agencies, non-governmental organizations (NGOs) and other civil society organizations. These dynamics also shape the ways in which aid actors respond to, and seek to influence, the context in which they operate. New key words used by aid agencies – *partnership, empowerment, ownership, participation, accountability and transparency* – all imply changes and levelling in the realm of power and relationships. Yet, these words are often applied in ways that do not acknowledge or address power. Throughout this book, diverse experiences involving a range of actors and contexts have all identified power as a common obstacle to making the rhetoric real. This suggests that from this diversity some common lessons and approaches to change may be derived.

In Chapter 2, Robb suggests that while donors aspire towards 'new, more open and collaborative power relationships…the necessary changes at the institutional, procedural and individual levels are likely to be achieved only progressively over time'. The World Bank and the International Monetary Fund

(IMF) have rolled out a raft of new procedures that are intended to reduce poverty through broader social participation, thus far with questionable integrity or impact. 'Although some have called recent changes radical', Robb concludes, 'power still lies in the North, a few people make the decisions and public dialogue is limited' (see Chapter 2). The poverty reduction strategy paper (PRSP) process, with a few exceptions, has exemplified this contradiction. Bolivia's PRSP, as described by Eyben in Chapter 4, was heavily influenced by 'structures of power and patterns of relationships between actors in government, the international cooperation community and civil society'. The process was skewed both by a domestic social context that is 'highly divided and unequal' and by a global political context in which 'mutual manipulative behaviour...results from this difficult and unequal relationship between donors and recipients' (see Chapter 4). The lack of trust and accountability in Uganda's aid partnerships, as Kakande (Chapter 6) explains, has also stemmed from inequality among partners. While Uganda's unique political system allowed some headway in improving donor–government partnerships, ultimately, the North–South divide remains and 'the choice of whom to be accountable to depends upon the power that the citizens in different locations wield'.

Some international NGOs, who act as donors to partner NGOs and community-based organizations (CBOs) in developing countries, are recognizing that similar dynamics of power and manipulation are embedded in their own practices. Staff of the international NGO ActionAid, as Owusu shows in Chapter 8, have been challenged by the realization that poor people and local NGOs 'feel far less in control of the development process than we ourselves had imagined... This feeling of disempowerment, in part, is traced to well-meaning but often constraining processes, procedures and attitudes that reinforce, in many instances, existing stereotypes and unbalanced power relations' (see Chapter 8). The negative influence of power on donor–NGO relationships, accountability and learning is also evident in Win's account of the 'nightmare' of donor-driven reporting systems (see Chapter 9). Hierarchy and power relations within development organizations, whether aid agencies, government or civil society, can restrict learning and change and give rise to procedures designed for control and upward accountability, rather than participation and innovation. An INTRAC (International NGO Training and Research Centre (at Oxford)) study of the UK Department for International Development (DFID) concluded that its internal structure, culture and procedures needed to change if stakeholder participation and partnership were to be realized (INTRAC, 1999; see also Chapter 13). Internal power dynamics and relationships are reflected in relationships with partners, as the same norms and procedures mediate external relations between aid agencies and recipients.

Action domains for change

The survival of hierarchical procedures and processes reflects the persistence of linear closed-system thinking, with its logical sequence of inputs, outputs and cause and effect. It conveniently avoids the complex interaction of variables and dynamics that can yield 'irrational' results. The central question, then, is what it takes to effect *systemic* change in the way that aid works, so that development organizations, procedures and relationships can become more inclusive. In our experience, sharp differences in power tend to exclude people, undermining trust and accountability, and driving a wedge between words and actions. This can work at many levels, sometimes in very obvious ways but also in hidden, unconscious ways – rooted in political and economic structures or embedded in social and cultural values (VeneKlasen with Miller, 2002). Narrowing the gap thus requires understanding power, in the first instance, and then seeking ways to challenge and alter the distribution of power among actors. What steps can be taken, then, to reveal and shift power, and to put concepts of trust, accountability and partnership into practice? There are implications for social, institutional, cultural and political change. There are no blueprints or quick 'off-the-shelf' solutions. The most effective strategies will not be 'toolkits' so much as diverse and complementary ways of addressing power relations in different domains.

Here we identify four action domains. The first is *understanding and analysing power* through methods that can help to reveal and 'make visible' the governing dynamics and leverage points of aid to those who seek to change it (see Chapter 3). The second is *narrowing the gaps between the words and actions*, recognizing that words themselves can be used to induce awareness and action. The third is *changing rules and procedures* by reforming or removing old ones and identifying new ones that can help to balance power relations and open up spaces for inclusion and diversity. And the fourth is *organizational learning and change*, using processes of internal reflection on values and principles to transform the way in which work is undertaken. Each of these, we suggest, can work in diverse but fundamental ways on the deeper governing dynamics of the aid system. Cutting across each of these four action domains is *personal agency and responsibility*. The attitudes, behaviours, commitments and actions of individuals, often neglected in development thinking, have a central role to play in shifting power and contributing to change.

Understanding and analysing power

The first action domain is exploring critical methods of reflection and analysis that can make the governing dynamics of power more visible and transparent, and expose optimal leverage points for action. Ultimately, as Eyben (see Chapter 4) notes, those with less power will have leading parts to play in transforming relationships, whether those with more power are ready or not. Yet, all actors committed to reducing poverty can make the aid system more inclusive by becoming more honest in acknowledging and naming differences in power. Donor agencies might learn to approach their work with a heightened awareness of the implications of power, both within their own organizations and in external relationships, and to find ways of supporting the efforts of others to gain voice and influence in decision-making. Intermediary organizations receiving aid can also examine the meaning of power for their work and partnerships, and learn to negotiate and refuse aid conditions that undermine their autonomy. Community-based organizations and social movements can analyse power structures and use this new understanding to develop their strategies and build alternative sources of power. This awareness can strengthen their capacities to advocate for rights and policy reforms, or to be in greater control of the support or services offered by governments, donors and intermediaries.

A growing body of practical literature offers insights into methods and approaches that can enhance awareness of power relations and their impact on aid and development (see VeneKlasen with Miller, 2002; Cohen et al, 2001; ActionAid, 2001b). The shift from 'projects' to engagement in wider processes of change, including citizenship, local governance, policy advocacy and rights-based approaches, is sparking demand for useful innovations that can help people to understand and address power more explicitly in their work. Some insights for doing this can be drawn from traditions of popular education, participatory action research and community organizing (for example, Freire, 1970; Fals-Borda and Rahman, 1991; Alinsky, 1989; Reason and Bradbury, 2001). What sets these traditions apart from more instrumental 'toolkits' is the value that they place on personal awareness and transformation as part of wider social and political change. Critical reflection or 'praxis' (action–reflection) is used to reveal and challenge structures that oppress, and to envision and promote alternatives.

A useful framework for this more comprehensive approach to understanding power in all of its dimensions is presented in an 'action guide' on advocacy and citizen participation (VeneKlasen with Miller, 2002). Based on extensive field-work, the authors propose methods for analysing the ways in which power operates on three levels: the 'visible power' of official rules, structures and procedures for decision-making; the 'hidden power' of people and institutions who can limit participation in decision-making; and the 'invisible power' of social beliefs, ideology, values and consciousness that define boundaries of debate and action (VeneKlasen with Miller, 2002, Chapter 3). Power at all three levels needs to be unpacked according to particular circumstances in order to develop effective strategies for change for particular contexts.

Awareness of power dynamics can also help actors to perceive the ways in which power is exercised beyond the financial dimensions of aid. 'Aid funding' is very small in comparison to the power dynamics of trade and macro-economic policies. Huge aid investments can be negated by the trade policies of donor countries, such as US and European Union (EU) agricultural subsidies. Aid and trade policies by the same Northern government may even work at cross purposes. Private financial flows to many countries of Asia and Latin America are also far larger than those of bilateral and multilateral aid combined; yet, systems for the governance and accountability of global capital markets – as they impact upon poverty and the environment – are nearly non-existent. These realities, and the role of powerful interest groups behind them, need to be better understood by development actors committed to inclusion and poverty reduction.

Tools for analysis can include the growing volume of approaches to 'economic literacy' employed by NGOs and advocacy groups to encourage citizen understanding and action on national and global economic policies (see, for example, Wilks and Lefrançois, 2002, Appendix). Such analysis can also examine how power is exercised through shaping the knowledge and discourse behind policy processes. While mechanisms such as the PRSPs have purported to make policy formulation more inclusive, most development knowledge is still largely shaped by powerful actors in the North (Brock and McGee, 2002). Lyla Mehta (2001, p195) has argued that 'knowledge has replaced lending capital as the bank's [World Bank's] greatest asset in the global market'. The World Bank, as shown in Box 11.1, is 'winning arguments upstream' through commissioning experts to review and recommend policies and giving it a 'near monopoly on development analysis' (Wilks and Lefrançois, 2002, pp8–9). Because other lenders and donors take so much of a lead from the World Bank, an 'intellectual hegemony' limits the terms of debate and crowds out alternative perspectives. The dominant development discourse can be understood as language, concepts, knowledge and thinking, expressing and reflecting the perceptions, interests and culture of powerful organizations. Methods for analysis have then to go beyond words and concepts to examine the motivations and relations of power that lie behind them.

Narrowing the gaps between words and actions

A second action domain for change is highlighting the gaps between language and practice. The new language of aid and development implies profound shifts in aid relationships and in the distribution of power and control among actors. Yet, in practice, a large gap remains between what is said and what is done (see Box 11.2). This stems, in part, from the integration of these words into what has been called the 'harmony' model of development (Alan Fowler, pers comm), in which poor people's voices, concerns and participation are viewed as technical inputs to rational decision-making processes – rather than as contending interests in processes characterized by highly unequal power relations. The proliferation of new words in the mainstreams of development can be regarded, with a cynicism that is often realistic, as a brute co-optation of language. Such hypocrisies, ambiguities and contradictions can, perhaps, never be fully eliminated.

There is, however, an obverse view. This recognizes the gaps between these words and actual practice as opportunities. As words are used, ways of seeing things can change. When the term 'primary stakeholder', for example, was introduced to describe the poor and marginalized, it served to jolt the user with its implication that poor people should come first. As words are introduced, the concepts and practices that they represent can be challenged and redefined. Gaps are exposed; ways of narrowing them can be sought. While a dominant discourse can co-opt or misuse language, it can also be turned on itself by efforts to reclaim the meanings behind words. *Thought* has long been recognized, in many philosophical and spiritual traditions, as an extremely powerful precursor and determinant of *action*. How people think and what they say do matter, and can become the groundwork for new ways of doing things. This is why discourse is so powerful, and worth unpacking, challenging and redefining.

BOX 11.1 WORLD BANK STUDIES AND ANALYSES

The extraordinary power of the World Bank to determine policy in developing countries cannot be explained alone or even, perhaps, primarily by the importance of its lending. A report from the Bretton Woods Project suggests that the bank's influence is due, in large part, to its capacity to demand processes and studies that generate knowledge and dominate debate (Wilks and Lefrançois, 2002). One dimension is the English language and new words and phrases: new terms and a plethora of acronyms are invented, adopted and used with confidence by World Bank staff, at least temporarily disarming and disempowering others.[2] Another dimension is the sheer number and volume of studies required. There are five core reports for all countries – poverty assessments; country economic memoranda or development policy reviews; public expenditure reviews; country financial accountability assessments; and country procurement assessment reviews. In addition, 16 sector or issue reports are prepared in selected countries (Wilks and Lefrançois, 2002, p13). Individually, any one requirement, such as the poverty reduction strategy paper (PRSP) or the poverty and social impact assessment (PSIA) can look a good thing to do, and a benefit side to the equation is not to be overlooked. At the same time, taken together, these multifarious studies and analyses become hegemonic, dominating countries through mandatory process and knowledge and information overload. Civil society is outpaced. Governments cannot keep up. The questions are, then, whose knowledge counts? Whose analysis? Whose priorities? Whose ideology? Demand generates supply, and much of the supply comes from those who demand it. As Robert Wade has put it: 'We would not want [cigarette transnational] Philip Morris research labs to be the only source of data on the effects of smoking, even if the research met professional standards' (Robert Wade, cited in Wilks and Lefrançois, 2002, p30).

In the words of the Bretton Woods Project:

> The bank most of the time no longer has to rely on its financial clout alone, as it is winning arguments upstream. Through its global- and national-level studies, and its extensive network of official, journalist and academic contacts, the bank has a strong influence on policy debates even where it is not lending (Wilks and Lefrançois, 2002, p8).

James Wolfensohn is proud of the World Bank's emerging influence as 'the knowledge bank', using its central research and policy units and extensive investments in the *World Development* reports and websites as ways of framing legitimate knowledge. The bank appears to remain on top now less through its lending, and more through its capacity to demand, generate and use knowledge, and to do this quickly – an area where it has a largely unchallenged comparative advantage in relation to many countries, especially in Africa, and where it can continually stay ahead of the rest of the field.

Seen in this way, hypocrisy in the use of words is not just a problem, but an opportunity. Indeed, one strategy for improving development practice is to introduce words, contribute to their definition, debate their practical implications, put them in goal and vision statements, and then identify and advocate measures to make them real. Such strategies can be inclusive, enabling people to define their own terminology and meanings and to resist interpretations imposed by others. There will never cease to be such opportunities. At the same time, the words of the new consensus provide a substantial agenda already. As conditions and understandings evolve, there may

---

BOX 11.2 THE GAP BETWEEN WORDS AND ACTIONS

Partnership implies collegial equality and mutual reciprocity; in reality, most lender–borrower and donor–recipient relationships are highly unequal and those who control the funding often call the shots.

Empowerment implies power to those who are subordinate and weak; but the usual practice between levels of hierarchy is control from above. Aid agencies impose conditionalities at the same time as they preach empowerment.

Ownership implies national and local autonomy; but this is limited by aid agencies' influence on policy, human rights and governance, whether this influence is exerted directly on governments or indirectly through citizens and civil society.

Participation is considered a means by some and an end by others, and is used to describe a wide range of practices, stretching from compulsory labour to public consultation to social empowerment and spontaneous self-organization.

Accountability between partners is described as mutual, and two-way up and down the aid chain; in practice, accountability downwards is rare and weak.

Transparency implies information shared between partners and accessible in the public domain; but aid agencies and governments often keep budget details and other information about decision-making confidential.

Primary stakeholder refers to the poor and marginalized; but though 'primary' they usually participate least and have least voice.

Source: adapted from Institute of Development Studies (2001)

---

always be a case for giving prominence to new words and concepts. Care is needed, however, to ensure that they do not distract attention and energy from narrowing current gaps. New fashions in aid, as Leslie Groves (see Chapter 5) has shown, can harm by undermining existing initiatives. To achieve inclusive aid, the major priority is commitment to making the current rhetoric real through changes in power and relationships.

Changing rules and procedures

A third action domain for change is in altering the internal rules and procedures that govern organizations and shape relationships within and between them. For aid agencies, much current practice stands in the way of practising what words imply. Hierarchy in organizations presents an embedded obstacle to change. It is reinforced by upward accountability in planning and reporting systems, by top-down development targets, and by pressures to scale up programmes and achieve wide impacts. Lending and funding invite constraints and conditionalities, such as those found in structural adjustment programmes and within the Heavily Indebted Poor Countries Initiative (HIPC) and the PRSPs. The systems and procedures set up to facilitate resource flows stem from deeper rules, such as goal imperatives handed down from above, that then reinforce hierarchical institutional cultures and relationships. Perhaps one of the most controversial examples has been the logical framework analysis (logframe), as illustrated in Box 11.3.

Box 11.3 Logical framework analysis (logframe)

Logical framework analysis[3] (logframe) and its variants as a required method for planning and monitoring illustrate how procedures can reinforce relationships of power and control (see also Chapters 7 and 8). With origins in management practices for infrastructure projects, the logframe embodies a linear logic associated with things rather than people, with simple and controlled conditions, and with closed systems. It has what has been called vertical and horizontal logic (Gasper, 2000), required in a matrix form. The vertical logic down the matrix is concerned with ends and means – with objectives, goals and purposes (the nomenclature varies), then outputs, then the activities intended to achieve the outputs. The horizontal logic across the matrix is from narrative summary to objectively verifiable indicators and means of verification. A final vertical column is used to identify assumptions about the external environment that enable or hinder the realization of activities, outputs and purpose.

In many instances, in its time, the logframe has served well to focus attention on the links between activities and their intended effects, and, hence, to sharpen interventions. For example, at the UK Department for International Development (DFID), the logframe was found to be useful in shifting the focus from technology toward people, and in demanding evidence of the connections between proposed activities and their impacts on poverty (Rosalind Eyben, pers comm). This signals that certain procedures have their time and place; but changing conditions may require their reassessment and replacement. In its heyday, the logframe gave rise to a small army of consultants who trained others in the technique, and then helped them to carry it out. Some agencies have now abandoned it or do not require it. At the same time, the European Union (EU) has been adopting it, even though during the late 1990s and early 2000s it has been increasingly challenged and resisted.

Most critics of the logframe recognize the value of thinking through some of the vertical logic of a project, but find the experience of using it costly and disempowering (see for example, Chapters 7 and 9; Rashida Dohad, pers comm, cited in Chambers, 1997a, pp43–44; Edington, 2001). Donor-induced logframe meetings rarely include poor people, yet participatory poverty assessments (see, for example, Norton et al, 2001) present much evidence that the priorities of poor people often differ from those perceived by outsiders and local elites. Often, expatriates dominate and the language is English. The idea in ZOPP (*Ziel-Orienterte Projekt Planung*), a close relative of the logframe developed by the German aid agency Deutsche Gesellschaft für Technische Zusammenarbeit (GTZ) (GTZ, 1996; Forster, 1996), is that stakeholders should brainstorm until they agree on one single core problem. This involves a reductionism that flies in the face of multiple and changing realities. Logframe analysis more generally inhibits process and participation and is often experienced as rigid and constraining. When the actual and sensible activities being undertaken differ from those in the frame, reporting can become a nightmare, and the eventual external 'purpose-to-outcome' evaluation can be perceived as a looming threat rather than an opportunity to learn and do better.

A few gifted facilitators have described requirements to make the logframe analysis process more participatory (for example, Samaranayake, 2001). The common experience, however, has been a control orientation that discourages innovation and learning, and reinforces unequal power relations. The reluctance of disempowered recipients to tell powerful donors how bad they find the logframe and how it generates frustration and anger seems likely to have been a factor in prolonging its life. External consultants, well-meaning intermediaries and some NGOs have found a niche industry in supplying expertise to prepare and report on logframes for others, sparing them those demotivating and time-consuming tasks. 'How to do it' guides have been produced for contexts, especially problematical for logframes (see, for example, Farrington and Nelson, 1997, for farmer participatory research). Whatever their merits, these are liable to perpetuate the logframe, the myths that surround it and the unequal power relationships that it induces and sustains.

The logframe demonstrates the ways in which procedures arise in response to a particular need and context. There are three reasons why the logframe may have had its day. In its time, and in appropriate contexts, logframe analysis was helpful in shifting the focus of development planners from technology to people. This mission having been largely accomplished, the logframe may have outlived its purpose. Second, as development shifts not only to people, but to the complex realm of relations among actors, and the need to understand and improve collaborative relationships, a linear planning tool may become dysfunctional. Third, donors have shifted from project funding to policy work and sector support, and project planning tools such as the logframe are simply less relevant. Ironically, the logframe has been abandoned by some donors for their policy and sector work, but is quite often still required for project recipients. Because procedures tend to be additive, and can be used as instruments of domination, one lesson to be drawn from this is to question the underlying reasons for given procedures, and to see if they should be revised or eliminated. It is a question of optimizing procedures for current needs. How should procedures be changed to make them more responsive to partnerships and relationships?

The same question could be posed with regard to aid relationships themselves. Before an aid agency–recipient relationship is entered into, there is a question of whether it is needed and by whom. Donors and lenders may need to be able to give and lend; but potential recipients may not need to receive or borrow. A first step is to establish, indeed, whether the potential recipient or borrower has a need. Voluntary Service Overseas (VSO), the international volunteer organization,[4] has pioneered and spread a workshop process in which a VSO staff member facilitates a potential partner who might wish to host a volunteer to develop its vision and review its resources and capabilities. Sometimes, by the end of the workshop, it emerges that a volunteer is not needed at all. The process empowers the potential partner and improves the prospects that volunteer placements will, indeed, be useful, appreciated and, in other senses, successful. But fewer volunteers may be placed. The institutional challenge is then to recognize, reward and value staff who place fewer volunteers because they facilitate this process well. This requires a rethink of evaluation norms, procedures, reporting and mindsets. The pressure and incentives for staff to disburse are problematic and can be difficult to resist (Blackburn et al, 2002).

Rules and procedures present one way toward systemic change in which the gap is narrowed between words and practice. Mutual accountability can be brought into both internal and external relationships. Examples include partnership agreements based upon shared principles; two-way and 360 degree reporting and accountability mechanisms; various forms of participatory planning, budgeting, monitoring and evaluation; and structural reforms such as decentralization, devolution to local control and decision-making, and the flattening of organizational hierarchies. In practice, however, new rules and procedures will rarely be enough alone. They may even reinforce existing power relations – for example, those at lower or local levels. They can, though, be a powerful tool for change.

Two innovations illustrate how power, relationships, rules and procedures interlink: the still evolving Accountability, Learning and Planning System (ALPS) of the international NGO ActionAid (discussed by Owusu in Chapter 8; see also Marsden, 2001; Scott-Villiers, 2002); and the non-negotiable principles of Mahila Samatha. While these examples are drawn from NGOs, they illustrate the basic principle of minimum enabling controls and of achieving congruence between culture, behaviour and values within organizations.

ActionAid's ALPS

ActionAid sought to reduce onerous procedures and requirements for reporting. One estimate was that staff were spending three months per year writing reports. For many of them, English was their second or third language; but it was the medium of reporting. On top of this, many reports were of little use and were little used. Attempts to reform and simplify the system were largely unsuccessful. Finally, in frustration, six international staff were given a week to come up with a solution. This resulted in the leaner, simpler and more radical Accountability, Learning and Planning System (ALPS).

Paradoxically, for an organization that prided itself on participatory approaches, the ALPS system was endorsed centrally and disseminated in a centre-outwards manner to ActionAid teams in some 30 countries. Teams were encouraged to explore and devise, with partners, their own processes. Reporting could be in new formats – by video, in local or national languages or in other forms. A key element was a series of annual participatory review and reflection processes at all levels, with multiple stakeholders, involving variously poor people, communities, partner organizations, staff and donors. Downward accountability was stressed, with transparency of budgets between all levels. Significantly, no single formula was laid down. Diversity was encouraged as an efficient way of learning, with exchanges of experience within and between countries. The manual *Notes to Accompany ALPS* carried at the head of each page: 'Health Warning: Ideas and Options Only'.

The early experience with ALPS was fascinating.[5] Some staff continued to prepare reports that had been abolished, saying that they needed them for various audiences. India produced its own independent manual. At a workshop in Bangalore, ActionAid's five local NGO partners were invited to a two-day workshop to evaluate ActionAid. Making the ActionAid budget transparent cleared the air and set an example for partners to follow in turn, sharing their budgets with communities (Bhattarcharjee, 2001). In Kenya, the finance officer, after meetings with villagers, set about radically restructuring the accounting system so that it would break down intelligibly for partners and communities. Elsewhere (see Chapter 8) many flowers bloomed.

The experiences with logframe analysis and ALPS illustrate how procedures influence behaviours, and how they both flow from, as well as influence, the cultures of organizations and their relationships. This also indicates that – more than has, perhaps, been generally recognized – procedures are tools that can be chosen, designed and used consciously to change cultures, relationships and actions.

Non-negotiables of the Andhra Pradesh Mahila Samatha Society

One promising approach is for negotiations between recipients and lenders or donors to focus less, or not at all, on outputs and indicators; instead, the focus is on principles, directions and process, with these subject to review, reflection, learning and adaptation. Principles can be values and objectives that are non-negotiable. If both parties in a relationship start by reflecting on and stating their non-negotiable principles, they may discover incompatibilities that prevent their working together, or they may gain from mutual learning and find ground and objectives in common. It may, then, be not just unnecessary but harmful to plan what outputs should occur. With shared non-negotiables, there is scope for targets to be replaced by trust.

For a less powerful party to an agreement, insisting on non-negotiables can become a source of power and a means of addressing the inequalities inherent in aid relationships. This is illustrated by the inspiring example of the Andhra Pradesh Mahila Samatha Society (APMSS) (see Box 11.4).[6] The society's objectives are manifold and include 'to create circumstances so that women have a better understanding of their predicament and move from a state of abject disempowerment towards a situation in which they can determine their own lives and, hence, influence the environment' (APMSS, undated). To achieve its objectives the society 'seeks guidance not from targets, but from certain inviolable principles' (APMSS, 1994, p2).

It is worth noting the nature and level of these non-negotiable principles. They are neither macro principles at the level of 'love they neighbour as thyself', nor micro principles at the level of 'identify the single most important problem'. They are, rather, meso principles that are special to the organization and its philosophy. They serve to indicate attitudes and guide behaviour without saying in detail what should be done. As such, they both express and reinforce an impressive culture and commitment.

Most strikingly, and some might think improbably, it has been on the basis of its non-negotiable principles that the society has been, from the beginning, funded through the Indian government, with substantial Dutch aid. This has been without a logframe, and without specification of outputs or targets. So inspiring has been its ethos and achievements that other aid agencies have repeatedly asked to be allowed to provide support, including the DFID and the World Bank. All have been refused. The non-negotiables accepted by the government and by others concerned have empowered the women, the staff and the organization. Perhaps because of the confidence and trust created by the non-negotiables, the Dutch are perceived as 'the most non-interfering donor'. This is efficient, leaving staff free from the distractions of multiple donors (travel, negotiations, visitors, report writing and the like) and able to devote more of their time and energy, which they do in full measure, to the substance of their work. The relationship with the donor is congruent with the relationships with poor women. The non-negotiable principles are polar and paradigmatic opposites of targets. Normal bureaucracies are driven by targets for disbursements and outputs that tend to destroy participation. Targets are incompatible with participatory actions in which poor women determine the pace.[7]

BOX 11.4 NON-NEGOTIABLE PRINCIPLES: ANDHRA PRADESH MAHILA SAMATHA SOCIETY

Since early in its history, the Mahila Samatha Society has adhered to a set of 'non-negotiable' principles as a point of constant reference in all negotiations:

- The initial phase when women are consolidating their independent time and space is not be to hurried or short-circuited.
- Village women determine the form, nature, content and timing of all activities in the village.
- The role of project functionaries, officials and other agencies is facilitative and not directive.
- Planning, decision-making and evaluation processes at all levels are accountable to the collective of village women.
- Education is understood as a process that enables women to question, conceptualize, seek answers, act and reflect upon their actions and raise new questions. It is not to be confused with mere literacy.
- The educational process and methodology must be based on respect for women's existing knowledge, experience and skill.

Additional principles were added later on, including:

- Every intervention and interaction occurring in the project must be a microcosm of the larger process of change – that is, the environment of learning; respect and equality; time and space; and room for individual uniqueness and variation must be experienced in every component of the project.
- A participatory selection process is followed to ensure that the project functionaries at all levels are committed to working amongst poor women and that they are free of caste/community prejudices.

Source: APMSS annual reports

The eternal struggle remains to achieve a balance between routines that are essential and those creative and flexible processes that are an essential part of good performance. There is a bottom line of minimum requirements of auditing and reporting, not least to ensure honest and transparent accounting. Almost always, though, more control and more information are demanded than needed, and that 'more' diminishes trust and motivation. Procedures and information systems quickly take on a life of their own, in defiance of their original purpose. More procedures and requirements are added than taken away. The ranks of development organizations are soon dominated by people able to manage and control these systems, at the expense of innovators and creative problem-solvers.

If there are any lessons from the experiences of logframe analysis, ALPS and Mahila Samatha, they are to explore and agree non-negotiables and process; to maintain only essential minimum controls; to invent and use rules and procedures that build-in learning and improved performance; and throughout to work to foster good, honest and transparent relationships and trust. Beyond these, there is scope for a diversity of procedures, as with ALPS, created by the stakeholders in each partnership or set of partnerships, with continuous lateral learning and evolution. Some procedures, by nature, lend themselves to hierarchy and control, while others provide openings for reversing power relations. It is not just a question of who is empowered and to do what; it is also a question of who has the space and discretion to determine and develop the ways things are done. A great challenge is to see how far down that space can be opened up and how creatively and well it can be occupied. The Mahila Samatha principle that women in a village determine the form, nature, content and timing of all activities in the village shows how far it is possible to go in reversing relationships of power. The ultimate achievement is when people devise good procedures for themselves.

Organizational learning and change

A fourth domain of action for change emerges from the growing interest within the development sector in organizational learning and change (see, for example, Edwards, 1997; Edwards and Hulme, 1996; Hobley, 2000; Minogue et al, 1998). Non-governmental and donor agencies alike are actively seeking ways to transform their institutions into 'learning organizations' that will be more innovative, responsive and internally democratic. To become a learning organization is often cast as a more virtuous and far-reaching process than reforming systems and procedures: it is about instilling new norms and behaviours that value critical reflection and enable fundamental changes in an organization's direction and strategy. The goal is not simply to improve effectiveness, but to create conditions for rethinking basic organizational principles and values. It is seen as a process approach, leading to better alignment with a rapidly changing environment and sparking innovation by valuing diverse sources of knowledge and learning. Teamwork and the upward flow of information from front-line workers and clients are encouraged, while excessive internal authority and power are viewed as barriers. Learning organizations seek to flatten hierarchies, reduce distinctions between staff and release untapped potential (Easterby-Smith, 1997).

The leading advocates and examples of organizational learning have come largely from private-sector experience (see, for example, Argyris and Schon, 1974; Senge, 1990; Argyris, 1993). But the concepts and practices have increasingly appealed to public- and voluntary-sector agencies looking for ways to improve performance. Many development organizations are now testing and experimenting with such internal learning processes (see Chapter 13; see also Roper and Pettit, 2002). Yet, in practice, there are many obstacles, and organizational learning – like so many concepts and tools for change – can be used superficially or mechanically. Methods of organizational learning have been criticized as a 'borrowed toolkit' with limited relevance for development (Kelleher and the Gender at Work Collaborative, 2002). What is the reason for these limitations?

One view is that aid organizations, whether public or voluntary, have fundamentally different incentives from for-profit companies. While much is said about the efforts of aid programmes to become accountable to their 'primary stakeholders', it is arguable that most businesses have far greater incentives to satisfy their immediate customers than aid organizations have to meet the needs of poor people (Power et al, 2002). Rhetoric aside, NGOs are generally more accountable to their donors than to the people whom they serve; and unlike businesses, they will usually survive regardless of the quality or impact of their work. And donors, whether public or private, have limited capacity or will to adequately monitor the performance of their recipients. They have strong upward accountabilities and, like NGOs, suffer from what Power et al (2002) call the 'alien hand syndrome', where priorities are influenced by donor demand. Aid agencies have little real incentive to facilitate learning from below; listening to poor people or including them in decision-making may even undermine the legitimacy and survival of the agency, and the careers invested in it. Upward-oriented accountability works for organizational survival, and this explains the resistance to 'learning from below' in the development field (Power et al, 2002).

Another limitation is that organizational learning has surprisingly little to say about power. For development agencies and donors, there is a need to ask *who* is involved in the learning, for *what purpose*, and what *power* or *special interests* may stand to gain or lose. There is a need to look beyond private-sector models, which have less need to grapple with the ways in which power mediates learning and change. As noted in the first action domain (understanding and analysing power), the development field has its own traditions to draw upon – such as popular and adult education – that see learning, in part, as a process of revealing and transforming power relations (Roper and Pettit, 2002). Paulo Freire's widely influential approach to literacy saw personal and collective critical reflection as instrumental to the process of social change (Freire, 1970; Cornwall, 2001). These notions are inherent in much current practice of participatory action research and participatory monitoring and evaluation – broad traditions that value diverse sources of knowledge and learning, and value the inclusion of many voices. Because learning takes place for both the 'participants' and the 'agents' of change, this learning can transform the organizations involved (Roper and Pettit, 2002). Participatory methodologies are now increasingly being adapted to processes of organizational learning and change (see, for example, Gubbels and Koss, 1999). This trend reflects a growing awareness of the need to make democratic and inclusive principles real within institutions and personal lives.

As experience builds in the field of organizational learning in the development sector, personal behaviour and individual leadership are emerging as key elements. An organization's ability to evolve depends greatly upon the capacity of its staff and volunteers to learn, reflect and envision change – not just on operational matters, but in shifting power, culture and values (Roper and Pettit, 2002). A recent study of South Asian NGOs found the role of leaders to be instrumental in enabling or inhibiting organizational learning (Hailey and James, 2002). But leaders, even those committed to egalitarian change, may also be threatened by enquiries into the power structures of which they are a part, including privileges based on gender or class. They may either be blind to the changes required or willingly obstruct meaningful analysis (Kelleher and the Gender at Work Collaborative, 2002). It is commonly observed that mid-level and senior managers can be among the most resistant to change. They often have responsibilities such as mortgages and children to educate, and do not want to take risks with their careers. So, they accept models of professionalism that emphasize authority and control, and that reward loyalty and conformity. This, in part, explains why in most aid organizations, accountability flows upwards rather than downwards to primary stakeholders.

This cultural and behavioural resistance is a key issue for Pasteur and Scott-Villiers (see Chapter 13) in seeking to 'mind the gap' between rhetoric and practice in aid organizations. Organizational learning methods can help to close this gap, they argue, but only if sufficient time and space is provided for staff reflection – not only on matters of practice, systems and procedures, or even principles and mission, but on the personal values, attitudes and behaviours of individuals. This approach calls for carefully designed processes of reflection and questioning that probe systematically, exploring the nature of culture and power both in individuals and society and recognizing their impact on ways of working and relating. The examples of two bilateral aid agencies' efforts to pursue organizational learning 'suggest a need to broaden the scope and nature of reflection, beyond seeking the immediate and most obvious causes of problems, in order to achieve a richer quality of learning' (see Chapter 13). The process needs to examine whether personal attitudes and behaviours are aligned with stated objectives. Organizational learning and change must stem from the personal lives of individual people. Here we turn, appropriately, to the role of agency and responsibility in effecting change.

Agency and responsibility

Personal agency

Much development thinking is beholden to a rather narrow and self-fulfilling model of what motivates individual and collective human behaviour. Rooted in neo-classical economic thinking, this model assumes rational self-interest as the driving force behind decision-making. Larger systemic changes are then viewed as aggregate expressions of many individual choices and preferences. Society and its institutions are seen to operate much like a market, and processes of social or organizational change are sought by adjusting incentives to modify individual actions and thus, incrementally, yield collective results. Whatever the merits of this model, particularly in economics, there is much human behaviour that it cannot explain.

Another view of human nature and society acknowledges agency, altruism and awareness, and the actions to which they give rise. Personal *agency* refers to the ability to choose, act and have effects. *Altruism* refers to actions where 'one considers oneself better off if others' welfare is being enhanced and acts accordingly' (Uphoff, 1992, p341). As Uphoff has argued and shown in detail in his case study of the Gal Oya irrigation scheme in Sri Lanka, altruism can be a strong motivation. *Awareness* includes insightful reflection on the effects of one's actions, including effects that are distant in time and space.

Champions

The scope and power of agency is most clearly indicated by the achievements of champions. These are individuals who, through their character, imagination, commitment and leadership, have pioneered change. For some this has been within bureaucracies and governments, aid agencies and NGOs. Recent research examining the origins of innovation and success of nine large South Asian NGOs emphasized the 'vision, commitment and character' of their founders, all of whom shared a leadership style that was 'value driven, knowledge based and responsive' (Hailey and James, 2002, p401). The study also identified the ways in which these individuals enabled learning and innovation to occur within their organizations, often through informal processes and as the result of personal engagement and example (Hailey and Smillie, 2001). Other champions, including political leaders, have reached beyond their institutions to influence policy and practice. Yet others span both organizational and policy change, as two examples illustrate.

From India, there is Anil C Shah. As senior civil servant turned civil society leader, he has been a key actor in major changes in government policy in irrigation, watershed management, and forestry (Blackburn, 1998; Iyengar and Hirway, 2001). His advice on how to influence policy (Shah, 1998), grounded in long experience in government, in the NGO sector and in direct field-work with poor people, demonstrates the importance of tenacity, patience, experience and a willingness to engage with the detail of negotiation, drafting, setting up working groups, arranging field visits and much else. One example was in forestry, where a long process over years led to a point at which he could draft for government an order that enabled NGOs and local communities to gain management control and usufruct of forest land (Blackburn, 1998; Iyengar and Hirway, 2001, pp292–322).

In Tanzania, the regional commissioners of Lindi and Mtwara, both colonels, were instrumental in supporting the introduction and spread of participatory processes in local administration and development in government (see Chapter 5). With consistent support from a Finnish-supported programme, their leadership played a significant part in moves to transform administrative culture and relationships. Through a series of participatory workshops, including retreats on participation, for permanent secretaries and then regional administrative secretaries, the innovations and practices in their regions came to influence policy at the national level (MRALG, 1999).

Alliances, networks and continuity

While leadership is often visible and recognized, single champions rarely achieve change on their own. More often it is combinations of leadership, networking and alliances within and between organizations, together with the actions and decisions of large numbers of 'ordinary' people that contribute synergy and momentum.

Change in big bureaucracies can start with informal groupings, alliances and networks of people who believe that they can make a difference. The ecumenical group of many religions meeting for breakfast on Friday mornings at the World Bank, and the rapid rural appraisal (RRA) group within the Food and Agricultural Organization (FAO) during the 1980s and 1990s are two examples that have been quietly influential when coming together in unofficial time. A participation group in the Swedish International Development Agency (Sida) has differed in having official blessing and time, but an informal spirit, involving individuals committed to enhancing their understanding and practice of participation. What begins small or informally can gradually permeate and transform the relationships and cultures of organizations through a synergy of committed individuals, alliances and networking.

Some of the most effective alliances have been partnerships between individuals in governments and in grant-making agencies. An outstanding example is Benjamin Bagadion of the National Irrigation Administration in the Philippines and Frances Korten of the Ford Foundation. Over some ten years, and with a stable network of colleagues, they were quietly instrumental in transforming much irrigation policy and practice (Bagadion and Korten, 1991; Korten and Siy, 1989). Another example is the Uganda Participatory Poverty Assessment Process (UPPAP). This was promoted and supported by an alliance of champions in both donor and recipient organizations, working closely together over a number of years (see Chapter 6; Bird and Kakande, 2001; Yates and Okello, 2002, pp90, 93).

In all four of these cases – from India, Tanzania, the Philippines and Uganda – two factors were crucial: continuity and commitment in relationships. The relationships could be strong because the key people remained where they were for years, came to know, understand and trust one another, and were respected. Conversely, rapid postings break relationships, which then have to be nurtured again from scratch. When ActionAid staff in an Indian region revealed that their salaries were higher than those of their partners, they were surprised and relieved to be told that it did not matter (Amar Jyoti, pers comm). What mattered to their partners was that they should stay in post and not keep on moving, so that they could get to know them and build up relationships of mutual trust and understanding. In practice, inclusiveness in aid is repeatedly undermined and fractured by reorganizations of agencies, and by personnel decisions to transfer staff. Alliances, networks and relationships need people to stay and work together not for months, but for substantial numbers of years.

The scale and scope for agency

For those faced with many demands, rigid procedures, multiple reporting requirements, hierarchical bureaucratic cultures, and personal and job insecurity, the temptation and (often) practice is to consent, conform and comply (see Chapter 9). There is a sense of impotence, of being powerless within a system. There are, however, three reasons why the potential for individuals to have an influence, wherever they are placed, may be greater than they suppose.

First, there is the understanding of causality from chaos and complexity theory that small changes in starting conditions can have big effects later. An early insight was C H Waddington's analogy of landscapes with marbles running down branching valleys, where a tiny push at the right time would determine which new valley was entered (Waddington, 1977). Paths and equilibria that seem inevitable after the fact may be only one of several or many alternatives (Waldrop, 1994). Sensitivity to starting conditions is borne out by the experience with participatory rural appraisal (PRA) in a number of countries. In both Kenya and Nepal, different traditions followed on from different early trainings (Cornwall et al, 2001; Pratt, 2001). In South Africa, the first PRA training, facilitated by Jimmy Mascarenhas at Stoffelton, Natal, in 1993 was enormously influential and appears to have affected much subsequent practice. The key is to be alert for moments and places when small actions can have big effects. These may occur when many people are able and willing to act together. Or they may be 'moments of competence' – times when a small push can move a marble into another and better groove. There are issues here not only of awareness, but of timing and decisiveness.

Second, there is scope for agency in empowering others. There is a resonance here between edge-of-chaos theory and field experience. In computer simulations, the edge of chaos is a border zone between control and chaos in which minimum rules can enable complex and diverse behaviour. This can mimic, for example, traffic jams, termites seeking food or the flocking of birds (Resnick, 1994). The edge of chaos is also a zone of emergent properties and self-organization. The pattern is similar with empowering ways of changing institutions, procedures, practices and behaviours through devolution and participation. Excessive top-down controls freeze systems, which then misfit local conditions. At the other extreme, no controls and no accountability may mean true chaos. In the words of Richard Edwards, the aim is not total control or total devolution, but 'managing diversity, coordinating variety and releasing potential' (Edwards, 2001, p26). For this, devolution with minimum controls can empower, creating space for participation and encouraging diverse, decentralized, dynamic behaviour that fits local conditions and enhances ownership. With the women's savings groups of Myrada, an NGO in south India, the only two conditions insisted on have been rotating the responsibilities and keeping transparent accounts (Aloysius Fernandez, pers comm, 1996); all other details are left to the groups to decide. The annual review and reflection meetings of ActionAid's ALPS system are a requirement; but what form they take is wide open: creativity and diversity have been encouraged and are manifest. The non-negotiable principles of Mahila Samatha are another and similar enabling structure. Myrada's women's savings groups, ActionAid's review and reflection meetings, and Mahila Samatha's principles thus illustrate the practical secret: to see and set only those minimum rules needed to enable people to combine and act in ways that they otherwise could not on their own.

Third, there is accelerating connectedness through communications. It took radio 38 years to reach 50 million people, television 13 years, and the internet only 5 years (Scandino, cited in Singer and Singer, 1999). Moreover, radio and television are largely one-way forms of communication with constrained choice, whereas internet and email are more empowering, presenting almost unlimited choices and opportunities. With greater connectedness, in whatever domain and through whatever medium, comes greater ability to have an impact and make a difference, especially at a distance. Email and the internet allow advocacy NGOs in different countries (Edwards and Gaventa, 2001) and staff in different agencies to communicate and coordinate their activities as never before. During the past decade, the information to which those with internet have access, and the range of actions that they can take, have risen exponentially. Alliances and networking have always been one means of exercising agency. Through electronic communications they have now gained dramatically, providing scope for quick and timely action.

In sum, the scope for action is now more widely spread and less limited to those who hold formal power. Many who are lower in hierarchies have been empowered by mobile phones and the speed and informality of email. It is now easier for them to form networks and alliances. They benefit, too, from the gradual spread of more egalitarian cultures in bureaucracies; through the indirect influence of democratic political systems; through the spread of participatory approaches and relationships; and more broadly through the growth of social movements and citizen advocacy. Conditions vary, and electronic inclusion has a downside in those who are on the excluded side of the digital divide. But the long-term trend is for more actors to have more agency, with more space for action and influence.

Power, awareness and responsibility

With power and agency comes responsibility. This requires personal awareness of the scope for agency and effects. It is difficult for actors in development to be fully aware of the scale of difference that they do and could make. This is more difficult the more powerful and the more distant they are: the more powerful they are the more far-reaching will be the effects of their decisions, actions and non-actions; and the more distant they are, whether the separation is spatial, social or temporal, the more difficult it is to know what effects there will be. Much of the challenge is to see beyond proximate responsibilities, effects and attributions (charity begins at home) to others that are equally real but less visible. People see and understand best what is close to them. Poor people tend not to attribute their poverty to global forces; to them, these are largely invisible, though the links are there for an outside analyst to see. Conversely, for those most in touch in the 'connected world', it is easier to recognize these macro factors than to see their direct effects on those who are poor and vulnerable. The challenge to the imagination is to see the links between the macro and micro worlds, and between the immediate and the distant, and to act to optimize these for changing relations of power.

For inclusive aid that is truly pro-poor, awareness of the realities of poor people has become more important than ever. There has been a sharp shift from supporting field projects to policy influence and budget support, to sector programmes and even to governments, as a whole. In Uganda, between only one financial year and the next, and with little change in the overall total, the ratio of DFID's project funding to programme funding switched from 5:2 to 2:5.[8] This shift has tended to isolate aid agency staff in capital cities and other central places, where they are trapped in meetings and social life, and meeting and dealing with visitors (see Chapters 4 and 5). Isolated and ignorant though they are of field realities, they are, at the same time, involved in policy dialogue.

Power is often spoken of like a commodity. This makes it easy to slip into a mindset that more power is good and less is bad. This perspective conflicts with common experiences: that decentralizing and devolving power diminishes stress; that there is fulfilment in empowering others and appreciating the capabilities they then develop and demonstrate; that being open, transparent and consistent contributes more to peace of mind and well-being than being closed, opaque and hypocritical; that good relations through mutual trust and accountability can reduce tension and anxiety. Furthermore, those who empower others may find their own personal well-being enhanced, and can find fulfilment in appreciating the capabilities others then develop and demonstrate.

Power and agency can then combine in responsible well-being (see Chapter 14; Chambers, 1997b). Fulfilment and well-being can be found in levelling and reversing relationships and empowering others. They can be sought, too, through narrowing the rhetoric–reality gaps of the words partnership, empowerment, ownership, participation, accountability and transparency. Responsible well-being also includes caring for one's own learning and improving one's own understanding and practice. In Mahila Samata (Andra Pradesh, India), one tenth of staff time is set aside for personal development. As the South African Community Development Resource Association's (CDRA's) report *Measuring Development* puts it:

> *There is a peculiar form of self-abasement amongst development workers – donors and practitioners alike. It begins with the fairly righteous stance that we may not spend money intended for the poor on our own development. So, we tend not to make time to learn. Yet, this lack of respect for ourselves as our most important 'instruments' in the development project results very quickly in a lack of respect-in-practice for those we claim to serve…we value action over learning, often doing things to the poor that are inappropriate, even destructive. The benign and laudable claim that resources should go to those they are intended for quickly becomes a more harmful refusal to learn from experience* (CDRA, 2001, pp10–11).

The personal dimension is then central for inclusive aid – in personal behaviour, attitudes and beliefs, in relationships, and in learning. The challenge is to overcome the disabilities of power and distance through realism and commitment. Here a new field of experiential learning and reflection is opening up (McGee, 2002). One set of initiatives has been the Exposure and Dialogue Programme (EDP) of the Association for the Promotion of North–South Dialogue, pioneered by Karl Osner, and adopted by SEWA (Self-Employed Women's Association) in India (Ledesma and Osner, 1988; SEWA and ASPNSD, 2002). In a typical EDP, a policy-maker spends several days living with a poor host and learning about her life history, and then several days reflecting on the experience. A second set of initiatives has been the one-week immersions of the World Bank. These immersions were introduced by James Wolfensohn for senior World Bank staff. Reportedly, these have been positive experiences for learning and for motivation. Following the World Bank's initiatives in much else, no other lender or donor agency is known to have followed suit in this regard. Enough is known about immersions, combined with self-critical reflexivity, to recognize their considerable promise as a means to personal learning and change, and to grounding policy in the experienced realities of poor people.

Actions for inclusive aid

As the potential for personal agency, awareness and responsibility is recognized more widely and put into practice, many pathways of action will open up for inclusive aid. The action domains explored in this book are suggested as places to start. These domains can be viewed as points of leverage within the aid system – entry points that hold promise for effecting change in the system's governing dynamics of power relations. All are domains in which individuals can act to make a difference. The first challenge for those seeking change is to take the necessary steps to *understand and analyse* power. We must develop the capacities and discipline to make power visible, including our own power, and to use this understanding to create more effective strategies. The second is to seek ways to *narrow the gaps between the words and actions* by asserting the meanings of these words in ways that are rooted in deeper understandings of power. In this way we can use the words more genuinely to induce awareness and leverage change. The third is to *change rules and procedures* by reforming or removing old ones and innovating new ones that encourage downward accountability, mutual transparency and learning. Such changes can help to reverse power relations and open up spaces for inclusion and diversity. The fourth is to engage in processes of *organizational learning and change* by reflecting on personal values, principles and responsibility to transform the way in which we behave and work.

Action in each of these domains can work in diverse but fundamental ways on the deeper governing dynamics of the aid system. Action on all four of them combined can alter power relations and enable a greater congruence of language, ideology, structure and action. Implicit throughout is the role of *personal agency, awareness and responsibility*. In the end, it is individuals who act, and it is our own attitudes, behaviours, decisions and commitments – often neglected in development thinking – that have a central role to play in shifting power relations and contributing to change. The way forward now is to share visions and experiences, to combine action, reflection, learning and change, and to help one another see how to do better. There is scope in this for all actors in the complex system of aid. In particular, it is those with less power whose agency will be most vital. But there is also scope for those with more power – for those who work in aid agencies, governments, civil society and universities and colleges; for officials, field-workers, researchers and teachers; and for other citizens, including the rich and the privileged. We can all develop awareness of our own power and its impact upon others, and in doing so open up spaces for those who are poor and excluded to act and claim their rights. We can all see what needs to be done to shift power and take responsibility to act. We can all make mistakes, and experience, reflect and learn. We can all find ways to make a difference.

Notes

1   This chapter was inspired by the workshop 'Power, Procedures and Relationships', held at the Institute of Development Studies, UK (IDS) in May 2001. The workshop's summary statement, entitled *The New Dynamics of Aid: Power, Procedures and Relationships* (IDS, 2001), compiled by Robert Chambers, Jethro Pettit and Patta Scott-Villiers, was a stage in the development of this chapter. The authors gratefully acknowledge the comments and advice of Rosalind Eyben, Patta Scott-Villiers and of the workshop participants and organizers, including the editors of this book, Leslie Groves and Rachel Hinton, who have contributed to the writing of this chapter. All the normal disclaimers apply.

2   Readers may wish to reflect on how they felt the first time they heard the (now common) terms of 'civil society', 'social capital', 'stakeholder', 'governance', 'rights-based approach', etc.

3   For authoritative reviews of the strengths and weaknesses of logical framework analysis, see Cracknell (2000, pp101–121) and Gasper (2000).

4   VSO is an international development organization that works through volunteers, with recruitment bases in five countries: Canada, Kenya, The Netherlands, the Philippines and the UK. VSO is also now using participatory evaluations, with partners, to assess the impact of volunteer placements.

5   The Participation Group at IDS was invited to provide a team, led by Patta Scott-Villiers and including Garett Pratt, Andrea Cornwall and, to a lesser degree, Robert Chambers, to accompany ALPS in India, Kenya, Ethiopia, The Gambia and Brazil. These summary remarks draw on this collective activity and on insights from the Impact Assessment Unit of ActionAid. ALPS (ActionAid, 2000) and *Notes to Accompany ALPS* (ActionAid, 2001a) are available on the ActionAid website at www.actionaid.org/policyandresearch/mae/oas.shtml. See also www.ids.ac.uk/ids/particip for other related materials.

6   For information about APMSS, we are indebted to personal communications from Y Padmavathy, Nandini Prasad and other staff, and have also drawn on annual reports.

7   In 2002, Mahila Samatha is, albeit with great caution, moving towards collaboration with a United Nations Development Programme (UNDP)/government of Andhra Pradesh programme with targets. Mahila Samatha recognizes the dangers and is resolutely determined not to compromise its principles. The collaboration promises to be fraught with interest and is a source of important learning.

8   From 1999–2000 to 2000–2001, DFID's project aid to Uganda dropped from UK£41.5 million to UK£17.7 million, while programme aid rose from UK£16 million to UK£45 million (compiled from statistics available at www.dfid.gov.uk).

References

ActionAid (2000) *ALPS: Accountability, Learning and Planning System*, ActionAid, London

ActionAid (2001a) *Notes to Accompany ALPS*, ActionAid, London

ActionAid (2001b) *Transforming Power: Report of the Participatory Methodologies Forum*, Bangladesh, February 2001, ActionAid, London

Alinsky, S (1989) *Rules for Radicals: A Practical Primer for Realistic Radicals*, Vintage, New York

APMSS (1994) *Andhra Pradesh Mahila Samatha Society Report 1993–1994, and Subsequent Years*, Andhra Pradesh Mahila Samatha Society, Hyderabad

APMSS (undated) *Mana Jaaga (Our Space)*, Andhra Pradesh Mahila Samatha Society, Hyderabad (text by V Lokesh Kumar and P Purandhar)

Argyris, C (1993) *Knowledge for Action: Guide for Overcoming Barriers to Organizational Change*, Jossey-Bass, San Francisco

Argyris, C and Schon, D (1974) *Theory and Practice: Increasing Professional Effectiveness*, Jossey-Bass, San Francisco

Bagadion, B and Korten, F (1991) 'Developing Irrigators' Organizations: A Learning Process Approach', in Cernea, M (ed) *Putting People First*, Oxford University Press, Oxford

Bhattarcharjee, P (2001) *Participatory Review and Reflection Process*, workshop report, 24–25 January 2001, ActionAid India, Bangalore Regional Office, Bangalore

Bird, B and Kakande, M (2001) 'The Uganda Participatory Poverty Assessment Process', in Norton, A with Bird, B, Brock, K, Kakande, M and Turk, C (eds) *A Rough Guide to PPAs – Participatory Poverty Assessment: An Introduction to Theory and Practice*, Overseas Development Institute, London

Blackburn, J (1998) 'Getting Policymakers to Move the Bricks Around: Advocacy and Participatory Irrigation Management in India', in Holland, J with Blackburn, J (eds), *Whose Voice? Participatory Research and Policy Change*, Intermediate Technology Publications, London

Blackburn, J, Chambers, R and Gaventa, J (2002) 'Mainstreaming Participation in Development', in Hanna, N and Picciotto, R (eds) *Making Development Work: Development Learning in a World of Poverty and Wealth*, World Bank Series on Evaluation and Development, vol 4, Tavistock, New Brunswick, and London

Brock, K and McGee, R (2002) *Knowing Poverty: Critical Reflections on Participatory Research and Policy*, Earthscan, London

CDRA (2001) *Measuring Development: Holding Infinity*, Community Development Resource Association, South Africa

Chambers, R (1997a) *Whose Reality Counts? Putting the First Last*, Intermediate Technology Publications, London

Chambers, R (1997b) 'Editorial: Responsible Well-Being – A Personal Agenda for Development', *World Development*, vol 25, no 11, pp1743–1754

Cohen, D, de la Vega, R and Watson, G (2001) *Advocacy for Social Justice: A Global Action and Reflection Guide*, Kumarian Press, Bloomfield, CT

Cornwall, A (2001) *Beneficiary, Consumer, Citizen: Perspectives on Participation for Poverty Reduction*, Sida Studies, no 2, Sida, Stockholm

Cornwall, A, Musyoki, S and Pratt, G (2001) *In Search of New Impetus: Practitioners' Reflections on PRA and Participation in Kenya*, Pathways to Participation, IDS Working Paper no 131, IDS, University of Sussex, Brighton

Cracknell, B (2000) *Evaluating Development Aid: Issues, Problems and Solutions*, Sage, Thousand Oaks, CA

Easterby-Smith, M (1997) 'Disciplines of Organizational Learning: Contributions and Critiques', *Human Relations*, vol 50, no 9, September, pp1085–2013

Edington, J (2001) 'Logical? Monitoring against Logical Frameworks', *IA Exchanges*, March, p9

Edwards, M (1997), *Organizational Learning in Non-Governmental Organizations: What Have We Learned?* World Bank, Washington, DC

Edwards, M and Gaventa, J (eds) (2001) *Global Citizen Action*, Lynne Rienner, Boulder, Colorado, and Earthscan, London

Edwards, M and Hulme, D (1996) *Beyond the Magic Bullet: NGO Performance and Accountability in the Post-Cold War World*, Kumarian Press, West Hartford, Connecticut

Edwards, R (2001) *Managing Participatory Development*, unpublished dissertation for MA (Econ) in Social Policy and Social Development, Institute of Development Policy and Management, University of Manchester, Manchester

Fals-Borda, O and Rahman, M (eds) (1991) *Action and Knowledge: Breaking the Monopoly with Participatory Action-Research*, Intermediate Technology Publications, London

Farrington, J and Nelson, J (1997) *Using Logframes to Monitor and Review Farmer Participatory Research*, Network Paper 73, Agricultural Research and Extension Network, Overseas Development Institute, London

Forster, R (ed) (1996) 'ZOPP marries PRA? Participatory Learning and Action: A Challenge for Our Services and Institutions', workshop documentation, GTZ, Eschborn, Germany

Freire, P (1970) *Pedagogy of the Oppressed*, The Seabury Press, New York

Gasper, D (2000) 'Evaluating the "Logical Framework Approach": Towards Learning-oriented Development Evaluation', *Public Administration and Development*, vol 20, no 1, pp17–28

GTZ (1996) *Project Cycle Management (PCM) and Objectives-oriented Project Planning (ZOPP): Guidelines*, GTZ, Eichborn

Gubbels, P and Koss, C (1999) *From the Roots Up: Organizational Capacity-building Through Guided Self-assessment*, World Neighbors, Oklahoma City

Hailey, J and James, R (2002) 'Learning Leaders: The Key to Learning Organizations', *Development in Practice*, vol 12, no 3, August, pp398–408

Hailey, J and Smillie, I (2001) *Managing for Change: Leadership, Strategy and Change in South Asian NGOs*, Earthscan, London

Hobley, M (2000) *Transformation of Organizations for Poverty Eradication: The Implications of Sustainable Livelihoods Approaches*, Sustainable Livelihoods Support Office, DFID, London; available from www.livelihoods.org.uk

Institute of Development Studies (IDS) (2001) *The New Dynamics of Aid: Power, Procedures and Relationships*, Policy Briefing 15, August, IDS, Brighton

INTRAC (1999) *The Participatory Approaches Learning Study (PALS) Overview Report*, Social Development Department, DFID, London

Iyengar, S and Hirway, I (eds) (2001) *In the Hands of the People: Selected Papers of Anil C Shah*, Gujarat Institute of Development Research and Gujarat Centre for Development Alternatives and Development Support Centre, Ahmedabad

Kelleher, D and the Gender at Work Collaborative (2002) 'Organizational Learning: A Borrowed Toolbox?' *Development in Practice*, vol 12, no 3, August, pp312–320

Korten, F and Siy, R (eds) (1989) *Transforming a Bureaucracy: The Experience of the Philippine National Irrigation Administration*, Kumarian Press, West Hartford, Connecticut, US, and Ateneo de Manila University Press, Quezon City

Ledesma, A and Osner, K (eds) (1988) *Ways and Steps Toward Solidarity: Experiences and Impetus from a German-Philippines Exposure and Dialogue Program*, The German Commission Justitia et Pax, Bonn, and Centre for the Development of Human Resources in Rural Asia, Manila

Marsden, R (2001) 'ALPS: Some Key Challenges', *IA Exchanges*, 7–8 March, ActionAid UK, London

McGee, R (2002) 'The Self in Participatory Poverty Research', in Brock, K and McGee, R (eds) *Knowing Poverty: Critical Reflections on Participatory Research and Policy*, Earthscan, London

Mehta, L (2001) 'Commentary: The World Bank and its Emerging Knowledge Empire,' *Human Organization*, vol 60, no 2, pp189–196

Minogue, M, Polidano, C and Hulme, D (eds) (1998) *Beyond the New Public Management: Changing Ideas and Practices in Governance*, Edward Elgar, Cheltenham

MRALG, Tanzania (1999) *Whose Priorities in Policy Making? Reflections from the Permanent Secretaries' Retreat on Participation in Tanzania*, held at Tarangire, Arusha, 10–11 February 1999, Ministry of Regional Administration and Local Government, Tanzania

Norton, A with Bird, B, Brock, K, Kakande, M and Turk, C (2001) *A Rough Guide to PPAs. Participatory Poverty Assessment: An Introduction to Theory and Practice*, Overseas Development Institute, London

Power, G, Maury, M and Maury, S (2002) 'Operationalizing Bottom-up Learning in International NGOs: Barriers and Alternatives', *Development in Practice*, vol 12, no 3, August, pp272–284

Pratt, G (2001) *Practitioners' Critical Reflections on PRA and Participation in Nepal: Pathways to Participation*, IDS Working Paper no 122, IDS, Brighton

Reason, P and Bradbury, H (2001) *Handbook of Action Research: Participative Inquiry and Practice*, Sage, London

Resnick, M (1994) *Turtles, Termites and Traffic Jams: Explorations in Massively Parallel Microworlds*, MIT Press, Cambridge, MA

Roper, L and Pettit, J (eds) (2002) 'Organizational Learning', Special Issue of *Development in Practice*, vol 12, no 3, August

Samaranayake, M (2001) 'How to Make Log-Frame Programming More Sensitive to Participatory Concerns', in IFAD et al, *Enhancing Ownership and Sustainability*, IFAD, Rome

Scott-Villiers, P (2002) 'How the ActionAid Accountability, Learning and Planning System emerged: The Struggle for an Organizational Change', *Development in Practice*, vol 12, no 3, August, pp424–35

Senge, P (1990) *The Fifth Discipline: The Art and Practice of the Learning Organization*, Doubleday, New York

SEWA and APNSD (2002) *'Tana Vana': Warp and Weft of Life*, Self-Employed Women's Association Academy, Ahmedabad, India, and Association for the Promotion of North–South Dialogue, Bonn

Shah, A (1998) 'Challenges in Influencing Policy: An NGO Perspective', in Holland, J with Blackburn, J (eds) *Whose Voice? Participatory Research and Policy Change*, Intermediate Technology Publications, London

Singer, N and Singer, J (1999) *The Little Book of the Millennium*, Headline, London, UK

Uphoff, N (1992) *Learning from Gal Oya: Possibilities for Participatory Development and Post-Newtonian Social Science*, Cornell University Press, Ithaca, and (1996) Intermediate Technology Publications, London

VeneKlasen, L with Miller, V (2002) *A New Weave of People, Power and Politics: The Action Guide for Advocacy and Citizen Participation*, World Neighbors, Oklahoma City

Waddington, C (1977) *Tools for Thought*, Paladin, St Albans

Waldrop, M (1994) *Complexity: The Emerging Science at the Edge of Order and Chaos*, Penguin Books, London

Wilks, A and Lefrançois, F (2002) *Blinding with Science or Encouraging Debate? How World Bank Analysis Determines PRSP Policies*, Bretton Woods Project, London, and World Vision International, Monrovia, California

Yates, J and Okello, L (2002) 'Learning from Uganda's Efforts to Learn from the Poor: Reflections and Lessons from the Uganda Participatory Poverty Assessment Project' in Brock, K and McGee, R (eds) *Knowing Poverty: Critical Reflections on Participatory Research and Policy*, Earthscan, London

12

How Can Donors Become More Accountable to Poor People?

Rosalind Eyben and Clare Ferguson[1]

Introduction

This chapter explores the new pressures placed on all stakeholders who have begun to adopt a rights-based approach in terms of power, procedures and relationships. It proposes that official bilateral aid agencies are starting to recognize and respond to multiple lines of accountability. The conflicts and challenges arising from this response are examined and discussed with examples from Bolivia and India. Although highly problematic, the chapter sees this process as a positive step towards Northern governments being prepared to be held accountable by poor people in the South.

Accountability and rights-based approaches

During recent years, a number of grant-giving official (government) donors, including the UK Department for International Development (DFID), have begun to incorporate rights-based approaches into their work. The cornerstone of this approach to development is the idea that all people are citizens with rights, rather than passive beneficiaries of aid. These rights are largely seen as being derived from international treaties, including the Universal Declaration of Human Rights, which have been agreed under the auspices of the United Nations (UN). One of the issues highlighted by a rights approach is that of accountability. The idea that individuals have rights implies that governments and others have corresponding legal and moral obligations, and that they can be held to account for their actions to fulfil those responsibilities. In particular, the emphasis on equality in rights-based approaches highlights the importance of accountability to the poorest. A rights perspective implies that poor people have entitlements to, among other things, political voice, equal treatment and certain levels of services, and that development aid is about meeting these rights rather than providing charity.

From a donor perspective, one of the key implications of a rights approach is that it may be accountable to more than one set of stakeholders, including stakeholders who currently have the least power and wealth in the world. This chapter focuses on some of the practical challenges that this recognition may create for official donors. Time and other constraints prevent any major academic review of the issues; rather, this chapter intends to establish an agenda for further research, exploration and discussion. That agenda concerns the need for official government donors to make their different lines of accountability explicit and manage them better, and to do so within the framework of a rights-based approach to development practice.

Such an agenda would provide some very modest and initial stepping stones to encourage donors to move in the right rather than the wrong direction. How may donors recognize and balance more equitably their different lines of accountability to the various parties who have an interest in donor action, and how can they do this in such a way that greater attention is paid to the primary stakeholders – those who today least enjoy their rights? Modesty is required because the rights-based approach in its entirety could never be *fully* realizable. Rather, it provides a vision that can help donor organizations make better practical choices in the here and now of messy day-to-day politics. They are 'better' choices because they are ones that can contribute, in Sen's (1999) terms, to the process of expanding the real freedoms that people in poorer countries enjoy.

The term 'a rights-based approach to development' is used variously by different actors involved in development practice, international non-governmental organizations (INGOs), local grassroots organizations, developing country governments and official development agencies, among others. We find that quite often we are talking about different kinds of practice, with the risk of unfruitful dialogue and misunderstanding. It would be erroneous to assume that all of these actors are in agreement regarding the definition and implications of such an approach.

We propose the following as the key elements of a rights-based approach for official bilateral and multilateral aid agencies:

- Frame our action within the moral statement of the Universal Declaration of Human Rights and the subsequent conventions.
- Perceive primary stakeholders as partner citizens with rights and responsibilities, rather than as voiceless beneficiaries of our aid.
- Promote equality and non-discrimination, and address the barriers that prevent the most marginalized from claiming their rights.
- Make explicit and put into practice the rules of engagement between donors and recipients, based on mutual accountability, responsiveness and transparency.
- Encourage partner governments to practise similar behaviour with their citizens.

- Work with governments and civil society to provide the enabling environment for citizens to acquire the voice and knowledge needed to improve their own lives and hold the state accountable for its obligations to respect, protect and fulfil their rights.
- Emphasize empowerment of those most deprived of voice, knowledge and the means of livelihood; this means donors assessing their support against the criterion of changing power relations in favour of poor people.
- Recognize the potential of legal systems as a means of promoting justice for people living in poverty.

This chapter will not explore all of the various facets of such an approach. Rather, it focuses on one important aspect that links to the other chapters in this book: the relations between accountability and power viewed through a rights lens. From this perspective we assess the changes currently taking place in donor–recipient relations, identifying how donors can reinforce and mainstream those emerging aspects of the relationship concerning mutual responsibilities that we would consider rights based.

This chapter proposes that *bilateral* aid agencies are accountable to five categories of institution or persons: taxpayers in the donor country; government in the donor country; government in the recipient country; poor people in the recipient country; and the international human rights framework.[2] We briefly comment on the current accountability status of donors with each of these stakeholders and point out the conflicts arising when agencies seek to respond to these different interests. We indicate possible steps that could be taken to minimize the conflicts and improve accountability with all of these different stakeholders to the benefit of the least empowered and most important, the primary stakeholders – that is, poor people in aid-recipient countries. Most of our examples are drawn from the perspective of the UK aid programme, and with particular reference to Eyben's experience in Bolivia (see Chapter 4). Nevertheless, we believe that many of the generic issues are relevant for all bilateral donors.

It takes two to tango. Without apology, this chapter is written from the donor perspective. We believe that donor efforts to establish lines of accountability through rights-based relationships will, in turn, produce positive changes in patterns of political and social relationships within the countries that donors are seeking to assist.

Conceiving accountability

The concept of accountability includes identifying responsibilities and measuring whether those responsibilities have been met. From a rights perspective, accountability requires that citizens, including the most marginalized people, engage in both defining governments' responsibilities and monitoring whether they have fulfilled their obligations. From this perspective, concepts of accountability are related to those of responsiveness and transparency.

In state–citizens relationships, *responsiveness* is about the capacity of the state to respond to citizens' legitimate and moral claims and to provide their statutory entitlements in a transparent and accountable manner. Responsiveness includes other characteristics, such as predictability (knowing that a certain service will be undertaken at a particular time and date) and flexibility (recognizing that different people have different needs in relation to their entitlement – for example, their entitlement to education).

A responsive organization recognizes differences among those with whom it relates and seeks to respond to these differences with an action that best fits the particular need. A challenge for any organization is to respond to these different identities, enabling those with whom it relates to define themselves as they wish, rather than to be ascribed definitions. In Bolivia, the Committee of Small Producers was seen by DFID and other donors as representing people engaged in micro- and small-scale enterprise – that is, 'businessmen'. On the other hand, many members of the organizations that made up the committee saw themselves as 'workers', with an associated traditional socialist class-consciousness. Many of these workers were seeking a return to a model of a state that manages the commanding heights of the economy, a quite different vision from that of official aid agencies who were promoting an agenda of strengthening competition and productivity.

Goetz and Gaventa (2001) define responsiveness in a slightly different but complementary way in the context of service delivery. This is the extent to which a public-service agency demonstrates receptivity to the views, complaints and suggestions of service users by implementing changes to its own structure, culture and service-delivery patterns in order to deliver a more appropriate product. A responsive aid agency encourages its partners to provide services that fit the specific needs, rights and interests of diverse citizens. For example, DFID in Bolivia was working with the Ministry of Health to adapt the basic health care programme to respond to the requirements of indigenous women when giving birth.

From the perspective of the state, *transparency* refers to making procedures clear and decision-making processes public (including the information that informed these decisions), and removing discretionary control of public officials in the exercise of public affairs. From the perspective of citizens, it means realizing the right to information so that all of the above are easily and freely accessible and citizens have the knowledge and skills required to make sense of the information.

In Bolivia, in preparation for possible support to strengthen the government's decentralization programme, aid agencies considered the implications of the government's commitment to greater transparency. They noted that to give practical effect to that requirement, possible action could include a wide variety of methods to ensure that dissemination of relevant information is not only limited to raw data or to channels accessible only to formally educated persons who read and/or understand the Spanish language. Such action could include:

- technical assistance to municipalities that lack sufficient administrative capacity to meet minimum transparency requirements and, if necessary, preparation and publication of required information;
- training of local newspaper, radio, television and selected non-governmental organization (NGO) staff in the analysis and interpretation of financial decisions and performance *in a manner that enables ordinary citizens to understand relevant consequences*;
- special quarterly print editions and radio/television broadcasts of relevant data and analyses in indigenous languages;
- quarterly 'town crier' visits by selected local NGOs to extend the dissemination of relevant data and analysis to isolated communities; and
- annual workshops for selected representatives of civil society and municipal governments to discuss and formulate appropriate operational responses to such data and analyses.

Such a broad-based communication strategy would ensure that the population, as a whole, and poor men and women, in particular, would be aware of the substantive intent and actual performance of programmes to support municipal infrastructure investment (Silverman, 2000).

Accountability includes transparency but also involves the creation of mechanisms to ensure transparency. Accountability is often used as a term without clarity concerning who is accountable to whom and in what domain of life (Cornwall and Gaventa, 2000). Thus, while many donor documents note the need for recipients to establish good governance and the modernization of the state, there are many references to the importance of enhancing accountability *without specifying to whom*. Abstract principles without practical and directed expression tend to benefit and sustain the status quo. In its 20/20 Vision initiative, the Andhra Pradesh state government in India emphasized the importance of strengthening accountability (DFID, 2001). Evidence from India indicates that it is poor people with the least power who are most vulnerable to demands from venal officials (Praxis, 2002). Nevertheless, examination of the measures proposed by the Andhra Pradesh government reveals that citizens are treated as an abstract homogeneous whole. For example, public opinion surveys are included as a means of tracking reduction in public-sector corruption. Other, more participatory, methods of enquiry would focus on whether excluded and marginalized groups report a reduction in demands for bribes.

Traditionally, official bilateral aid agencies have seen themselves as strictly accountable only to their own governance structure, as established by procedures. In recent years, they have sought to become more responsive to other stakeholders – for example, to recipient governments and to the citizens back home, as well as to primary stakeholders. Where, how and when does responsiveness develop into accountability and why does this matter? Responsiveness is basically instrumental: it ensures a more efficient and effective service. Nevertheless, responsiveness depends upon the goodwill of the more powerful to the less powerful. Should the service deliverer decide to stop the service or be inadequate in its delivery, the recipient cannot hold the deliverer to account. Lipsky (cited in Norton and Elson, 2002) believes that efforts to improve transparency and client-orientation in delivery will be likely to fail in the absence of broader social change.

In their study of client focus in service delivery, Goetz and Gaventa (2001) demonstrate that the line between responsiveness and accountability becomes blurred. Many citizens' voice initiatives imply expectations that civil servants can be held to account directly to clients for their actions, rather than through the established governance procedures of mediation through elected officials. In the case of development aid, the challenge for citizens' voice is much greater. This is because those receiving services are a different set of citizens and in another part of the world from those who can formally hold the bureaucracy accountable through their elected officials, but have no direct experience of the service that is meant to be delivered.

Despite the ambiguities of the term, and the fact that in many situations it may have little meaning for poor people claiming their rights (Jones and Gaventa, 2002), *citizenship* is an important word for donors. It transforms conceptually the nature of the relationship between donors, the recipient government and the people. People become agents and subjects, rather than objects, of their own development. This is why, as is argued in the United Nations Development Programme (UNDP) *Human Development Report* (2000), the evolving international human rights agenda brings principles of accountability and social justice to the process of human development.

Horizontal accountability relates to one part of the state system monitoring another part – for example, the legislative public accounts committees, a national audit office, courts of law and formal reporting requirements within the executive (such as within a ministry responsible for development aid). *Vertical accountability* includes the citizens' voice through representative democracy and the collective voice of civil society pressure. Goetz and Jenkins (2001) comment that efforts in many countries to strengthen these two kinds of accountability have tended to proceed independently of one another and argue for more joined-up efforts towards what they term 'diagonal accountability' – that is, citizens engaging directly in the workings of horizontal accountability mechanisms. We discuss later how these ideas of diagonal accountability, developed in relation to what takes place inside one country, can be relevant for the development of transnational accountability mechanisms, as in the provision of development aid.

Another model of accountability has been developed within the corporate sector in response to citizens' concerns about the behaviour of big business. Formally, corporate governance procedures make a company's board of directors responsible to their shareholders. Many businesses insist that there is no need to change these procedures. Others are developing and implementing *social accounting* procedures to respond to the concerns of their customers and the wider community about the impact of business on society and the environment. Thus, Shell refers to its triple bottom line of profits, people and planet. The procedures have also been adopted by a number of organizations in the voluntary sector.

A social audit identifies the extent to which those with a stake in the business (all of the people associated with or affected by it) believe that it is achieving its objectives, whether it is living up to its values and if those objectives and values are relevant and appropriate. That is what the social accounting process aims to facilitate. Social accounting and audit together comprise a framework that allows an organization to build on existing documentation and reporting, and to develop a process where it can *account* for its social performance, *report* on that performance and draw up an action plan to improve that performance. Through this framework, the organization can understand its *impact* on the community and be *accountable* to its key stakeholders (Zadek et al, 1999).

Some donor agencies, including DFID, have explored the possibility of adopting the social audit procedure as one way of strengthening their different lines of accountability. It would appear to have greatest potential at the country-programme level; but we know of few serious attempts to put it into practice. Effective social audits require a sustained and repeated social accounting effort over a considerable period of time, and the rapid turnover of donor staff in country offices may be a serious constraint on the capacity to carry through the procedure. Nevertheless, the initial stakeholder analysis required to undertake a social audit has helped us to identify and explore the principal lines of accountability of an official bilateral donor agency. The following section examines these lines of accountability.

Lines of accountability

Taxpayers in the donor country

In terms of accountability procedures, government donor agencies usually see taxpayers as the principal stakeholder. In many donor countries, parliaments scrutinize and approve not only budgets, but also policies and programmes. For these reasons, donor agencies are keen to build up and maintain interested constituencies back home in order to help preserve donor budgets. Until very recently, DFID's Information Department saw its responsibility solely in terms of communicating with UK taxpayers and not with stakeholders in recipient countries.

The resistance of many donor countries to untying aid is related to nurturing special interests in business and elsewhere so that they, in return, will provide political support for the wider aid programme. Most donor governments maintain earmarked funds for Northern NGOs to spend in the South as another means of building and maintaining a constituency for aid. Finally, immigrant communities with citizen status in the donor country may take a lively interest in how much and what kind of aid their government delivers in their original home country. Responding to all of these special interests creates potential conflict with donors' other lines of accountability. For example, an immigrant community can seek to procure additional funds for their country of origin, even though on grounds of global equity and levels of poverty this country may not merit such levels of aid. Nevertheless, there are also interesting examples of immigrant communities taking advantage of the formal accountability procedures to challenge the agency on the extent to which it is implementing its human rights agenda in the recipient country. In the UK parliament, for example, in response to concerns of British citizens of Dalit origin (scheduled caste), questions have been asked concerning the extent to which UK aid is championing the rights of Dalits in India.

Swedish parliamentarians have taken a radical approach of encouraging their own constituents to recognize the competing claims of poor people in the South. In recommendations for a new Swedish policy for global development, the report states that 'Sometimes it will be necessary to weigh the respective claims of the aim to raise our own standard of living and the need to refrain from pursuing this goal for the benefit of poor people in other parts of the world' (Parliamentary Commission, 2002).

Governments in the donor country

Conventionally, official donors have defined their accountability back to their own taxpayers through the democratically elected government, via the responsible minister. Generally, no accountability distinction is made between these two. In the UK, for example, an official in DFID is accountable to the permanent secretary who delivers what the minister requires. The minister, in turn, is accountable to parliament. However, the permanent secretary is also the principal accounting officer with a direct responsibility for expenditure to parliament (the legislature representing the taxpayers, rather than the minister representing the executive). As accounting officer, he or she can object to a ministerial political decision if it is deemed to be outside the law. This is what happened some years ago when the permanent secretary at that time challenged the ministerial decision to finance the construction of the Pergau Dam in Malaysia in exchange for the Malaysian government buying UK arms.

In 2002, the UK parliament passed the International Development Act as a step towards greater accountability to poor people in recipient countries and a reduction in the power of ministers to decide how aid money should be spent. The act replaces and repeals the outdated 1980 Overseas Development and Cooperation Act, reflecting in law for the first time the centrality of poverty elimination in DFID's work and ensuring that future governments will not be able to use development assistance for other purposes.

Politicians (ministers) tend to operate within a short time frame, and one of the challenges for donor agency staff is to manage ministerial expectations concerning the agency's capacity to deliver real world change. The use of targets and other measuring instruments are as much a political instrument for the domestic constituency as a means of putting pressure on recipient governments.

Governments have established a system of horizontal accountability in their performance as donors. This is through a peer review mechanism of the Development Assistance Committee (DAC) of the Organisation for Economic Co-operation and Development (OECD). The DAC is one of the key forums in which the major bilateral donors work together to increase the effectiveness of their common efforts to support sustainable development. Members of the DAC are expected to have certain common objectives concerning the conduct of their aid programmes. To this end, guidelines have been prepared for development practitioners in capitals and in the field. Every two years, each member's performance is reviewed by two other members against agreed guiding principles. Senior staff in the donor agency under review use this mechanism to bring to the attention of their own minister aspects of the agency's work that they would like to see changed.

Governments in the recipient country

Traditionally, human rights relations are thought about in terms of citizens and states. However, we now recognize that relationships are more complex. Societies and communities are not homogeneous and there are competing interests within communities. Patron–client relationships exist between citizens – for example, between landlords and peasants. Patron–client relationships may also exist between government workers and citizens. Access to services and resources, for example, may be based on political support or extraction of rent. Within governments, there is evidence to suggest that ministers may operate line ministries on the basis of patron–client relationships.

Donors who operate at the country level become an integral part of the existing and complex patterns of patronage that already exist in that society and political economy. From the recipient's point of view, they are just one particular kind of patron. Paradoxically, donors may be contributing to the reproduction and reinforcement of the prevailing patterns of patronage that they are trying to eliminate through their good governance agendas. Can they shift from a patronage to a rights-based relationship and thus become part of the solution, rather than remain part of the problem?

The last few years have produced important changes in development policy and practice, both by developing country governments and by donor countries and the multilateral agencies that these donors support. The promotion of 'good governance' has come to be seen as a fundamental part of donor assistance. In Bolivia, the World Bank judged clientelism as the principal cause of poor public-sector performance and lack of responsiveness to poor people's needs and demands. Recipient governments are encouraged to move from 'a patronage to a professional state' (World Bank, 2000). Public-sector reform programmes promote the rule of law with greater accountability and transparency of the state towards its citizens.

After a certain time lag, aid agencies appreciated that they should try to practise what they preach. They have been developing a sense of responsibility, verging on accountability, towards recipient governments. This was noted by the change of language in the late 1990s to that of 'partnership', with a recognition of the mutual responsibilities that a partnership implies and an emphasis on the recipient country being the owner of the policies that the country was implementing with donor money. The DAC noted in May 2000 that an agenda for strengthening ownership and partnership has already emerged in recent years (DAC, 2000):

> *…common frameworks for programme implementation; partner-led coordination; transparency, simplification and, wherever feasible, sustained progress towards*

harmonizing donor procedures, in particular those concerning auditing and procurement of goods and services; continuing efforts toward untying; discouraging the proliferation of isolated projects; enhanced use of local capacities; joint monitoring and evaluation; improved coherence; and innovative ways of financing.

Donors hope that this new approach will result in considerable strengthening of the quality, effectiveness and accountability of the institutions in recipient countries. Improvements in the quality of governance would thus allow donors to put finances directly into government budgets – thereby helping to fund rapid improvements in health, education, water and other services that contribute to poverty reduction and fulfilment of rights.

While this move to greater harmonization, coordination and mutual accountability is encouraging, there are two inherent problems that, paradoxically, can constrain this attempt to shift to a more rights-based approach. First, as a result of this change, whereas previously donors spent most of their time designing and managing projects in particular urban or rural locations, today donors are in the capital city discussing policy issues with each other and with recipient government officials and national representatives of civil society organizations. While more focused on how to influence or persuade recipient governments to implement accountable and transparent policies for sustainable poverty reduction and the fulfilment of rights, donors are further removed from the poor people whom they are seeking to help. They risk living in a world of 'what should be', detached from any knowledge of the reality on the ground. Means to tackle this problem include the 'exposure and dialogue visits' developed by the Self-Employed Women's Association (SEWA) in India and described by McGee (2002).

In Bolivia, DFID began to tackle this challenge by developing and implementing 'reality checks' as a means of staying in touch. If well designed, such visits can be more effective than the traditional project monitoring visit that has specific terms of reference, possibly constraining the visitor from being open to issues beyond predetermined boundaries. Conditions for an effective reality check include travelling with companions who have pre-established access to local communities and institutions; when feasible, making return visits to these same communities and institutions in order to understand local dynamics, rather than just taking a snapshot; bringing a fellow visitor, such as a senior government official who may be equally suffering from reality deprivation; having no responsibility during the visit for any specific action or task; a frame of mind ready to absorb the unexpected and digest the unpalatable; reporting back to government and donor colleagues in the capital and at head office; and using the experience to inform policy debates.

Second, and even more serious, this change reduces the recipient's room for manoeuvre and, thus, freedom to act. The mutual accountability and responsibility is weighted in favour of the donor who always has the option to walk away. In the present world, donors have more power of choice as to whether or not to stay in the relationship than do the clients. The current tendency for greater official donor coordination through the OECD DAC and the Comprehensive Development Framework (CDF)/poverty reduction strategy (PRS) approaches limits the recipient's choice even further. No longer can the recipient 'play off' one donor against another. The relationship remains fundamentally one of patron and client, where now the client cannot choose, as before, who will be his patron. Governments have to dance to the different tunes of donors and the multilaterals – even if they do not agree with them – in order to get aid and debt relief. This can often lead to situations where governments are saying the right things in order to please donors, but then not substantially changing policy or practice (see Chapter 2).

Poor people in recipient countries

Generally, donor governments consider their accountability to poor people in recipient countries to be mediated through elected governments. For this premise to be sustained, such governments must be sufficiently accountable to their citizens. Donors judge this not to be the case in most aid-recipient countries and conceive empowered citizens as their allies in the struggle for greater state accountability. Citizens can be empowered through enhancing their direct capacity to influence the state through civil society action or through improving representative democracy.

Empowered citizens can also help donors to be accountable for their actions to the citizens (taxpayers) in the donor country. One of the reasons for earlier project-based funding was donors' concern about recipient government corruption. The shift to policy-based funding of recipient government budgets means that donors must rely more on the recipient country's citizens to hold their government accountable for donor funds; how to do this has become an important topic for aid practice (Norton and Elson, 2002). Thus, the shift to budget support was a way of reducing conflicting donor projects, but also acted to strengthen state–citizen relationships. The PRS process places very considerable emphasis on citizens' participation, although the requirements for participation are not always met, in practice. While it does not always happen as much in practice as had been hoped for in theory, it does, at least, open up new spaces for dialogue (see Chapter 4).

How do donors improve efforts to enhance citizens' direct and representative participation in policy processes without upsetting recipient governments? The overarching human rights framework provides a justification for donors to stand up for the interests of poor people; but how do they do this without imposing their views and conditions on governments? The adoption of a rights-based approach by donors makes explicit the importance of politics, power and voice, and not just income, in addressing poverty. It is a recognition that discrimination and other forms of exclusion – including exclusion from political and policy processes – are an important part of the agenda.

Donors' efforts to support citizens to hold the state more accountable have taken a number of approaches. The US Agency for International Development (USAID) and Germany, for example, have focused on strengthening democracy per se, without necessarily specific reference to those most excluded or disempowered (although USAID has had a strong gender equality dimension in its work). This has resulted in the growth of advocacy NGOs who, as noted by

Carothers (1999) and others, face a number of problems that donors have been reluctant to confront. These include lack of financial accountability, not representing the people on whose behalf they claim to advocate and the illusion of non-partisanship. Many of these problems are due to such NGOs being part of the general patronage social system where accountability mechanisms are weak and civil society concerns are often channelled to bureaucrats through patron–client relations.

Donors have tended to understand civil society as voluntary associations organized according to democratic principles, rather than adopt a broader understanding of civil society as a social arena between family and state. This definition tends to ignore the darker side of civil society – the fact that civil society organizations may, themselves, be oppressive, exclusive and violent.

If donors wish to encourage democratization, they must work out whether it is better to support small elite networks that promote discourses of democratic rights but have virtually no political leverage (other than through undesirable patronage links), or large socially embedded organizations, such as trade unions or religious organizations, that have political leverage but may reinforce existing social hierarchies.

A further and even riskier alternative is to support non-membership-based social movements that – as, for example, in Bolivia – may most represent the voice of the excluded. Such a shift not only raises major problems of financial and political accountability but is also most likely to bring donors into direct conflict with the recipient government, particularly if the movement turns violent and authoritarian when pushing for more responsiveness and better accountability from the state. Donors may find themselves accused of bias, of getting involved in political processes about which they know nothing and of fuelling the opposition. While this may cause some embarrassment for the donor, with a loss of credibility with the recipient government, it may also undermine the credibility of organizations being supported.

This challenge confronted aid agencies in Bolivia during the preparations for the 2002 national elections. All agencies shared a similar diagnosis of the problem of poor people, particularly women and those of indigenous origin, of being deprived of their rights as informed voters. One agency concluded that the best means to tackle this problem was to support advocacy and research organizations in the capital city, encouraging them to investigate the causes and scale of the problem. Others decided to support grassroots organizations that directly represented the deprived groups and to help them find out from the people themselves why it was that they were not voting. Whereas the first option was fully approved by the Bolivian authorities, the second was seen as unacceptable interference in national political processes. By seeking to respond more directly to the primary stakeholders, the agencies were accused of becoming unaccountable to the recipient government.

Finally, according to Tendler (1997), while current wisdom sees civil society's special advantage as lying in its outsider status or independence from government, there has been a tendency to exaggerate the extent to which civil society can counteract the rent-seeking tendencies of government. Civil society is not all virtue and government all vices. Tendler (1997) argues that successful examples of achieving good government show that the state itself plays an important role in fostering civil society's capacity to hold the state accountable, and that alliances between reformers in civil society and government may be an important key to better government.

In addition to all of these problems, we believe that when donors fund civil society to make the state more accountable, they run a serious risk of distorting the very lines of accountability that they want to reinforce. Donor procedures and reporting requirements, and their accountability to politicians and taxpayers back home result in the imposition of new forms of conditionality on these organizations. Through the application of logical frameworks (logframes) and other requirements, this means that organizations become shaped by the aims of the donor and that donors want to fund civil society organizations that mirror their own agendas.

Some bilateral programmes have tried to move away from this fundamental problem of distorted lines of accountability by setting up locally appointed management boards for civil society funding. These shift the opportunity costs of management from the donor to the board and thus enable the funding of smaller organizations. Furthermore, because the donor is one step removed, it means that it may be able to fund more radical organizations without losing its credibility with the recipient government. DFID has done this, for example, in Bangladesh and Peru. Unfortunately, every solution breeds its own problems. By being one step removed, the donor may not so easily be able to facilitate civil society–government dialogue and may become disconnected from the reality of poor people's lives through lack of direct contact with civil society organizations that represent poor people.

The role and reaction of Northern NGOs brings another dimension to the distorted lines of accountability. Many donor governments support civil society in recipient countries by channelling money through their own countries' development NGOs, which may be an important political constituency back home for aid. This can result in the right hand not knowing what the left hand is doing; in some cases, a donor government may be indirectly supporting actions in the recipient country that run completely contrary to the agenda it is promoting with the recipient government. In other cases, donor and recipient governments may be complicit in the lack of transparency in such arrangements. Back home, the donor can declare that it is supporting human rights efforts of poor people, while in the recipient country the local donor representative can declare total ignorance of what the Northern NGO is doing ('not my department'). We believe that these arrangements are unhelpful in efforts to help establish alliances between reformers in government and advocates for change in civil society. With greater consistency and transparency in what it funds, a donor government can make a useful contribution to facilitating dialogue. Nevertheless, in the recipient country itself those civil society organizations benefiting from a privileged special relationship with Northern NGOs, and through them with a particular donor government, might well be reluctant to switch to a more transparent and equitable arrangement. Eyben (2003) describes the resistance encountered when some official aid agencies tried to change the way in which donors were funding Bolivian civil society.

One way in which donors can avoid these problems is not to fund civil society, but simply to provide support to the strengthening of the formal democratic machinery, through support to political parties, the legislature and election processes. This kind of support has been a significant aspect of some donor portfolios, but has generally not been successful in enhancing the capacity of poor and excluded people to have a greater voice in the state's affairs. In response to that problem, donors have turned to civil society organizations to support their efforts to make formal democracy more inclusive. In so doing, donors face the various challenges described earlier in this section.

Finally, donors are developing a greater sense of accountability directly to the citizens of recipient countries, bypassing the mediation of elected governments. Evidence of this comes from efforts to establish information services in donor country offices and to hold consultation meetings with civil society organizations during the design and evaluation of country assistance strategies. Participatory poverty assessments are more common among multilateral organizations that face rather different accountability challenges; but bilateral donors draw on the findings from such assessments to justify their own strategies.

The international human rights framework

The interest in the idea of rights and, in particular, the overarching human rights framework has developed among donors as a way of standing up for the interests of poor people without imposing their views and conditions on governments. The internationally agreed human rights framework theoretically provides a basis for engaging with other governments. It provides a set of internationally agreed treaties that governments, including donor governments, have signed up to and against which they can be monitored. The casuistic argument is that as recipient governments have generally ratified these human rights agreements, donors are simply helping them to do what they have already declared they want to do.

The UN conferences of the first half of the 1990s put flesh to these human rights agreements by identifying specific time-bound targets that the world's governments should aim to meet. These targets and specifically a subset of these, the Millennium Development Goals (MDGs), endorsed by the UN General Assembly in 2000, is an outcome of the most global democratic process currently available. Whatever their faults, the MDGs are a set of rights that everyone can agree on and should provide a normative basis for the objectives of development. A rights-based relationship between donors and recipients is one that recognizes and makes explicit the principles of mutual obligation and entitlement within this shared normative framework.

Some challenge this framework on the grounds of not being genuinely universal, but derived from the European Enlightenment and thus an ideological expression of the hegemony of the North. It is not our intention here to review these debates that have produced a substantial body of academic literature.[3] What interests us is that a shared normative framework for action is now becoming a legitimate subject on the agenda of official development assistance.

That such a framework exists as the basis for donor–recipient accountability is still a relatively new idea and remains contested inside donor organizations. Until recently, aid was seen as a technical issue, a matter of what can be done rather than what ought to be done. Resource transfers from the North to the South were 'developmental', along the lines of contributing to economic growth as an end in itself, or of meeting 'basic needs' as a welfare measure. The introduction of a normative framework since the mid 1990s has led to an approach to action that was stated by Kofi Annan: 'not simply in terms of human needs, or developmental requirements, but in terms of society's obligations to respond to inalienable rights of individuals, it empowers people to demand justice as a right, not as charity, and gives communities a moral basis from which to claim international assistance when needed'.[4]

The international human rights framework therefore raises the issue of whether donor governments are duty bearers in relation to realizing the rights of poor people in other countries. Can poor people either directly, or through their elected governments, hold richer countries accountable for the poverty and misery in the rest of the world? This is the basic premise of the right to development. There have been many sterile arguments in international forums concerning aid flows that continue to keep it a contested issue, which is why it has only the status of a declaration rather than of a legally binding convention or covenant. Nevertheless, we note a gradual shift in the position of donor governments. The commitment to the MDGs and the outcome of the Monterrey Conference on Financing for Development are symptoms of such a shift. Other signs include the broadening of donor perspective from considering aid as the single instrument of poverty reduction. As DFID's White Paper on globalization (2000) made clear, issues for donors include exploring how to achieve fairer trade rules that allow developing countries to access rich countries' markets, how to encourage greater transnational corporate responsibility and how to secure reduction in global conflict. Finally, even without the right to development, some of the existing conventions and covenants do include a reference to the responsibilities of all governments in relation to rights. Thus, if they wish, donor governments can use the mechanism of reporting to the UN human rights commissions in order to include a report on how they are contributing to the realization of rights in other countries, as well as in their own. Global civil society action, an issue not explored in this chapter, is potentially a key means of holding donors more accountable within the international human rights framework.

Conclusions

Official bilateral donor agencies in the past were principally accountable to the taxpayers who provided the aid funds. Unlike other government spending departments, the services provided by the agency were not provided to those who paid the taxes but to people in another part of the world. Since the end of the Cold War, donor agencies have been gradually recognizing and responding to other lines of accountability.

In one sense, the last decade has seen a shift in balance of power *towards* the donors as recipient governments are no longer able to use Cold War politics to play one donor off against the other. At the same time, however, the end of the Cold War removed some of the *realpolitik* from donor behaviour. While it is true that aid budgets were cut, the aid that remained began to take its job more seriously. There was a new opportunity to consider the purpose of aid and to develop a shared goal of improved global well-being and the elimination of poverty.

The rights-based approach to development has been part of this shift in donor perspective. Even donors without such a perspective have had to engage in the issues of accountability. It became much more important that donor funds were used for their intended purpose and recipient governments found that they had to be more accountable to donors for those funds. It was a logical development that donors have now started to enlist the primary stakeholders as allies in holding recipient governments accountable, usually to the discomfiture of these governments who, as we have seen, may challenge donors' right to do this.

Today, on the whole, we are witnessing greater responsiveness rather than, as yet, genuine accountability. Nevertheless, donor procedures are changing. Principles of accountability, once recognized, seem to generate their own momentum and processes of change. Donor governments are finding the need to establish relations of mutual responsibility with recipient governments through compacts such as the New Partnership for African Development. Those donor governments who have most embraced rights-based approaches, such as Sweden, are asking recipient governments to evaluate their aid programmes. Efforts at donor basket-funding and direct purchase of technical assistance by the recipients are other signs of genuine efforts to 'put the recipient government in the driving seat'. Donors are becoming prepared to be held accountable to that government for delivering on donor promises.

It may well be that in their enthusiasm for such instruments as direct budgetary support, donors are making heroic assumptions about the recipient government's capacity or will to be accountable to their citizens, particularly to those with least voice and wealth. There is an impression of attempting to run before having learned properly to walk. In these challenging circumstances, staff in donor agencies need to map out and seek to manage in an equitable and transparent manner all of the institutions to whom their agency is accountable. They can do this more easily by welcoming and facilitating alliances within and across these sets of institutions – for example, encouraging links between citizens in donor countries and citizens in recipient countries, or supporting joined-up efforts by recipient governments when they struggle for fairer rules of the game in international trade negotiations.

Can donor governments become more accountable to poor people? Our answer is perhaps they can – provided they meet two conditions. The first is that they hold this vision of accountability to poor people as central to all of their work, their procedures and their relationships The second is that they persuade their own citizens that the donor agencies should be held accountable by them in working towards this vision, as in the case of the parliamentary questions in the UK concerning excluded poor people in India.

The evolving policy and practice of official donor agencies are not entirely a dependent variable of developments in the global political economy. Donor agencies can be genuine *agents* and influence that political economy in favour of a more just world. Nevertheless, any gains they make will be small, and incremental achievements in the power of ideas and changed personal behaviour are likely to be more significant than the power of money. This is not to disparage the effort. On the contrary, when staff in donor agencies realize that there is no overnight solution but, at best, a slow and modest progress, then they may move faster than they have during the past 40 years.

Notes

1 The views presented here are the authors' own and do not in any way represent the policy of DFID or any other aid agency.
2 Multilateral agencies, such as the UNDP or World Bank, have rather different upward lines of accountability from those of governing bodies made up of country representatives or shareholders. In our view, the tendency to distinguish donors on the grounds of whether they make grants or loans (and some, such as the German and Japanese governments and the World Bank, do both) may obscure the – perhaps more important – differences between donors in their accountability relationships.
3 There is an excellent summary of these in Nyamu-Musembi (2002).
4 Kofi Annan in a speech to the UN General Assembly in 1998.

References

Carothers, T (1999) *Aiding Democracy Abroad, the Learning Curve*, Carnegie Endowment for International Peace, Washington, DC

Cornwall, A and Gaventa, J (2000) 'From Users and Choosers to Makers and Shapers: Repositioning Participation in Social Policy', *IDS Bulletin*, vol 31, no 4, pp50–62

DAC (2000) *Partnership for Poverty Reduction*, Statement by the DAC High Level Meeting, Paris, 11–12 May

DFID (2000) *Making Globalization Work for Poor People*, Government White Paper, HMSO, London

DFID (2001) *Andhra Pradesh, State Strategy Paper*, DFID, New Delhi

Eyben, R (2003) *Donors as Political Actors: Fighting the Thirty Years War in Bolivia*, IDS Working Paper, no 183, IDS, Brighton

Goetz, A-M and Gaventa, J (2001) *Bringing Citizen Voice and Client Focus into Service Delivery*, IDS Working Paper, no 138, IDS, Brighton

Goetz, A-M and Jenkins, R (2001) 'Hybrid Forms of Accountability, Citizen Engagement in Institutions of Public Sector Oversight in India', *Public Management Review*, vol 3, no 3, pp363–383

Jones, E and Gaventa, J (2002) *Concepts of Citizenship: A Review*, IDS Development Bibliography, no 19, IDS, Brighton

McGee, R (2002) 'The Self in Participatory Poverty Research', in Brock, K and McGee, R (eds) *Knowing Poverty: Critical Reflections on Participatory Research and Policy*, Earthscan, London

Norton, A and Elson, D (2002) *What's Behind the Budget? Politics, Rights and Accountability in the Budget Process*, ODI, London

Nyamu-Musembi, C (2002) *Toward an Actor-Oriented Perspective on Human Rights*, IDS Working Paper, no 169, IDS, Brighton

Parliamentary Commission on Swedish Policy for Global Development (Sweden) (2002) *Towards a More Equitable World Free from Poverty*, Swedish Government Official Reports, Stockholm

Praxis (2002) *Participatory Assessment of Government of Orissa's Delivery of Services that Impact at the Village Level*, report prepared for the Poverty Task Force, Government of Orissa, India

Sen, A (1999) *Development as Freedom*, Oxford University Press, Oxford

Silverman, J (2000) Unpublished draft annex to World Bank project appraisal document on strengthening decentralization in Bolivia, commissioned by DFID, La Paz, Bolivia

Tendler, J (1997) *Good Government in the Tropics*, Johns Hopkins University Press, Baltimore and London

UNDP (2000) *Human Development Report: Human Rights and Human Development*, United Nations Development Programme/Oxford University Press, New York

World Bank (2000) *Bolivia from Patronage to a Professional State*, Institutional and Governance Review Report, World Bank, Washington, DC

Zadek, S, Evans, R and Reynard, P (1999) *Value-based Effectiveness: A Scoping Study for a Social Audit for DFID*, unpublished report, New Economics Foundation, London

13

Minding the Gap through Organizational Learning

Katherine Pasteur and Patta Scott-Villiers

Introduction

The new language of development stresses the importance of more inclusive systems of aid. However, new challenges are presented by aid policies and projects that advocate participation of a broader range of stakeholders. The new development orthodoxies are highly value laden and, as such, are difficult to enact, both at a personal and at an organizational level.

Experiences in the UK Department for International Development (DFID) and the Swedish International Development Agency (Sida) illustrate how, in instances where such value-laden policies are being promoted, gaps often emerge between what is being said or prescribed, and what is actually happening in practice. Ownership is often absent among government and non-government partners. These cases also illustrate processes whereby groups of agency and project staff have come to realize a need for better learning in order to understand and close those gaps.

This chapter proposes that the gaps that frequently emerge between words and practice can be narrowed, and that implementation of the new development agenda can be improved through learning and change. Organizational learning involves taking time to reflect upon action and experience in order to reframe the problem or issue and gain relevant insights, leading to improved future action and performance. To understand more fully why gaps are occurring requires processes of reflection and questioning that probe more systemically, and that look at personal, organizational and institutional systems. Sub-cultural factors, such as values, goals, attitudes and behaviours, influence individuals' capacity to work with partners in new ways and should not be ignored; they should be analysed and brought to the centre. Broadening understanding of how different organizational systems (organizational structure, procedures, culture and power), as well as the wider institutional environment, interact and make up the whole will help to draw attention to critical factors that influence or inhibit change towards new goals.

Mind the gap!

As described in the introduction to this book (see Chapter 1), development agencies now propose to deliver social goods with greater ownership, participation, partnership and accountability to the poor. But if these ideas are going to play any useful part in reducing poverty, they have to be imbued with realism and energy. Reality is not as glib as theory. The words of the new agenda are abstract and idealistic; the actions are driven by context and expediency. The language and ideas of the new agenda have been introduced; but corresponding changes to underlying behaviours and organizational procedures at different levels are slow in materializing. What development agencies say, the language they use and the policies they propose are still out of alignment with what they do.

Some incongruity between ideals and reality is inevitable and a degree of tension can create desirable debate. An exact match of rhetoric and practice would be excessively fundamentalist, closing any space for initiative and challenge to the status quo. It is only when the gulf becomes wide and goes unrecognized that problems result. For instance, if we claim to our partners that we believe in their participation, but then do not give them relevant information or access to our decision processes, our misleading messages will lead to conflict. If we believe that people have rights to a share in decision-making, then we have an obligation to close the gap.

The complex implications for individuals and the organization are seldom made explicit when new value-based aid delivery policies are introduced. Enacting policies of participation, accountability, transparency, ownership, empowerment and partnership means changing the nature of the relationship between individual development professionals, their bosses and their counterparts in the government and community. It also implies similar relational shifts between an agency, its funders, partners and poor people. Individuals need to be willing to form new types of relationship. In addition to adjustments to organizational procedures, structures and power relations, these policies imply a need for personal changes in attitudes and behaviour.

In this chapter it is argued that the gaps between words and action can best be narrowed through developing new forms of learning. The literature on organizational learning has grown rapidly during recent years (Davies, 1998), and the topic covers a whole range of disciplines, goals and approaches, as usefully outlined in a literature review by Easterby-Smith (1997). It is useful here to make a distinction between organizational learning and knowledge management in order to clarify our perspective. This can also be seen as a distinction between learning from action (tacit knowledge, based on experience and remaining in people's heads) and learning from other sources (explicit knowledge, which can be documented or clearly articulated; Nonaka et al, 1996).

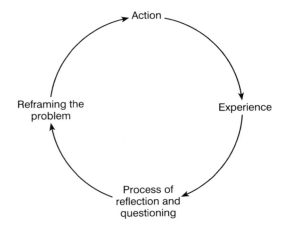

Figure 13.1 *A cycle of learning and action*

Organizational learning and, in particular, literature on the learning organization, occupies itself more with the processes and environment for effective knowledge creation and knowledge application for improved performance. Knowledge management concerns itself with the capture, storage, communication and retrieval of information that tends to be explicit. This includes documentation, information technology (IT) systems and databases, as well as conferences and meetings.

This chapter is concerned principally with organizational learning: improved reflection around, and learning from, action. This type of learning process is illustrated in Figure 13.1. Ensuring that experience leads to appropriate actions to close the gaps between rhetoric and reality requires not only *time and space* for reflection, but also more effective *processes* of reflection and reframing in order to achieve relevant insights for redirecting action.

To understand more clearly why policy–practice gaps are occurring requires more systemic processes of reflection and questioning. There is a tendency to seek immediate sources of explanation when challenges are encountered. Case examples illustrate that adjustments to a range of organizational structures, procedures and organizational culture are necessary. They also show that, despite organizational will, wider institutional factors can limit the capacity for change. Greater understanding of how organizational systems and subsystems interact and make up the whole will help to draw attention to critical factors that influence or inhibit change towards new goals. This framework for learning helps one to notice, understand, internalize and act upon the gaps continuously. It helps to create an active dialogue between practice and policy.

If learning from action is based around the forms of reflection described above, then the lessons learned will be more apposite and relevant. Learning and sharing both require a supportive environment, in terms of time and space for reflection, but also appropriate incentives and conditions that encourage openness, risk-taking and creativity:

We have been talking about partnership for about ten years now but we still don't know exactly what we mean by it (DFID adviser Brazil, pers comm).

The analysis presented in this chapter is based principally on the early stages of work on organizational learning in DFID and Sida.[1] This chapter draws on literature and case study illustrations to show ways of reflecting that lead to more realistic and appropriate options for change. Unless otherwise stated, the quotations and stories that are used in this chapter illustrate the authors' understanding of learning and the case for change, and draw on interactions and activities that have formed part of this work. The chapter starts by presenting two examples that illustrate some of the challenges, as well as positive responses to develop new ways of learning. It then looks at the literature to provide insights and theories that argue for systemic thinking as a vital component of reflection and learning. Finally, we reflect on ways to create the supportive environment required for this new type of organizational learning.

Recognizing and acting on the gap

The following two examples highlight some of the new types of problems and issues that arise when implementing value-laden development goals such as 'ownership' in the DFID case and 'participation' in the Sida case. They also illustrate new ways of learning, developed to help address some of those challenges. In DFID Uganda, the original stimulus for reflection was a desire to share lessons on institutional and policy reform. A process of retrospective review by external consultants drew attention to the need to understand issues concerning ownership, and was effective in broadening and deepening stakeholders' perspectives of this issue, as explored below. At Sida, the need to gain a better understanding of participation had been recognized for some time, and a process of reflection was organized to address that need.

Retrospective learning in the Uganda forest sector

DFID Uganda has been supporting policy and institutional reform in the Ugandan government's forest sector since 1997. Although the support programme has been subject to the usual reviews and evaluations, in September 2001 DFID Uganda commissioned local consultants to carry out a 'retrospective learning' engagement with a range of stakeholders. The aim was to draw lessons from the reform and stimulate new action. The commissioning of this work indicated that, despite the general success of the programmed activities, there was some discomfort among DFID staff that certain aspects of the reform process were presenting tough challenges that were not easy to explain or resolve. They felt that the reform experiences needed to be understood, shared and followed by timely action and ongoing learning. The call for a new method for reflection also indicated that traditional forms of monitoring and review had not proved entirely effective in ensuring the appropriate lessons were applied, and that something different needed to be tried. A growing interest across DFID, more generally, in improving 'lesson learning' – particularly concerning issues of policy reform – provided the space and legitimacy for experimenting with a new idea such as this one.

What was the gap and what were the effects?

The ownership of the reform by the Ugandan government was hypothetical. It is only stated in the project document (view of one stakeholder in the forest-sector learning study, cited in Kazoora et al, 2002, p20).

An issue of particular importance to DFID was that of shifting ownership of the reform to the Ugandan government and other forest stakeholders before the end of the funding period. The goal of local, particularly government, ownership was spoken of in the project documents, speeches and meetings. But, in practice, it was proving difficult to achieve. The expectation of DFID staff was that achieving a shift towards government ownership was the responsibility of the change agents contracted by DFID to manage the reform process. The contractors are, ultimately, accountable to DFID for the spending of funds and for achieving outputs (a new forest policy, a new forest agency, etc) and project goals (government ownership). It became clear that rapid progress on outputs had a tendency to compromise progress on the ownership goal, and the contractors argued that the same would have been true the other way round – government ownership of the process might have delayed the actual achievement of new agencies and policies as they would have been subject to normal politics, rather than looked after by an external agent.

Discussions revealed a complex set of cultural, political and procedural issues around achieving government ownership. The relationship between DFID and government was equivocal: there was never enough time to commit to building a strong relationship between them; some distrust existed on both sides; and the systems in place for sharing control (particularly financial) were imperfect. Meanwhile, the contractors being funded by DFID to work with the government in delivering the outputs found themselves servants of two masters whose wishes did not always match. Since they were primarily accountable to their paymasters, DFID, for the outputs, there was a tendency to focus on these (the new forest agency, for example) rather than on the ownership question. In addition, it could be argued that the contractors, who were from the North, felt more comfortable working closely with DFID staff in order to achieve the DFID outputs because communication, in terms of language and socio-cultural backgrounds, was simpler. Furthermore, there was a feeling of mistrust of the government, which re-emphasized the focus on DFID's outputs as opposed to government ownership. The outputs were therefore achieved with admirable efficiency, the policy statement was elegant, the agency planned and the law drafted. But without ownership by government, the whole effort was in jeopardy.

Understanding the gap through a process of reflection

The interview has triggered a lot of questions in my mind that previously I had not considered regarding this project (Kazoora et al, 2002, p8).

A 'retrospective learning study' was undertaken by local external consultants about half way through the three-year reform process (Kazoora et al, 2002). It involved interviews with around 70 stakeholders: government (ministry, department and district levels); civil society representatives; the DFID-funded contractors working on the project; and DFID office staff linked to it. The local consultants were skilled in gaining the confidence of these stakeholders and allowed participants to take time to reflect and consider the whole story of the reform process, and their role in it, rather than focusing on isolated incidents or problems. Thus, the exercise revealed areas of agreement and progress, but also differences of opinion, frustrations and dissatisfaction. It also revealed the extent of differences between what had been and was being said, and what was, in practice, being done. Most importantly, several of the discussions motivated people to question their personal responsibility and to think about how to improve their role and relationship-building:

[The workshop] helped them to lift their vision out of the sea of details and decisions at the top of the minds of anyone involved in a complex project to focus, instead, on the 'big picture' and learning lessons for the future (Workshop participants, DFID, 2002a).

Issues arising from this and other institutional change projects in forestry in Africa stimulated the organization of a workshop for DFID and some of its forest reform contractors to try to seek concrete solutions and guidance. This was beneficial in drawing attention from the particulars of individual projects to the broader determinants of the problems that were being encountered. These included issues governed by procurement and contracting procedures, questions of skills for managing change among contracted staff, and the role of personal factors in shaping or hindering project success.

Closing the gap

It is common for consultants to have big egos… They can also come to projects with family pressures, past experiences or other personal agendas that might conflict with or undermine the project (workshop participants, DFID, 2002b).

As outcomes of both the learning study and the workshop, many procedural, personal, political and cultural obstacles to shifting ownership were made explicit. Some early steps have been taken towards addressing some of these obstacles. Shifts have been made in the reform project accountability structure. Proposals have also been drafted to the DFID permanent secretary and DFID's procurement department outlining suggested alterations to the procedures for the delivery of, and accountability for, funds so that national governments have stronger control.

With respect to personal and cultural obstacles, some staff members involved in the study have started to question their personal assumptions and goals, and thus begin to think about appropriate changes in their own behaviour and to improve their relationships with partners and colleagues. One staff member suggested the idea of 'personal' and 'relationship-building' sessions so that outsiders might help the various key players to understand how others interpret their behaviour, and help them to learn to work together better in the future. While these are small steps, they are significant. The challenge will be whether these initiatives continue and grow over the long term. This case study illustrates that traditional forms of monitoring and review do not necessarily draw appropriate lessons and that new methods are being experimented with. The learning process used here illustrated that the issues involved in achieving a goal such as ownership are complex and diverse. They are not merely technical or procedural issues, but can also be traced to relationships, politics and even personalities.

Participatory enquiry at Sida

In September 2001 a group of managers at Sida's headquarters in Stockholm and another group at the Swedish embassy in Nairobi, Kenya, started a learning project with a team from the participation group at the Institute of Development Studies (IDS).[2] They embarked on a process of iterative enquiry into the practicalities and meanings of people's participation in development. The individuals felt that they did not know enough about participation and wished to understand why their efforts had not always been successful.

The reflection process

In this form of enquiry, small groups come together to learn from each other and deepen their understanding of a central, commonly agreed theme, generating new issues and questions for further investigation and action. Between meetings, individuals try things out, carry out enquiries with colleagues or analyse records and documents to produce findings and insights that they bring to the process.

The groups decided to balance theoretical and practical concerns in a way that is thorough enough, but does not take up excessive time. The Stockholm group called this *Lagom*: 'not too much and not too little'. They met regularly over eight months and explored conceptual, practical and personal views on participation. Both groups started by looking at practical participation in their own projects and programmes. They questioned who participates, why, when, how much and what for, and examined activities as diverse as participation in the Mekong River Authority, human rights in Kenya, police reform in Honduras and evaluation and internal policy-making in Sida. In doing this they also looked at the theories and practices of participation, and its meanings among themselves, their colleagues and in the broader environment. They touched on the extent to which participation was one of their values, discovering, for example, how the culture and history of Sweden and of Sida has tended to promote complementary values among its citizens, such as solidarity.

Closing the gap

During a brief follow-up review with the participants, almost everyone said that they have gone about their work in a subtly different way as a result of their involvement in the reflection process. They have begun to question their actions more frequently and are more willing to seek different opinions before taking decisions. They have, in essence, begun to hold a new attitude to learning. While they had hoped to arrive at a single definition of, and approach to, participation, many have now arrived at an understanding of its diverse manifestations in the organization and feel comfortable with this realization.

They have put into practice new approaches to participation, both internal to Sida and in their external relations. For example, during a mid-term review of a sector-support programme, other stakeholders were asked to design and run the review with Sida, resulting in a more collegial process and outcome. In another example, a cross-sectoral group put together terms of reference for a participatory urban-planning exercise. The terms of reference reflected the different angles of importance brought by different Sida participants, from technical excellence in design to issues of gender. Making the terms of reference practical and coherent was a struggle. As the group said:

> On a practical level, we debated the question of how to reduce the ever increasing number of policies that a staff member must include in every terms of reference and project to ensure that it is correct and holistic, including concerns for the environment, gender, diversity, democracy, rights, participation and more. If each of these is seen as implying a separate layer of requirements, the activity becomes overwhelmed with good intentions and is practically impossible to implement. The organization needs to look at how these various themes are integrated in any given context in order that all are achieved, but a simplicity of approach is maintained (Sida, 2002).

Although the process was not as time efficient as the participants desired, there are plans in both Nairobi and Stockholm to continue in a streamlined form:

> The Lagom way of learning helps to deepen understanding of a subject and links it directly and practically to our ongoing work. It is also very useful for staff members to do their own research and cooperate with one another – the resulting learning is better embedded inside Sida than would be the case if consultants were asked to do a study... In proposing mini-Lagoms in various divisions, we plan to take into account all we have learned about making the process effective by choosing a mix of activities that is suited to the particular division and subject. Live debate on policy issues linked to practice could be a significant addition to Sida's way of working, resulting in a better-integrated organization (Sida, 2002).

Lessons from new ways of learning about gaps

What can we learn from these experiences that ensures a better understanding of the gaps between words and practice, and moves practitioners towards closing those gaps? Principally, the examples suggest a need to broaden the scope and nature of reflection, beyond seeking the immediate and most obvious causes of problems, in order to achieve a richer quality of learning. They also reveal the need for an improved organizational environment, including time and space, for learning. The following section highlights some organizational learning theories that add insight to an understanding of learning and how it can be made more effective.

Improving the quality of reflection

In their introduction to this book, Hinton and Groves (see Chapter 1) highlighted the complexity of the human and social world. Infinite numbers of variables interrelate, and multiple levels of feedback, both spatial and temporal, are in operation, thus making outcomes hard to predict. Traditional forms of analysis focus on separating problems or issues out into individual pieces and considering them in isolation. Systems thinking highlights the need to see or think in wholes rather than in parts, drawing attention to the importance of interrelationships and feedback loops in the complex and dynamic environments in which we work, interact and learn (Senge, 1990; Checkland and Scholes, 1990; Flood, 1999). In the case of complex issues that involve multiple stakeholders and are influenced by a history of past actions and policies, taking a more systemic approach is hugely valuable. Systems thinking can aid learning by expanding the 'mental maps' that people use to understand problems or opportunities – in other words, it provides people with a broader and more complex picture of all the patterns and relationships that surround the particular issue that they wish to address.

The work of Argyris and Schon (1978) argues for greater depth of thinking in order to gain relevant insights that aid learning and change. They distinguish between 'single-loop' and 'double-loop' learning. Single-loop learning tends to focus on understanding an issue in terms of project or programme strategy and the procedures that surround it. The types of solutions sought revolve around changing existing organizational rules largely at the programme level – that is, a general tightening and improvement in current procedures. Double-loop learning, however, focuses on 'insight' – understanding reasons for current rules and then questioning these reasons. It enquires more deeply into the variables that originally determined that choice of strategy – for example, personal or organizational values, norms or broader policies. An exploration of the role of these variables, which shape and determine particular actions and choices, brings one closer to a potential rethinking and re-orienting of individual and organizational behaviour, culture and systems.

Figures 13.2 and 13.3 illustrate two key interlocking systems that should be put under the lens of greater scrutiny. Although organizational factors are key in achieving policy goals, both personal factors (attitudes, values and behaviours)

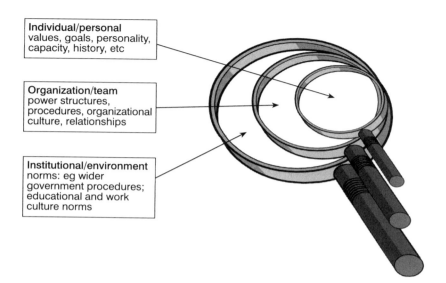

Figure 13.2 *Looking more closely at individual, organizational and institutional systems*

and broader institutional or environmental factors can also have a huge role to play. The significance of each of these is discussed in more detail in the following three sections. Homing in on the organizational level, it is important to look at the interplay between structures, procedures and cultures, as well as at the influence of the broader power and political dynamics that shape them. This is dealt with below.

Looking within: reflecting on the personal

Individual development professionals have their own way of understanding and viewing the world, as well as their own personal goals and priorities (see also Chapters 4 and 14). There is a tendency, however, for people not to reflect on the significance of personal goals and values, and the way in which they may influence their capacity to achieve organizational goals. It is relatively easy to espouse certain values or goals, but much harder to put them into practice, particularly in the face of other work and private pressures. At one level, we may feel deeply committed to values such as participation, equity or strengthening local ownership; but when it comes down to practice, the way in which we tend to work and live can give the impression of contradictory values. When the power is in our hands, or we are accountable for the money, how easy is it to truly relinquish control? When we consider ourselves well educated and have achieved position in a hierarchy, how easy is it to invite others to join us as equals (see Chapter 4)? When given the chance of an exclusive lifestyle in developing country capitals, how can we argue against excessive differences between rich and poor?

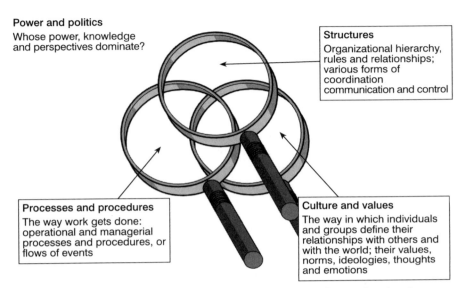

Power and politics
Whose power, knowledge and perspectives dominate?

Structures
Organizational hierarchy, rules and relationships; various forms of coordination communication and control

Processes and procedures
The way work gets done: operational and managerial processes and procedures, or flows of events

Culture and values
The way in which individuals and groups define their relationships with others and with the world; their values, norms, ideologies, thoughts and emotions

Figure 13.3 *Looking more closely at structural, cultural, procedural and power dimensions of organizations and groups or teams within organizations*

Typically, we avoid looking inwardly at ourselves for possible explanations as a defence mechanism against uncomfortable feelings of incompetence or personal incongruence. Argyris (1982) notes that people are highly resistant to recognizing and admitting any inconsistency between their goals and their actual behaviour, and that both individuals and organizations establish 'defensive routines' that make it hard for people to challenge the status quo and for the organization, as a whole, to recognize that it has a problem. These include incentive systems that do not reward personal reflection or encourage a critique of attitudes or behaviour:

> *You think how you act as a person. It's so easy to pick up a paper and write comments on it without thinking; but now I've got some tools to work with myself and to start to reflect in my office* (Scott-Villiers, 2002).

The DFID and Sida cases illustrate, to differing degrees, the importance of personal reflection and learning in order to achieve a better understanding of the gaps and our personal role in maintaining or closing them. Recognizing and exploring the personal influences on achieving participation has been a critical aspect of the learning process in Sida; people realized that it was not just 'the system' that makes it hard to allow participation, it is one's own behaviour.

In the DFID Uganda case, too, after initially perceiving the problems as external to their own behaviour, the donor professionals and contractors began to realize the significance of their own responses and attitudes in hindering relationships that would facilitate a smoother project and greater government ownership. When things became difficult, there was a tendency for DFID to adopt a 'hands-off' approach – thus avoiding conflict, but also failing to resolve particular challenges. The retrospective learning study helped some of the key players to realize the implications of their own behaviour, and they began to think about how to improve, thus illustrating a shift in the conventional understanding of the scope of learning and change.

Organizational systems

When analysing the challenge of achieving a particular policy goal, it is useful to expand one's 'mental map' of the relevant issues to encompass the following groups of organizational factors: structures (for example, hierarchy) and relationships; organizational culture[3] and values; and processes and procedures. These are all influenced and bounded by dynamics of power – who has ultimate control or dominance in relation to knowledge, goals, decisions and understandings of outcomes (see Figure 13.3). A consideration of all of these factors can lead to a more fruitful questioning of the compatibility between the policies and approaches professed by the organization, and the underlying values of an organization, as reflected in its patterns of control, its ways of allocating resources, and its ways of rewarding (or punishing) performance. It is not uncommon that the cultural norms of the organization reward and reinforce certain forms of expected behaviour that are not compatible with the new development agenda.

The learning process described in the Uganda example allowed the participants to take time to reflect and consider their perspectives on the project in some detail. It also introduced the perspectives of a wide range of stakeholders, and revealed the ways in which they viewed donor–contractor–government relationships, procedures, roles and power dynamics. Both of these factors led to a far more complex understanding of the reform and its challenges. Carrying out the retrospective learning has helped to build a more comprehensive multidimensional understanding of, and commitment to, the ownership issue, based on the views of a large number of stakeholders.

It highlighted that achieving the ideal of ownership requires more than a simple statement of policy. It also implies changes in procedures for the delivery of funds; greater equality in power relationships between donors and government; an adjustment in the location of control and flows of accountability; and a greater respect for the capacity of local staff to own and implement plans, trusting that they will be fulfilled (see also Chapter 8). Some of the issues emerging from the Uganda study are presented diagrammatically in Figure 13.4, illustrating the need to achieve congruence between structures, organizational culture and procedures in support of the policy goal.

The wider institutional context

Organizations exist within a wider institutional environment that influences their activities and ability to change. For example, Northern bilateral donor agencies are, ultimately, accountable to their taxpayers, and non-governmental organizations (NGOs) need to be accountable to their funders. This leads to a

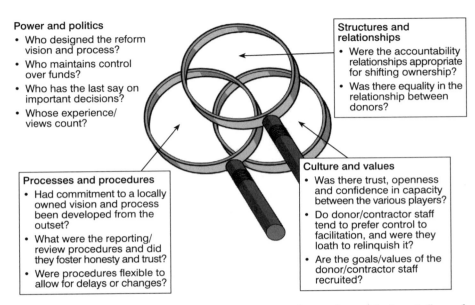

Power and politics
- Who designed the reform vision and process?
- Who maintains control over funds?
- Who has the last say on important decisions?
- Whose experience/ views count?

Structures and relationships
- Were the accountability relationships appropriate for shifting ownership?
- Was there equality in the relationship between donors?

Processes and procedures
- Had commitment to a locally owned vision and process been developed from the outset?
- What were the reporting/ review procedures and did they foster honesty and trust?
- Were procedures flexible to allow for delays or changes?

Culture and values
- Was there trust, openness and confidence in capacity between the various players?
- Do donor/contractor staff tend to prefer control to facilitation, and were they loath to relinquish it?
- Are the goals/values of the donor/contractor staff recruited?

Figure 13.4 *Questioning a wider range of systemic factors that might have influenced the transfer of ownership in the Uganda Forest Reform Programme*

dilemma between espoused drives towards greater ownership and downward accountability, and the political necessity of upward accountability.

There is also an inherent inequality in the nature of the relationship between donors and aid recipients (see also Chapter 9). Although aid policy is moving away from a 'top-down' transfer of information and technology, and the funding of particular projects or activities, towards more 'horizontal' provision of advice on policy and governance processes and basket-funding at the sectoral or even national budget level, donor agencies still maintain principle control over the use of resources. Furthermore, there is still an underlying cultural notion that developed nations 'know best'. The line between policy advice, policy influence and funding conditions can easily become blurred. This is rarely resisted effectively by aid recipients because they are acutely aware that you don't bite the hand that feeds you. This unavoidable power dynamic between donor and recipient makes many of even the best intentions hard to achieve. The complex alliances between one donor and another also influence the degree of real equality in the relationship with recipients. For example, a Sida manager describes how the involvement of the World Bank on a budget support programme has introduced levels of external conditionality that were not in accordance with Sida principles, but which, nonetheless, have been accepted by the recipients and Sida.

There are contradictions between what a development agency, as a value-driven organization, would like to achieve and what they, as a politically bounded government department, are expected to do. Trade, for example, is hugely important to development; but trade policy often works against the very objectives of aid (see also Chapter 5). Meeting disbursement targets is key to ensuring that government budget allocations are renewed, however much the 'push to spend' is an inappropriate indicator of achievement.

Pressures from the global, national and organizational arenas limit the capacity of individuals to close their own gap between ideals and action. But the influence of these large structures is no reason to abandon learning and change at an individual and organizational level. Individuals and organizations have agency and power, and this can be strengthened through networking and influence in order to build a momentum for change. The organizational and institutional variables that facilitate or constrain change towards the new development goals are many. Seeing more clearly the underlying and interconnected systemic factors that cause certain patterns of behaviour, or the formation of assumptions, helps to generate more appropriate responses and more realistic approaches to the new agenda.

Creating an environment and space to reflect

> *We are rewarded for innovation and proliferation* (DFID staff London, pers comm).

Interviews and exchanges with staff in DFID and Sida reveal frustrations and concerns regarding the achievement of the new goals and expectations, many of which relate directly or indirectly to the organizational and personal contexts within which people work. Many of these frustrations relate to particular barriers to better learning. Commitment, time and trust are three critical factors.

Development agencies have a tendency towards 'fads' – frequent changes in priorities and agendas – often with little lesson-learning. Many donor organizations strive to work at the 'cutting edge', developing new and better ways of working for poverty reduction (see also Chapter 5). They are also keen to spend budgets and produce results. Development professionals therefore tend to be rewarded for looking forward and coming up with new initiatives, and for ensuring that budgets are spent. Less value is given to the actual achievement of outcomes, or to reflecting upon and sharing experiences:

> *I have a sense of not taking time to reflect – why didn't it work. Instead, we just throw it out and do something new* (DFID staff London, pers comm).

The lack of time for reflection is a common complaint among development professionals. They find themselves so caught up in the practicalities of their daily work schedules (endlessly meeting, reporting and managing) that they simply cannot find the necessary hours or days to spend upon thinking and clarifying. Taking time for reflection without concrete output tends not to be encouraged.

Trust is critical to honest reflection of the type described in this chapter. Learning requires people to admit to themselves, as well as to others, that things are not necessarily going entirely according to plan. It implies honesty and

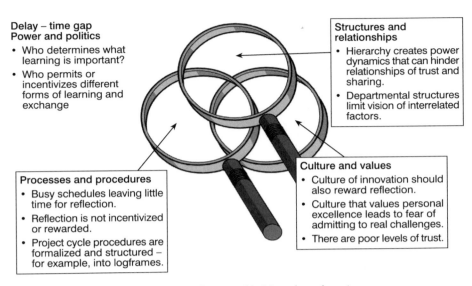

**Delay – time gap
Power and politics**

- Who determines what learning is important?
- Who permits or incentivizes different forms of learning and exchange

Structures and relationships

- Hierarchy creates power dynamics that can hinder relationships of trust and sharing.
- Departmental structures limit vision of interrelated factors.

Processes and procedures

- Busy schedules leaving little time for reflection.
- Reflection is not incentivized or rewarded.
- Project cycle procedures are formalized and structured – for example, into logframes.

Culture and values

- Culture of innovation should also reward reflection.
- Culture that values personal excellence leads to fear of admitting to real challenges.
- There are poor levels of trust.

Figure 13.5 *Systems thinking about learning*

freedom from fear of negative consequences. Power dynamics, accountability structures, organizational hierarchies, incentive and reward structures, and even personal behaviours all influence an environment that is conducive to trust. In the Uganda example, the accountability arrangements between DFID and the contractors created a power dynamic that inevitably made it difficult for them to establish an honest relationship. Even in the case of the participatory enquiry group in Sida, whose members were all from a similar level within the organizational hierarchy, open communication took time to build.

Using the systems approach, it is valuable to consider the structural, cultural, procedural and power factors that might facilitate or hinder the establishment of trust, time and commitment to learning within an organization. Some of the relevant issues are highlighted in Figure 13.5.

For the cycle of learning and action described in 'Mind the gap!' (see also Figure 13.1) to be effective, staff within development organizations need to have the time and a supportive environment for learning. Finger and Brand (1999) argue that unless the organization provides an environment and incentives that support learning, then the ultimate goal of becoming a learning organization is unlikely to be achieved. Thus, the process of learning and the environment in which it happens must be mutually supportive. As outlined in Table 13.1, integrated learning must occur at all levels, and the organizational structure, culture and procedures must facilitate these processes.

Table 13.1 *Support to learning at different levels*

Society	• Connect the organization to its environment
Organization	• Empower people in a collective vision • Establish systems to capture and share learning
Teams	• Encourage collaboration and team learning
Individuals	• Promote enquiry and dialogue • Create continuous learning opportunities

Source: Watkins and Marsick (1993)

Conclusions

Taking in information is only distantly related to real learning. It would be nonsensical to say, 'I just read a great book about bicycle riding – I've now learned that'... Through learning we re-perceive the world and our relationship to it (Senge, 1990, p13).

The implementation of value-based policy goals cannot be learned by simply reading books and guidelines. As the examples in this chapter have illustrated, learning requires ongoing, honest reflection on the kinds of personal, organizational and institutional assumptions that underlie programme goals. It involves a deep questioning of personal attitudes and behaviours and whether they are congruent with espoused objectives. It also requires a broader reflection on whether procedures, cultures and relationships are supportive of the expressed goals. Expressed goals also need to be realistic within the cultural context and organizational power dynamics. Development takes place within a wider global environment that must be understood in order to capitalize on its opportunities and evade its negative influences.

Few development agencies equip their staff with the necessary skills and capacities for organizational learning. The competencies are rarely analysed and assessed. The role that external facilitators play in helping staff to acquire new learning skills is significant. The case studies demonstrate that the most effective learning takes place when development staff work alongside the outside professionals to deepen their understanding of gap issues, and to build their capacity to think and learn in new ways as an integral part of their working life.

The type of learning we describe in this chapter is not an add-on of new tools, activities or information systems. It is a way of learning that will, ultimately, lighten the development professional's load by increasing efficiency and effectiveness. Through new forms of reflection at a personal level, people can shed light on the nature of their social, political and technical relationships. Through such enquiry, individuals and the organization can then respond more swiftly and appropriately to both subtle and dramatic developments – understanding better the underlying, as well as the superficial, elements of their working environment and achieving greater congruence between what is said and what is done.

Notes

1   The analysis of work underway in these agencies is described from the authors' perspective only and does not necessarily reflect the opinions of the agencies or individuals within them.
2   The IDS is a UK-based research institute. Within the institute, the participation group links research to learning and practice, aiming to strengthen the quality and critique of participatory processes in development.
3   Organizational culture is the personality of the organization. It is determined by historically transmitted beliefs, behaviours and values dominant within an organization, which are manifested as a collective mindset of 'the way we do things round here'. Many functions of human resource departments reflect and reinforce culture. The type of staff recruited is influential in maintaining the culture, reinforced through training and processes of socialization. Reward and appraisal are all key to revealing and shaping values.

References

Argyris, C (1982) *Reasoning, Learning, and Action: Individual and Organizational*, Jossey-Bass, San Francisco

Argyris, C and Schon, D (1978) *Organizational Learning: A Theory of Action Perspective*, Addison-Wesley, Reading, MA

Checkland, P and Scholes, J (1990) *Soft Systems Methodology in Action*, John Wiley and Sons, Chichester

Davies, R (1998) 'Order and Diversity: Representing and Assisting Organizational Learning in Non Government Aid Organizations', unpublished PhD thesis, Centre for Development Studies, University of Wales, Bangor

DFID (2002a) *Process Reflections on the Munyonyo Learning Event*, mimeo, DFID Forestry Group and DFID Sustainable livelihoods Support Office

DFID (2002b) *Egos, Heroes and Champions: Some Best Practice in Change Management. Learning from three institutional change programmes in the forest sector*, mimeo, DFID Forestry Group and DFID Sustainable Livelihoods Support Office

Easterby-Smith, M (1997) 'Disciplines of Organizational Learning, Contributions and Critiques', *Human Relations*, vol 50, no 9, pp1085–1114

Finger, M and Brand, S B (1999) 'The Concept of the "Learning Organization" Applied to the Transformation of the Public Sector', in Easterby-Smith, M, Araujo, L and Burgoyne, J (eds) *Organizational Learning and the Learning Organization*, Sage, London

Flood, R L (1999) *Rethinking the Fifth Discipline: Learning within the Unknowable*, Routledge, London

Kazoora, C, Sekabanja, F and Kabumba, I (2002) 'Organizational Learning from Forestry Policy and Institutional Reform in Uganda', mimeo, 20 May, Sustainable Development Centre, Kampala

Nonaka, I, Takeuchi, H and Umemoto, K (1996) 'A Theory of Organizational Knowledge Creation', *International Journal of Information Management*, vol 11, no 7–8, pp833–845

Scott-Villiers, P (2002) *Internal Review of the Sida-IDS learning project*, unpublished document, IDS

Senge, P (1990) *The Fifth Discipline: The Art and Practice of the Learning Organization*, Doubleday, New York

Sida (2002) 'The Lagom Group on Participation at Sida: A Report on our Progress', mimeo, Sida, Stockholm

Watkins, K and Marsick, V (eds) (1993) *Sculpting the Learning Organization: Lessons in the Art and Science of Systematic Change*, Jossey-Bass, San Fransisco

14

Personal Change and Responsible Well-Being

Patta Scott-Villiers

Introduction

Uprooting a prejudice is as painful as extracting a nerve (Primo Levi, 1987, p103).

When it comes to improving development policy and practice, individual learning and change is as important as organizational learning and change, and the organization depends upon the individual. At both of these levels, an understanding of internal perspectives is required in order to explain external perspectives and vice versa. Using the concept of responsible well-being is one way of achieving this balance of internal and external awareness and of individual and organizational levels of learning and change. This chapter introduces this concept and then uses an individual story to describe how a failure of self-awareness and self-responsibility led to contradictory relationships and less than perfect progress in combating poverty. It goes on to argue that understanding one's own worldview, and that of development organizations, is a crucial step towards improving relationships and effectiveness in development. Action research is one way of approaching this understanding; but there are many more.

Individuals, organizations and relationships

Traditionally, development policy has focused on the organization as the primary entity for delivering solutions to poverty and has viewed the individual staff member as a component of the organization. As a result, the focus of attention on change has been at an organizational level, and personal or individual change has been subservient and largely ignored. Individual learning and change, beyond the kind of moulding that training can provide, has been considered an unnecessary diversion from real business. An alternative view of the system, however, as a dynamic flux in which boundaries between one organization and another are not as clear and constant as we have previously supposed, results in a different view of change. If we were to accept that the important element in the aid system is not so much its entities, but its relationships, our approach would be different. Margaret Wheatley (1992) outlines how the disciplines of physics, biology and chemistry and theories of evolution and chaos all moved during the 20th century from materialism and reductionism to relativity and holism. She asks, 'If the physics of our universe is revealing the primacy of relationships, is it any wonder that we are beginning to reconfigure our ideas about management in relational terms' (Wheatley, 1992, p13)? Since individuals are the ones who mediate relationships, with support from their organizations, then personal development becomes a central focus of good development.

Responsible well-being

Each of us is different; we have different purposes, talents, cultures and approaches. We share an ability to act, as well as a collective responsibility for our own, our planet's and one another's well-being. We all, rich or poor, have agency and power, and small actions can lead to significant results (see Chapter 11). So, how is it that these actions can be made significant? What advice can we give ourselves to optimize our contribution?

It is worth considering the concept of responsible well-being, an idea proposed by Robert Chambers. Amartya Sen (1993) describes well-being as 'the wellness of a person's state of being', and he argues that it is arrived at from a person's capability or 'actual ability to achieve various valuable functionings as a part of living'. This is influenced, he says, by his or her choice, as well as his or her freedom to be and to act (Sen, 1993, p30). Responsible well-being builds on this idea, agreeing that each individual, rich or poor, should have such capabilities, and emphasizing that one cannot be responsible for others' well-being without being responsible for one's own; but neither can one be well on one's own, without taking some responsibility for the well-being of others. In this chapter I argue that in order to deliver this responsibility for oneself and others, one has to understand oneself. Though a simple concept, responsible well-being could be powerful for development policy and decision-makers because it advises people to look not just outwards, towards solutions for 'the poor', but also inwards towards personal development.

A short story

When I was growing up, my favourite books were adventure stories. Tintin was the best of all: small intelligent person travels the world sorting things out through a mix of intelligence, luck and being polite. Later at school I did science and history, all in a vein of sorting things out through the technology and intelligence of man.

I set off for Africa in 1983 and arrived in Darfur in western Sudan for my first job in the aid business. My task was to help establish whether or not local farming practices were causing desertification. It was a big World Bank project involving agronomic trials for higher-yielding crops, supplies of fertilizer and deep wells. I spent a happy time roving about the woods, fields and villages of that beautiful and far-off place, learning from farmers how they made decisions about crop rotation and how they knew about soil fertility. I took samples of the different soils they pointed out – sands and clays and sandy clays, cropped and fallow. I spread out my satellite photos of the region and matched what they said to what I saw. I concluded that the farmers knew their ecology. Around each deep well there was a village and around that, an area of near desert about 6.5 kilometres across. They could crop that land one year in ten. There was a sinister plant called *usher* with white irritant sap that showed the state of that soil. Beyond that zone were the real fields, which the farmers cropped for 5 years and fallowed for 15 or 20 years in a prettier equilibrium. A fallow had done its work when a certain hardwood, *babanus*, re-established. It was a useful wood. Beyond that zone was savannah forest, through which nomadic pastoralists moved. While the farmers and pastoralists and their various communities were each managing elegantly, there was, indeed, a problem. The more frequently that deep wells were drilled, the more frequently villages appeared and the more their spheres began to overlap. And who was putting in the wells? We were.

The seduction of our gifts (or loans, in this case) was palpable. Local politicians gained power, as we did, from the sinking of those wells. And the water was good, cool, clear and clean. But there is a slow acting poison in that water, in environmental and social terms. (I heard that in 2000 during a drought, local people in northern Kenya stopped international agencies and government drilling new wells. I imagine them lining up in front of the rigs refusing to move. The people now know the rough science and politics of deep wells and they want water on their own terms.)

When I left Darfur nine months later I was convinced that the farmers knew what was what. It wasn't an idea that I had arrived with, but I left with it. I moved east to Kordofan, starting work on mapping nomad routes across the rapidly enclosing cotton lands of that region. And then, quite suddenly it seemed to me, the whole of northern Sudan fell into famine. Harsh, harsh famine. The sky turned brown, the grass brown, everything was brown. Children turned to sticks, old eyes in tiny bodies, and died everywhere. Grandparents stopped eating and faded away. Men disappeared to Khartoum or the cotton fields in the east, promising to find work and send money, food or whatever they could. I was shocked. I joined an international non-governmental organization (INGO) to help with food distribution. I ran around in small circles trying to be useful, working long hours organizing trucks, warehouses, waybills, loaders and unloaders. We foreigners took charge of thousands of tonnes of sorghum shipped in from the US and delivered it to stores in hundreds of towns and villages up the endless desert tracks and muddy black cotton roads. We handed it over to government and monitored it. We were exhausted.

One of the things that we did was look for nomads to see if they needed and had received a share of the relief food. One late afternoon our team reached a small camp 48 kilometres south of El Obeid. There were some sticks and bits of old plastic sorghum sack that made up the house. A woman came and greeted us with a few children behind her. Her husband and older sons then arrived. We explained our intent, asked questions and measured the children's arms for our nutrition survey (so thin, so sweet). We talked about what they'd do now and after the drought. They showed us their supplies, two or three kid goats and a pan of *mukhet*, a wild berry that tastes foul, soaking in water. Whenever I see that plant now I think of those days. The savannah sun was going down. No more animals arrived, as they do with pastoralists at dusk. So there were only three kid goats.

We asked if we could camp with them that night. They were very welcoming. We said, 'You mustn't give us food, we have some rice and beans in the car.' They said, of course, they would give us food, we were their guests. We squirmed. Oh, we should have gone; we shouldn't have imposed our fat selves on their thin place. I cry whenever I think of this, even now. They killed one of their goats for us that night.

We brought our rice and beans and together we had a feast. The food was good, the company so merry. They said we shouldn't worry about the goat: 'We had to eat it some time; you were a good reason.' It was a fine party. We left in the morning and they waved us away in the bleak harsh light of the famine sun. Who died; who survived? I don't know. But what I do know is that those people knew how to live with their humanity and we, with our clipboards and arm measurements, had to have it dragged out of us. Our way of organizing everything, directing and controlling, distributing and monitoring was nowhere near as powerful in the story of people's survival during that famine as was their own way of managing it. We contributed, no doubt, to saving lives; but we also contributed to a subtle loss of humanity in that place because our system didn't have a box marked humanity. It only had food, medicine and money.

A few months later, standing in a dusty displaced person's camp on the edge of town, watching George Bush, senior, dispensing platitudes to bereft women and a pack of journalists, I resolved that I would never treat people as less then me, as victims or numbers of annoying aberrations to my perfect plans. They and I were in this together: I, from my worldview, my history and my power and they from theirs. My belief in participation starts there.

Domineering or participatory?

In the development system of which I am a part, a rationalist view predominates over a participatory view. We have, for example, the logical framework (logframe), in which we lay out our goals, purpose, activities and indicators of success. We imply that by drilling a well we will create health and wealth, which is our goal. But if you look at the history of the development project over the last 40 years, you will see that no project ever turned out as expected. Where wells were drilled, some people got healthy, others dispossessed; while the immediate environment degraded, the vegetable garden flourished. The dynamic complexity of the result of any action is huge. It seems to me that this complexity is an argument for a participatory view – not only that people have a right to participate, or that it may be more effective if they do, but that *people and the environment already do participate and control is not possible – only engagement.*

If people are already participating (rather than the quaint idea that they participate when we give them a chance to do so), then it makes sense to participate with them, not treat them as controllable units in our calculations. From my perspective, in that nomad place in Sudan, they were running the relief programme, not us. The farmers of southern Darfur were managing the land. It worked best when we took our part. It didn't work at all well when we tried to push people around. In my view, it is not enough just to listen to others, 'understand' them and then invite them to participate in our decision-making. I would like to participate in theirs. I would like to do things differently.

Looking at what I actually did in Sudan, and later in my continued attempts to 'do' development, I can see approaches that are opaque, distrustful, arrogant and a bit selfish. To borrow from E Ike Udogu's fine phrase about bureaucracy in Africa, we are 'capricious and parasitic' (Udogu, 2001, p5). These approaches demonstrate a lack of respect for the poor as a whole sector of society, a disrespect that only serves to further undermine the position of the poor and deepen their anger towards us. Our approaches, therefore, do little to eradicate the elements of poverty that are about position and voice. Neither do they build on the innate strengths of humanity and love. Would it be possible to be different? Powerful people are the most disabled in this regard because dominance is difficult to change. Our culture applauds it and, in a rational world, we crave control and fear uncertainty.

The dominant culture of aid is materialist and rooted in an ideology of charity and disrespect. As Nancy Fraser (1989) has pointed out, in the welfare state societies (particularly in the US and western Europe):

> *'needs' approach has become the only way to think about development and 'needs talk' has been institutionalized as a major vocabulary of political discourse. It co-exists, albeit often uneasily, with talk about rights and interests at the very centre of political life* (Fraser, 1989, p162).

Much of what we do in development is based on our apparent expert ability to define, interpret and deliver to the 'needs' of the poor. Robert Chambers calls this expertise culture 'uppers and lowers', where people dominate one another, and professional knowledge, though often erroneous or inadequate, is considered superior to poor people's knowledge (Chambers, 1996).

In my own view, no amount of changing our approaches and procedures will make any real difference to poverty if we believe that poor people are 'below' us, that they are lesser beings. Thinking this way means, essentially, that we agree we *should* be more powerful than them and that relationships between us should be more uncomfortable for them than for us. If we help to meet needs, while undermining people, material improvements are hard to sustain. At its more extreme, this can be seen in the famine camp, where a hungry family is given a sack of grain, but submits to degrading treatment by workers trying to organize the distribution. The same happens in the welfare lines of Europe and the states where welfare workers, disrespected and underpaid, treat their clients with rudeness and exasperation. But even in the more 'participatory' development approaches there is still an element of removing from people their right to debate, negotiation and accountability. Participation is usually a superficial gloss over the same old story. Like receiving a false smile, you are left disconcerted.

Development is not only about interpreting and delivering the things that people need; it is about the people themselves. David Crocker (1995), drawing on Sen, argues that development is about realizing our capabilities to function as full human beings:

> *A focus on functioning enables us to keep very clear about the constant ends and the variable means of development. The welfarist perspective, concerned only with the goal of utilities, neglects or 'muffles' all other sorts of human functioning. Happiness may be coupled with malfunctioning and discontent may accompany or spurt the most important of activities. Even the discipline of development economics has been one sided, for it has emphasized quantity of life (longevity) and neglected the quality of the lives that are led, for example being healthy and being educated* (Crocker, 1995, p156).

In the barrios, slums, desert villages and urban housing projects are poor people who have not just needs, but also unique existences, expertise and cultures as powerful – in many ways, more powerful – than those of richer peoples. If development cared to recognize this, then it would be run differently. We would not only seek to interpret the needs of poor people, but to compare worldviews and co-develop our *mutual well-being and responsibility*. We would not allow ourselves to dominate and control the anti-poverty process, but would want to share that responsibility with the poor.

Learning worldviews

That is my view. I may wish to explain my version of the participatory worldview; but I would also like to persuade you to be clear about what your own view is. Our worldview moulds the actions we take, the rules that we follow and the goals that we set. In his book *Cosmopolis*, Stephen Toulmin (1990) describes how, during the 17th century, Europeans adopted a rationalist worldview as described by Descartes, a mode of thinking that is still dominant today. He argues that this worldview was cemented in a state of crisis during the 30 years' war in Europe. Two theologies, the Protestant and Catholic, were fighting for supremacy and devastating Europe in the process. People wanted a new certainty, not plurality. So when Descartes put forward a worldview that 'promoted theory, devalued practice and insisted equally on the need to find foundations for knowledge that were clear, distinct and certain' (Toulmin, 1990, p72), Europe took up the idea with enthusiasm. Many Europeans and North

Americans today operate on the basis that once we *understand* the world, we can manipulate it to our will.

Each particular worldview, which is rooted in history and culture, has a radical effect on what each person sees, interprets and decides. As development decision-makers, examining our basic beliefs about development is, therefore, important. I suspect that a lot of attempts to create change have foundered on the lack of ability to truly understand ourselves and what we want. Sadly, I can't say that my great resolution in that Sudanese displaced camp made a huge amount of difference to my work in the years that followed. Although I tried repeatedly to create participatory projects of one sort or another, I made a mistake. I looked outwards without looking inwards. The old sages, manipulative warlords and admirable women of Africa entranced me. The landscape captured me under its huge skies. I thought that if I listened, looked and learned more and more about them, I would eventually be able to come up with a way of doing development that actually worked. I just forgot one thing – to look at myself and what it was about my worldview, my culture and my organizations that made things happen as they did. I had been watching Africa through my particular pair of glasses without really realizing that I was wearing them.[1] By looking only outwards, I was hoping for participation without taking responsibility for my own participation, so I was not being participatory. Naturally, my efforts failed. As Primo Levi has pointed out, uprooting prejudice is no easy thing.

Enacting responsible well-being

So it is that the idea of responsible well-being comes back into the picture. If one cannot be responsible for others' well-being without being responsible for one's own, then each of us has to make as much effort to understand what is inside ourselves (our beliefs about what is right and wrong) as to be aware of, and consonant with, the quite extraordinary diversity that is outside (cultures, politics, environments and people). To achieve this I argue that we must start with investigating our own philosophies. This is both a lifetime's effort and an instantaneous transformation of attitude. Enquiry into oneself as a thinker and actor may follow numerous paths, involving thinking, acting, observing, experiencing, conversing, reading and feeling in infinite varieties and combinations. Rather than supply a list of approaches, I will describe a route that I have taken. Although it is not necessarily relevant to others, it is just one example of a way of developing clarity.

Action research

Until recently, I had only managed an incremental and partial realization of my philosophy. It has been through a study of action research that my perspectives have crystallized enough for me to be able to say that I understand a little about how I construct the world, how I know it and how I interact. Action research has proved useful at this juncture because of its insistence on looking, first, at one's own worldview before proceeding to those of others. It is a way of engaging in reflection and action that has multiple origins, including Paulo Freire's conscientization; Kurt Lewin's organizational experiments; thoughts of philosophers such as Michel Foucault on power and knowledge; and Jurgen Habermas on communicative action; and the work and experience of many others in numerous cultures, traditions and centuries. Action research requires active recognition of relationships. Individuals and groups cannot just affect others; they are affected by them at the same time, so process cannot be linear, only circular or cyclical. It is a form of participatory enquiry in which people examine their own issues, rather than examine those of others. The ideas and knowledge developed are directly relevant to the lives of the people who researched them. Thus, 'action research is conducted by, *with* and *for* people, rather than [being] research *on* people' (Reason and McArdle, 2003). It is described as:

> ...*a participatory, democratic process concerned with developing practical knowing in the pursuit of worthwhile human purposes, grounded in a participatory worldview... It seeks to bring together action and reflection, theory and practice, in participation with others, in the pursuit of practical solutions to issues of pressing concern to people, and more generally the flourishing of individual persons and their communities* (Reason and Bradbury, 2001, p1).

I enrolled in a part-time course in action research in early 2002. We started with first-person enquiry, which involved looking at ourselves, a seemingly self-indulgent process. The idea is to 'foster an enquiring approach to their own lives, to act awarely and choicefully, and to assess effects in the outside world while acting. First person enquiry skills are essential for those who would provide leadership in any social enterprise' (Reason and McArdle, 2003, p1). In writing down stories about my own life, I began to clarify my worldview. The way in which I told a story on paper turned out to be different than the way in which I might have told it to friends, as it had a different purpose. It was longer and more questioning. Then, in reading and hearing the astonishingly honest stories of my co-researchers, I learned more, because their perspectives and insights were so startlingly different from my own. This is second-person enquiry, a practice that increases understanding of the self *and* others through conversation.

As well as doing this with my fellow students, I was facilitating a learning group in the Swedish International Development Agency (Sida). It was a form of co-operative enquiry in which a group of peers come together in cycles of action and reflection to develop understanding of a chosen subject for themselves and to deliver some learning externally (Heron, 1996). Our subject was participation – why is it so difficult to achieve in practice? We met several times over a period of a year and followed an iterative course of investigation, looking at individual projects and collective efforts. It helped us substantially to deepen our understandings of participation and to communicate these ideas more cogently. This was the beginning of third-person enquiry, where not only do you learn about yourself and your peers, but you interact with a wider community.

By starting the learning process I describe above, I started to work differently: making changes that were qualitatively different from changes I had made before. This time, I was not only thinking about changes I could make to things external; I was beginning to develop myself in order to make things work better. Perhaps I am finally getting around to becoming a more fully human person, one who is fulfilling her capabilities. As a result, I noticed that I had found a new way of interacting in which responsible well-being emerged as an important idea. I now argue that learning about oneself, while holding the idea of responsible well-being, creates learning about and better interaction with others.

From personal to organizational change

Many development organizations have the same problem as I did: looking out a long way and not very far in – seldom linking the two together. As I began to develop the idea of looking first at your own agency so that you can be a better participant with others, I began to shift my own working approach. After many years in Africa, I came back to the UK during the late 1990s and started to work with managers and policy-makers of Northern development organizations. Many donors, NGOs and government departments profess, with seriousness, a belief in participation; but they seldom take the time to truly examine their own cultures and underlying worldviews. Many of the people working in these institutions are educated in a rationalist worldview and their politics, procedures and cultures reflect that. They generally care very much for the success of what they do; yet, many are frustrated by lack of progress. They live in a kind of contradictory tension, not sure of where the problem is coming from. Having watched a number of good organizational change ideas lose momentum, I wonder if one reason is that the organizational worldview doesn't let it happen. The work that ActionAid is doing with the idea of downward accountability (see Chapter 8) is of interest here, as it offers an opportunity for ActionAid's staff and their interlocutors to understand themselves and one another and, therefore, to cooperate better. But I can also see ActionAid's Accountability, Learning and Planning System (ALPS) failing if it adopts the prevailing worldview that the organization or its sponsors have the last word. Are the people taking part in ALPS being consulted for ActionAid's upward accountability or for learning and participation? Just as I decided to be participatory, and then consistently failed to achieve it for 15 years, people in an organization might find themselves trying to do one thing but, essentially, believing another.

How does an organization find out and work on its worldview in order to improve its relationships and effectiveness? Since this view is held within its people, an organization has a critical role in supporting and encouraging individuals to clarify it. Ways of making this happen will vary, but will be bound by the principle that individuals should have the freedom and responsibility to discover. They need opportunities (in the broadest sense of time, space, security and validation) to enquire, reflect and take action on worldviews and relationships, as well as on programmes, policies and procedures.

This sort of learning is not comfortable, as it highlights the inconsistencies in relationships between the individual, the organization and the world. It demands a new clarity on beliefs that we gloss over and fundamental changes in attitudes and action. It may seem unrealistic to expect people in the aid industry to adopt concepts of self-awareness and responsible well-being. But it is a matter of some urgency that we do, as things cannot stay as they are. The wastage and ill-being over which the aid industry presides, both internally and externally, calls for radical change.

Conclusions

Responsible well-being based on self-awareness is a desirable end for development as it implies material and mental wellness, nursed by taking a responsible part in the development process. It applies to all of us, rich and poor, the providers and recipients of development, and it turns the idea of giver and taker into a spiral of reciprocity. It is achieved through individual learning. This is not a call for an idealized approach to development only applicable to residents of ivory towers. This is about each individual within their sphere using the space around them to consider both the 'without' and the 'within', and in so doing making their work and its relationships a little more enjoyable and congruent, a touch more energized and spiced with an edge of questioning and creativity.

Note

1   Thanks to Steve Taylor and Peter Reason, at the Bath University Centre for Action Research in Professional Practice, for pointing this simple thing out to me.

References

Chambers, R (1996) *Whose Reality Counts?* Intermediate Technology Publications, London

Crocker, D A (1995) 'Foundations of Development Ethics', in Nussbaum, M and Glover, J (eds) *Women, Culture and Development: A Study of Human Capabilities*, Clarendon Press, Oxford

Fraser, N (1989) *Unruly Practices: Power Discourse and Gender in Contemporary Social Theory*, Polity Press, Cambridge

Heron, J (1996) *Cooperative Inquiry: Research into the Human Condition*, Sage, London

Levi, P (1987) *If Not Now, When?* translated from the Italian by William Weaver, Sphere, London

Reason, P and Bradbury, H (2001) 'Introduction: Inquiry and Participation in Search of a World Worthy of Human Aspiration', in Reason, P and Bradbury, H (eds), *Handbook of Action Research: Participative Inquiry and Practice*, Sage, London

Reason, P and McArdle, K (2003) 'Brief Notes on the Theory and Practice of Action Research', in Becker, S and Bryman, A (eds) *Understanding Research Methods for Social Policy and Practice*, Polity Press, Bristol

Sen, A (1993) 'Capability and Well-being', in Nussbaum, M C and Sen, A (eds) *The Quality of Life*, Oxford University Press, Oxford

Toulmin, S (1990) *Cosmopolis: The Hidden Agenda of Modernity*, Chicago University Press, Chicago

Udogu, E Ike (ed) (2001) *The Issue of Political Ethnicity in Africa*, Ashgate, Aldershot

Wheatley, M J (1992) *Leadership and the New Science: Learning about Organization from an Orderly Universe*, Berret Koehler, San Francisco

15

Enabling Inclusive Aid: Changing Power and Relationships in International Development[1]

Rachel Hinton

Development is essentially a local affair; a marathon dogged by unexpected twists and turns rather than a rush to a nearby summit (Rihani, 2002, pxvi).

The development community has set an ambitious agenda with the Millennium Development Goals (MDGs). The commitments are long term. There are multiple frameworks for action that demand more strategic and reflective interventions than before. Many of them highlight the complexity of the new aid environment (Brock and McGee, 2002). Yet procedures and models for change continue to be based on reductionist paradigms that fail to embrace international development as a complex system. Planning continues as though it were a predictable process free of internal unpredictable interactions between stakeholders, where certain inputs produce set results to specified time frames. In contrast, the authors in this book suggest that there is a need to recognize the complex, nonlinear nature of the aid system and in doing so make aid more inclusive.

By inclusive aid we mean both an increase in the diversity of relationships, and an increased understanding of the power dynamics between key stakeholders. In the past, partnerships have often focused on the most visible players. When addressing issues of girls' education, for example, key donor interactions might primarily be between the World Bank and the Ministry of Education. Inclusive aid seeks to engage a wider range of stakeholders, primarily poor people, but also elites within society who, among others, have considerable power to make a difference. This volume reveals how awareness of the dynamics of power and relationships among actors is too often lacking, and that shifts in attention to personal attitudes and behaviour are a missing link in enabling institutional and professional commitment to making development more inclusive. Accounts from authors in this book highlight new initiatives and approaches that signal promising ways forward.

The rise of participatory rhetoric

Language can contribute to, or undermine, efforts to achieve inclusive aid. The past two decades have seen growing support for concepts of *participation and partnership*[2], yet key decisions that affect people's lives continue to be made without sufficient attention to local, national and global socio-political realities. So, has the rise in participatory rhetoric increased the degree to which poor people's voices are actually heard? The rise of participatory terminology *has* coincided with some significant advances in methods and approaches designed for listening to poor people, such as participatory poverty assessments (PPAs), citizens' juries and the World Bank Voices of the Poor initiative. These organizational initiatives have reinforced understanding of poor people's realities as multidimensional and dynamic. There is, however, great variability in the extent to which the conclusions of participatory assessments have been internalized and acted upon, for example, the degree to which the results have influenced policy and budget allocations.

New language can be used to disempower as often as it is used to empower. It can sometimes widen the gap between 'insiders' and 'outsiders'. The new rhetoric used by the international development community can be intimidating and may prevent the broad and meaningful involvement of citizens that is so genuinely sought.[3] In Chapter 6, Kakande highlights the problem of new vocabulary reinforcing status and emphasizing the difference between the expert and novice, creating an 'inner circle' of people who share a common language. Beneath the new rhetoric are embedded structures of power, specific to each context and highly resistant to change. Many poor people are reluctant to share their insights in contexts where they lack confidence or fear the consequences of greater transparency – for example, a reduction in financial support if weaknesses are revealed. The existing dynamics are reinforced by both institutional and personal norms and by fear of challenging the status quo. These, combined with established personal behaviour and attitudes, mean that technical and procedural solutions alone will have limited impact.

However, new language can also have positive outcomes. At an individual and institutional level language can act as a catalyst for gradual change in behaviour. The focus on mission statements is recognition of the importance of using language to create a common organizational identity. At an individual level, people are uncomfortable saying one thing and doing another – for example, arguing for 'partnership' and yet acting independently. This is a recognized phenomenon, described as cognitive dissonance, where people experience a disjunction between their stated attitudes or beliefs and actual behaviour (Festinger, 1957). When such dissonance arises, either the individual's stated attitude or their behaviour shifts. In Chapter 7, Marsden documents such a transition where an aid worker's adoption of the participatory terminology required a greater commitment to learning the local language and embracing appropriate behaviour when visiting communities. Language that signals a united goal, such as the terms 'partnership' and 'transparency', requires discussion to establish joint agreement of meanings and implications. Use of these terms can encourage trust if citizens see that there is a genuine desire to listen to their views as a key part of the development process. Such language implies profound shifts in aid relationships and in the distribution of power and control among actors.[4] If the new language of partnership continues not only to be used, but reflected upon, negotiated and redefined by key actors it is possible that over time people will alter their ways of behaving to make the current rhetoric real.

The impact of procedures and new aid modalities

In Chapter 8, Owusu shows that it is not only language but procedures that can exclude. He provides an example from Kenya where the community's experience was not one of 'ownership' and 'empowerment' but a 'conceptual maze' created by complex donor procedures that constrained decision-making at the local level and excluded those who were unfamiliar with the specific donor tools. Limited stakeholder participation may have exacerbated the absence of potentially significant political and cultural analysis. New procedures could help to balance relationships of power and open up space for risk-taking and the involvement of key stakeholders. The creation of clear principles for action, such as Mahila Samatha's 'non-negotiable' principles provides one example. They can serve to guide behaviour and attitudes without being dogmatic about specific practice, such as their principle that 'the initial phase where women are consolidating their independent time and space is not be to hurried or short-circuited.' (see Chambers and Pettit, Chapter 11). Such principles may reinforce organizational commitment to shared goals. When implemented effectively, such principles can level and reverse relationships of power and provide the foundations for democratic decision-making and more inclusive partnerships.

Many procedures exclude individuals and organizations who have the potential to promote change. Traditionally, the onus has been on the recipients of aid to 'take' the power, rather than understand the barriers that preclude their participation. Many individuals and organizations with the potential to promote change are isolated and lack the influence to bring it about. There are many barriers that prevent their active participation in decision-making. It is not always those with the interests of the community at heart who act as spokespeople. In donor forums, it is regularly the individuals with Western language skills or familiarity with accepted procedures who are selected as beneficiary representatives. The dilemma is that those in control may have limited knowledge of local power dynamics, even when they recognize that these spokespeople do not represent the 'voices of the poor'.[5] Current tools fail to include a reflexive and historical perspective that is required to enable an understanding of current power and relationships.

Another factor that can undermine inclusive aid is the increasing need for donors to show immediate results. There is a mounting tension between the pressure to show results of poverty reduction interventions and the need to allow time for inclusive processes of reflection, analysis and policy formulation. The consequence of imposed time frames is often a loss of local ownership. A dramatic illustration is the well-intentioned commitment from Northern governments to ensure that 'no countries seriously committed to education for all will be thwarted in their achievement of this goal by a lack of resources'.[6] Yet, the recent push for the World Bank-led Fast Track initiative on education has had the unintended consequence of several governments submitting national education plans for funding according to an external timetable, bypassing ongoing in-country consultative processes. There is a real danger that this type of high-profile initiative can create parallel processes that undermine the efforts of multiple stakeholders who are working to ensure national ownership of plans and budgets.

New aid modalities are having a variety of impacts, yet there is insufficient evidence at present to assess the long-term implications. For example, direct budget support can help move development assistance away from isolated, donor-led projects to helping governments implement long-term programmes for poverty reduction and strengthen country planning, financial and procurement systems. However, there is some preliminary evidence that direct budget support may have shifted the balance of resources away from work with civil-society organizations, work that was providing an essential element in the foundations for democracy. This is an important factor that will need to be tracked, since many civil society initiatives are helping to build citizens' confidence and raise their expectations in terms of the potential for influencing pro-poor reform. Learning lessons from these experiences is critical as there is limited understanding of how these initiatives can be scaled up to establish increased community confidence and voice. It is hoped that such programmes are not being cut since citizens are being urged to play an increasing role in ensuring good governance and improving government accountability.[7] In Chapter 5, Groves provides two examples from Tanzania in which the community has neither the capacity nor the mechanisms to achieve this effectively. The lack of demand for change from poor people, in the appropriate forum or form, emerges time and again as a central obstacle to pro-poor reform (Duncan et al, 2002). Poor people's low status and lack of political patronage may also mean that their voices remain unheard. Governments in turn may not prioritize the resources needed to redress these issues. As a result, most countries lack the means to facilitate upward accountability through the dissemination of detailed information to the grassroots. Focusing on strengthening demand through work to support champions for change is an important way forward.[8]

Rights, accountability and the stakeholder web

The move away from funding discrete country projects in favour of support for broad-sector programmes and addressing global policy concerns demands a greater understanding of the overall development system. As such, policy-makers and development practitioners need to be more aware of the bigger stakeholder web and recognise the power relations within it. Too often, aid is regarded as though it were apolitical, without winners and losers (hence the term 'beneficiary') yet it is often a zero-sum game. Contributors argue that the power differentials need to be exposed, understood and addressed. In Chapter 2, Robb provides a comprehensive account of the changing power relations in the history of aid. Her account reveals that the web of development is complex: in order to influence the system, attention must be paid to the multifaceted power dynamics that govern the relationships between actors. There are many types of power at work and an equally diverse range of modes of resistance. She argues that people need to be aware of how global, national and sub-national policies and interventions can affect their work at all levels, including the community level. For example, Bush's withdrawal of money for family planning can have devastating effects on certain communities. Further, an International Monetary Fund (IMF)-supported programme that devalues a currency, increases VAT or a fuel tax, or deregulates a market can affect farmers. But do we know or understand these links? The powerful institutions (such as the World Bank, IMF, European Union) must make more transparent the positive and negative impacts of their policy advice for a more informed government-led public debate (see Robb, this volume).

In understanding the big picture we also need to understand its component parts. The case studies in Part Two provide the points of illustration from a range of players belonging to institutions that make up the aid system: the international financial institutions; bilateral donors; international non-government organizations and local civil-society organizations. Written from such varied vantage points, the accounts highlight similarities and differences and show how different actors may attribute the same problem to distinct causes and consequently propose divergent solutions (as seen in the case studies in Part Two). The interpretation of motivations and incentives also differs greatly, depending upon the actor's own perspective (compare, for example, Chapters 9 and 10 by Win and Jassey respectively). It becomes clear that each organization operates according to its organizational culture and particular behavioural features (see Figure 1.1). Thus each has specific organizational challenges for reform.

Taking a global view of development has focused attention on issues of accountability. Donors have recognized their responsibility, as they adopt rights-based approaches, to become more accountable to the citizens in poor countries (not just their own citizens) as well as to the international human rights framework (see Chapter 12). Examples from India and Bolivia in Chapter 12 show that a great deal can be achieved within a supportive environment. However, one of the barriers to improved accountability is that the relationships, and most notably those with poor people, are not in place. Evidence from the authors' accounts indicates that people are generally better at forming relationships with those with whom they share common behavioural traits. Where there are significant differences it appears to be more difficult to develop relationships grounded in trust and transparency. This seems to be the case even when the same overall 'mission' is shared. This could go some way to explain why the rights agenda has not been more actively implemented. Staff in donor agencies could welcome and facilitate alliances within and across the sets of institutions to whom they are accountable – for example, encouraging links between citizens in donor countries with citizens in recipient countries, or supporting joined-up efforts by recipient governments when negotiating fairer international trade agreements. Global forms of citizen action can also contribute to greater awareness of rights, which can in turn lead to new international agreements or conventions (Gaventa, 2001). Transparency acts as a critical catalyst for new forms of accountability. The media and policy research centres have a crucial role to play in disseminating public information, a role that has yet to be fully exploited. Increased global communications and new forms of technology provide new opportunities for the poor to access information and engage in international debate.[9] Yet, the challenge remains how to harness this opportunity and link it to donors' articulated desire for change.

Inter-organizational dynamics and partnerships

Recent years have witnessed an increase in organizational assessments and the restructuring of aid agencies. Consultancy firms have been employed by aid agencies at great expense. Most of the attention has been devoted to intra-organizational issues with attempts to improve internal efficiency. Inter-organizational issues and partnerships have not been prioritized. What is required now is to address the critical gaps that prevent effective development of the relationships among actors that can ensure inclusive aid. We argue that past analysis of donor effectiveness has failed to recognize sufficiently the importance of the personal skills and competencies required to achieve a change in the dynamics among key actors. Policy-makers require time and opportunities to negotiate their own solutions. We need to recognize the powerful ways in which individual attitudes, behaviours and beliefs can either hinder or encourage wider systemic change. In Chapter 11, Chambers and Pettit argue that all actors 'can make the aid system more inclusive by becoming more honest in acknowledging and naming differences in power'.

All actors require a heightened awareness of the implications of power, both within organizations and in external relations. For example, most civil-society organizations are under pressure to accept funds regardless of the conditions. The existence of multiple donors and the lack of coordination between them places pressure on civil-society partners in terms of extra travel, arrangements for visitors, report writing and accounting. This burden has been widely acknowledged at a national level and a commitment made to reduce pressures on government through the introduction of aid modalities such as sector-wide approaches (SWAPs). The Development Assistance Committee (DAC) has also established a special task force on harmonizing donor procedures.[10] However, equivalent energy has not been given to applying the international agreements to civil society. Where a non-governmental organization (NGO) has the capacity and strength to negotiate and mediate donor power, coordination can occur, as with the Forum for African Women Educationionalists Zambia (FAWEZA). FAWEZA has developed transparent relationships and built trust with key donors who have agreed to a process of reporting and accounting that maintains essential minimum controls. FAWEZA personnel can thus devote their time and energy to the substance of their work. This is an exception: donors almost always demand more control and more information than needed, diverting energy and resources away from the achievement of organizational objectives. Motivation decreases and trust diminishes as the recipient interprets the demands as an abuse of power.

The era of directly funded project service-delivery work had three distinct advantages for developing inter-organizational relationships. First, it provided policy-makers with first-hand knowledge of the country reality and local socio-political interests, an important resource that could be drawn on at the national level. Secondly, direct engagement in the implementation of projects was a practical demonstration of donors' commitment to improving services for the poor and reduced beneficiaries' scepticism about donors' underlying motivations. Finally, working in partnerships with local people provided the scope to build trust and mutual respect and gave access to relationships and networks important to open dialogue at the macro level. Research on organizations shows that established relationships provide critical entry points for discussion based on trust that enable 'negotiated implementation' of programmes.[11] Without these opportunities donors' influence at the national level will remain limited.

It is often those with resources who dominate the decisions. This is not only a problem between the donors and citizens. The same dynamic is observed within the powerful donor community. The United Nations, for example, often has a weak voice at the donor table because, though it may bring experience, it does not bring financial resources. Improving the knowledge base of those with power is important; but the time required to develop a culture that is conducive to democratic diversity, and to invite and be open to all perspectives, is also crucial. While the exclusion of the poor is widely recognized, interestingly new debate is emerging around the relative neglect of elites, who have significant influence to mobilize change. An open attitude to diversity requires a concerted commitment to change by actors at various levels, as individuals and within our organizations. Implementing the new agreements on international cooperation and harmonization demands a spirit of cooperation between actors. The process can serve as a catalyst for increased communication. Through negotiation around concrete policies, new understanding may develop and unexpected relationships materialize. While these harmonization agreements have the potential to support greater government ownership, they may also create new power structures. Eyben's experience of the participatory poverty reduction strategy process in Bolivia warns of the possibility of donor coordination actually undermining the agreed principle of government ownership (see Chapter 4). If the international community becomes too powerful it may displace the recipient government from the driving seat (Eyben, this volume).

Personal agency and responsible well-being

There has been a call for increased understanding of the social and cultural factors influencing development and the need to approach government reform with full awareness of the local incentives for change (see Unsworth, forthcoming). Yet an understanding of what motivates individual citizens and their local socio-political realities remains weak.[12] Why has this not been part of mainstream development practice? Typically, these issues have been the responsibility of the organizations' 'anthropologists' or 'social development advisers'. There are encouraging signs that organizations wish to extend this beyond the domain of the 'specialist'. Another move forward is the agenda of identifying and working with champions; yet, this strategy stresses the role of others to make the difference. There is a danger of seeing this as an alternative, rather than in addition, to the personal responsibility to build an extended knowledge base. Sensitivity to local culture, understanding the motivations of others and embracing local language all demonstrate an attitude of respect towards local people's beliefs and perspectives that is essential if the new ambitious agenda is to be embraced. A degree of reflexivity would enable staff to situate themselves with respect to personal and institutional values and relationships and thus more easily explore taken-for-granted assumptions.[13] People need incentives to change. Organizations can support critical questioning and provide positive feedback to individuals who invest the energy in an examination of personal and professional standpoints and biases (Chapter 13).

Of crucial importance are the perspectives of the poor 'beneficiaries'. There are difficulties in developing the trust and relationships fundamental to an open discussion and a sharing of their views. Long histories of mistrust exist in many contexts; so it is often an onerous challenge to establish that poor peoples' multiple opinions and realities are valued. It takes time and space to reflect on how power, attitudes and behaviour interact. Investment in these relationships is critical; yet, the new environment puts pressures on staff to be 'strategic', which limits the extent and nature of these more reflective interactions. Donor staff find themselves trapped in capital cities with limited time to connect with poor people. Personal critical reflection is also required (see Chapter 14) and can be actively encouraged by organizations.[14] Relationships and local knowledge develop over time yet the relatively rapid turnover among donor staff in country offices hinders the development of socio-political expertise. There is evidence that aid organizations are transforming through changing rewards and incentives and building new alliances and networks (see Chapter 8).

Organizations as enabling environments

Organizations have unexploited potential to provide the foundation for effective development. There is increasing evidence that organizations play a critical role in providing an enabling environment for change.[15] Those that provide a secure context, in which staff can be more reflective and take risks, encourage innovation (see Chapter 10). The effects are rarely immediate, and organizations need to allow a degree of failure. In time, the impact is seen in terms of more highly motivated staff and more effective development interventions (see Chapter 3). In parallel, enabling staff to take time to understand local dynamics will ultimately help broaden and deepen the interaction with critical stakeholders. Learning about the recipient's history can enable outsiders to play an important facilitating role, by using the knowledge sensitively as a contribution to a country's effort to build consensus (see Chapter 4). The value of the local knowledge and network base that local staff members bring is also being reassessed by many donor agencies. It is only when donors are aware of the web of relationships and patterns of exclusion that they have the opportunity to use their power to encourage and provide entry points to groups that might otherwise be excluded from national decision-making forums.

Organizations can equally serve to exclude alternative perspectives and reinforce existing patterns of dominance. This is one aspect of organizations' failure to embrace complexity. There is a tendency to apply analytical models beyond their sphere for explanation, creating standard portfolios of aid projects.[16] Procedures may also be applied inappropriately; Marsden shows, in Chapter 7, how well-intentioned use of the logical framework, far from introducing clarity and shared objectives, served to reinforce existing power relations, both between donor and project implementers and local NGO staff and the village community. In contrast, where an organization is able to provide sufficient support and guidance through flexible rules that recognize the complexity of the context, innovation and learning are enabled. In Chapter 8, Owusu provides us with an example of ActionAid's evolving Accountability Learning and Planning System (ALPS), where the involvement of multiple stakeholders was central to the process. Diversity is encouraged with exchanges of experience within and between organizations. New approaches are thus needed to help staff build on and develop new models and procedures for the complex environments in which they work.

Inclusive aid

In inclusive aid, all actors can identify and expand the domains in which their attitudes, beliefs and behaviour can make a difference. Through personal accounts across 16 countries, the authors in this book have illustrated that development is, indeed, a complex system. Their experiences offer important lessons for a new approach to development. It is by embracing, rather than simplifying, this complexity that development practitioners will be able to use the power that they have to achieve the goal of poverty elimination.

If aid is to be viewed as a complex system, the governing dynamics of power and relationships need to be better understood. Inclusive aid will demand change to organizational norms and procedures, closely linked to changes in personal behaviour, attitudes and beliefs, to enable the inclusion of currently marginalized actors in decision-making processes. Systemic change cannot be achieved by applying a 'blueprint': it will require diverse and flexible approaches and a time frame that allows shifts in power differentials.

The authors do not offer any prescriptions for action; rather, the challenge is to recognize that the process of development is unpredictable and fluid and so demands flexible and adaptive procedures. Breaking the barriers to ensure meaningful engagement among donors, lenders and partner citizens is an even greater challenge. Institutionally, this will require visionary leadership and a courageous commitment to change. It means embracing diversity and transforming hierarchies into participatory spaces for reflection, learning and action. It requires us to take the time to understand local socio-political realities and to include a wider range of people in the planning and implementation of policies. Only then are we likely to meet the Millennium Development Goals.

Notes

1   I am grateful to Robert Chambers, Leslie Groves, Matt Pearce, Jethro Pettit, and Caroline Robb for their insights and input on a draft of this chapter. The usual disclaimers apply.
2   Cornwall (2000) provides a comprehensive critique of the changing development language.
3   Morgan (1998) provides an interesting discussion of the insights and distortions created by the images and metaphors used in organizations.
4   See Korten, Robert and Siy (1989) for an example of local empowerment by a large government organization.
5   See Unsworth (forthcoming) for a discussion of 'political culture' and the extent to which concepts such as citizenship and accountability were historically constructed in the North.
6   World Education Forum commitments at Dakar. See UNESCO (2000, p5).
7   Golub (forthcoming) maintains that most funding organizations active in the legal field downplay civil-society initiatives grounded in the poor's legal needs and priorities.
8   See Eyben (2003a) regarding the need for donor agencies to work with both governments and civil society.
9   Rick Davies has developed a website to facilitate civil-society participation in global debate in an attempt to improve outward accountability. See www.mande.co.uk/news.htm.
10 See DAC (2002) for a discussion on development cooperation.
11 See the work by Griffith (1996).
12 See recent work by Heath (1999), who argues that when assessing people's motivations people overestimate the importance of extrinsic factors.
13 See Eyben (2003b) for a discussion of these issues in the context of Bolivia.
14 Chambers (2001) argues for 'self-doubting pluralism' – to reflect on personal and professional predispositions and biases and be open to other perspectives.
15 See Fowler (2000) on how non-governmental development organizations can negotiate relationships.
16 For example, see Carothers (2002) on the overuse of the model for democratic transition.

References

Brock, K and McGee, R (2002) *Knowing Poverty: Critical Reflections on Participatory Research and Policy*, Earthscan, London

Carothers, T (2002) 'The End of The Transition Paradigm', *Journal of Democracy*, vol 12, pp6–21

Chambers, R (2001) 'The World Development Report: Concepts, Content and a Chapter 12', *Journal of International Development*, vol 13, pp299–306

Cornwall, A (2000) *Beneficiary, Consumer, Citizen: Perspectives on Participation for Poverty Reduction*, Sida Studies Series, no 2, Sida, Stockholm, Sweden

DAC (2002) *Development Co-operation in Difficult Partnerships*, DAC DCD/DAC 11

Duncan, A, Sharif, I, Landell-Mills, P, Hulme, D and Roy, J (2002) *Bangladesh: Supporting the Drivers of Pro-poor Change*, Department for International Development, London

Eyben, R (2003a) *The Rise of Rights: Rights-based Approaches to International Development*, IDS Policy Briefing, no 17, IDS, Brighton

Eyben, R (2003b) *Donors as Political Actors: Fighting the Thirty Years War in Bolivia*, IDS Working Paper, no 183, IDS, Brighton

Festinger, L (1957) *A Theory of Cognitive Dissonance*, Stanford University Press, Stanford, CA

Fowler, A (2000) *Partnerships: Negotiating Relationships – A Resource for Non-governmental Development Organisations*, Occasional Paper, no 32, International NGO Training and Research Centre, Oxford

Gaventa, J (2001) 'Global Citizen Action: Lessons and Challenges', in Edwards, M and Gaventa, J (eds) *Global Citizen Action*, Earthscan, London

Golub, S (forthcoming) 'Beyond Rule of Law Orthodoxy: The Legal Empowerment Alternative', Rule of Law Series of the Endowment's Democracy and Rule of Law Project, Washington

Griffith, T (1996) Negotiating Successful Technology Implementation: A Motivation Perspective, *Journal of Engineering and Technology Management*, vol 131, pp224–248

Heath, C (1999) 'On the Social Psychology of Agency Relationships: Lay Theories of Motivation Overemphasise Extrinsic Incentives', *Organisational Behaviour and Human Decision Processes*, vol 78, pp25–62

Korten, F F, Robert, J and Siy, Y (1989) *Transforming A Bureaucracy: The Experience of The Philippine National Irrigation Administration*, Kumarian Press, Connecticut

Morgan, G (1998) *Images of Organization: The Executive Edition*, Sage, London

Rihani, S (2002) *Complex Systems Theory and Development Practice: Understanding Non-Linear Realities*, Zed Books, London

UNESCO (2000) *The Dakar Framework for Action. Education for All: Meeting our Collective Commitments*, World Education Forum, Document no ED-2000/CONF/211/1, UNESCO

Unsworth, S (forthcoming) *Better Government for Poverty Reduction: More Effective Partnerships for Change*, DFID, London

The Dynamics of Aid: Power, Procedures and Relationships Timeline

Time frame	Changes in the world environment that have influenced development and aid	Changes in aided governments and their actions	Changes in aid agencies' policies and procedures	Changing aid-related activities and relationships
1946–1960 **End of World War II, colonialism and the onset of the Cold War**	• Need to promote stability in international monetary affairs and the expansion of world trade after World War II • Marshall Plan, 1947 • Independence for Indonesia (1945), India (1947), Pakistan (1947), Ghana (1957) and Algeria (1962) • Competitive devaluations; world trade slumped • Onset of the Cold War • Establishment of the UN (1942) and its specialized agencies (ILO, 1919; WHO, 1946; FAO, 1945; UNICEF, 1946) • Bandung Conference, 1955, launched the Non-Aligned Movement (1961)	• Africa and Asian governments attempt to promote economic and cultural cooperation and oppose colonialism • The term 'third world' emerged from the Bandung Conference; originally intended to distinguish non-aligned nations that gained independence from colonial rule after World War II from Western nations and the former Eastern bloc (the first and second worlds, respectively)	• Infrastructure projects dominate; blueprint approach • Financial aid and technical cooperation to colonies • Technical assistance, the rise of economic planning and five-year plans • US aid more politically focused • World Bank lending through IBRD at market rates • Co-operatives and community development projects (especially in India, with much US/Ford Foundation support)	• Struggles for independence • Decolonizing conflicts, negotiations, transitions and constitutional arrangements • Colonial governments handing over formal power • Ex-colonial sense of guilt, permissive aid agency goodwill, and confidence of leaders to independence together minimize conditionality in aid • Expansion of colonial and post-colonial state with socialism, parastatals, protection and controls (Africa and Asia)
1960s **Rise of the nation state**	• Post-colonialism • Pearson Commission led to a UN target of 1% of national income on aid (0.7% as official aid) • NGOs campaign for 'trade not aid' • Increasing public concern in Northern countries	• Rise of the nation state in Africa • Political ideology, especially in India, of self-reliance and collective action; many countries aim to shift from exporters of raw materials to import substitution. • Soviet Union emerges as a	• World Bank IDA established in 1960; interest-free loans • Aid agencies influenced by modernization theory and the focus on growth • Increase in technical projects leads to an increase in 'technical dependency' of developing countries	• Shift in aid agency behaviour from being colonial powers to negotiating with independent states • African Financial Community franc zone established by the French enabled them to support/control former colonies

regarding development issues
- G77 established in 1964
- Vietnam War (1954–1975)
- Green Revolution in north-west India leads to dramatic increases in yields; importance of US foundations (Ford and Rockefeller) in the research and spread of Green Revolution

world superpower; the Soviet model influences other countries

- Manpower planning prominent

- World Bank lending to poor countries increased through IDA (1960)
- Some aid agencies' governments concerned about influence of Soviet Union; this concern affects the focus of development assistance

1970s
Oil crisis and focus on poverty

- End of gold standard, 1971
- CGIAR established, 1971, with a focus on research in food security and poverty; supported by Ford and Rockefeller Foundations
- UN Stockholm conference on environment, 1972
- **Oil crisis.** OPEC increases price of crude oil in 1973; OPEC countries' monetary reserves accumulated rapidly
- 1973 break up of the Bretton Woods system
- **G7** established, Rambouillet 1975, to promote better coordination
- **Feminist movement.** 1975 Mexico City, UN Conference on Women; Women's organizations begin to work more globally

- Huge increase in borrowing because of oil crisis
- Many of the developing countries turned to IMF and commercial banks, where a flood of OPEC petrol dollars lead to widespread lending, especially in Latin America
- Heavy role of the state
- 1974 New International Economic Order demanded by developing countries to balance power
- Dictatorships in Latin America and single-party governments in Africa

- Basic needs approach; household surveys dominate poverty analysis; integrated rural development projects
- Redistribution with growth promoted
- 1973 Nairobi, World Bank President McNamara states that World Bank mission is poverty reduction, as well as growth; World Bank education lending increases and moves from tertiary to primary; World Bank health lending starts at the end of the 1970s
- Infrastructure projects still dominate; high dependence of aid agencies on agriculturalists and engineers
- Women in development discussions by aid agencies

- US aid (and also World Bank and IMF) precipitated on Cold War alliances (for example, Honduras, Zaire, the Philippines, Israel)
- Aid agencies, in general, shift focus to poorer countries and increase grant aid
- Limited focus on borrowing government ownership

Time frame	Changes in the world environment that have influenced development and aid	Changes in aided governments and their actions	Changes in aid agencies' policies and procedures	Changing aid-related activities and relationships
	• Club of Rome, 1974 • Increase in **popular organizations** and social movements • 1974 IFAD established • 1977 Lome Convention (Agreement between the European Union and African, Caribbean and Pacific (ACP) states on development cooperation) • International Conference on Primary Health Care, Alma-Ata, 1978			
1980s The 'lost decade' and the emergence of debt crisis	• **Brandt Commission**, 1980 • Early 1980s world recession • **Africa** gets poorer – the 'lost decade' • 1982 **Mexico debt crisis.** Mexico threatened to default; world monetary community realized the extent and depth of the crisis • Emergence of **HIV/AIDS** • During the mid 1980s, the **debt crisis** deepened, especially in Latin America	• Borrowing countries accumulate debts • Wave of democratization in Africa and end of some dictatorships in Latin America • Central planning less dominant • Macro-economic instability • Conditions of structural adjustment impact on national politics • Focus on infrastructure projects and the introduction of structural adjustment	• From Brandt report aid agencies make recognition of the structural reasons for poverty • Move away from projects to balance-of-payments support and transfer of funds attached to policy reform; large increase in IMF's and World Bank's **structural adjustment** lending • More focus on effective **projects** that make an	• Aid agencies very confident; try to increase control over development planning through **conditionality** • Aid agencies retain primary control over what to fund and where • Increased aid agency focus on supervision of projects • World Bank begins to acknowledge the importance of the policy environment for increasing impacts of projects

- Brady Plan (commercial banks encouraged to write off some of the debt with some funding from the IMF and World Bank)
- The growth of service delivery **NGOs**. NGOs start to influence environmental projects and increase support in debt campaigns
- Environmental movement focuses on projects such as the Narmada Dam
- UN conference – 'Education for All', Thailand, 1988

- programmes (SAPs) lead to a neglect of health and education sectors
- US and Russia support Cold War countries, allowing many repressive regimes to continue

- impact; some concern over limiting harm done to people and environment; increase in 'people-centred' development
- **Logical framework** introduced by some aid agencies, especially USAID and DFID; overseas training opportunities; consultants assigned to specific projects
- 1987 onwards, **social investment funds**
- Aid agencies continue to support countries with weak governance; aid in many countries was political, not developmental, in nature
- 1987, Adjustment with a Human Face, UNICEF
- Aid agencies support growth of service delivery NGOs in response to the negative impacts of SAPs
- 1989 UNDP, *Human Development Report* challenges the narrow income-based poverty definition of the World Bank
- In 1989 the IMF developed new **debt reduction guidelines**, providing IMF

- More diversity in new and middle managers in some aid organizations

Time frame	Changes in the world environment that have influenced development and aid	Changes in aided governments and their actions	Changes in aid agencies' policies and procedures	Changing aid-related activities and relationships
1990s *The end of the Cold War and the origins of debt relief*	• End of **Cold War** and rise in instability • Increasing awareness of number of regional and local **conflicts** in developing countries • **HIV/AIDs** threat increases • **Conditionality** questioned • Rio 1992. **Climate change** emerges as a problem • Emergence of **global civil society**. NGO boom • Increasing **complexity and scale of aid** • Development of **technology** • NGOs influence policy (for example, debt) • **UN conferences** – UN Convention on the Rights of the Child, New York, 1990; Population and Development,	• More developing countries adopted SAPs, but later unable to meet the terms of the agreement • NGO boom partly due to the government's inability to use available resources; aid agencies channelling money through NGOs as a response; and government retrenchment through SAPs • Collapse of Soviet Union leads to large decreases in aid to some developing country governments	support for commercial bank debt and debt service-reduction operations; ESAF introduced • Gender as opposed to women in development emphasized • Emphasis on **democracy and good governance**; aid agencies less willing to support countries with poor governance; some shift support to NGOs and strengthening civil society • Many new aid agency procedures introduced, but old ones continue leading to heavier workloads • Spread of **logframe** and strategic planning; PRA, stakeholder analysis and workshops; process projects; overseas training; TCOs in decline but more consultancies • Some consideration of **gender and environment** in projects; environmental	• Aid agency language introduces many new words, such as empowerment, but with limited understanding and a lack of consensus around meanings; change in language not matched by change in procedures • Accumulation of 'un-valuable' formal knowledge and the disappearance of valuable informal knowledge • Some aid agencies more responsive to country needs – not assuming that they know best • Some aid agencies control decreases with decline of old-style projects; but policy conditionality continues • Some aid agencies work with

End of 1990s onwards **Globalization and is poverty on the agenda?**						
• **Globalization.** New world of integrated global markets for goods, services and capital • **East Asia crisis**, 1998 • The mounting influence of the **international debt campaign**; endorsement of this campaign by prominent religious leaders, and growing parliamentary and political support	• Governments demand greater ownership of policies • Failure of most of the former **Soviet Union** to make successful transition to Western-style democracy with regulated market economy • Huge adjustment lending to East Asian governments and Soviet Union • Some governments more able to negotiate because of	• Taxpayers in aid agency countries demand **results-based accounting** • Recognition of **corruption and governance** as a development issue • **Enhanced HIPC** links debt relief to poverty • World Bank Comprehensive Development Framework • World Bank and IMF **poverty reduction strategy** papers	• Cairo, 1994; Social Summit, Copenhagen, 1995; Fourth World Conference on Women, Beijing, 1995; World Food Summit, Rome, 1996 • Territorial integrity of weak countries diminishes	assessments and other safeguard policies introduced in the World Bank • Know-how fund approach spreads to LDCs from former communist countries • Early 1990s, boom in **participatory planning** and participatory rural appraisals • **1996 HIPC** introduced • Policy-related consultancies; **sector-wide approaches** and basket-funding • **Poverty redefined** • Expansion of **social funds** in response to growing negative impacts of SAPs • World Bank increasingly accepts the importance of participation in projects	• Aid agencies becoming **less confident; accountable to multiple stakeholders,** including the poor • Some aid agencies have a **wider mandate** leading to confusion; international debate about the mandate of the IMF and World Bank reopened • Some aid agencies **less cautious/'secretive'**; more	NGOs as advocates for their policy objectives • Aid agency coordination increases and so does their influence over national politics

Time frame	Changes in the world environment that have influenced development and aid	Changes in aided governments and their actions	Changes in aid agencies' policies and procedures	Changing aid-related activities and relationships
	• The launch of enhanced **HIPC Initiative** at the G7 Summit in Cologne in mid 1999 made debt relief conditional on formulation of a poverty-reduction framework • Increased global migration; increased spread of diseases across international boundaries; increased size of youth populations in developing countries; booming ageing populations in Northern countries • **World Trade Organization** starts to make an impact. Seattle, 1999, marks the beginning of mass globalization demonstration • Fair Trade Movement • Increased use of email and boom in websites • Debate on doubling of aid • Globalization of terrorist activities; 11 September 2001; suicide bombing and terrorism as a means of protest; war in Afghanistan	increased technical capacity • Limited **sustainability of policy change** driven by external conditionality	• World Bank poverty reduction strategy credits • Linking the **IMF's PRGF** with poverty through the introduction of PRSPs and development of poverty impact assessments of macro and structural reforms • Bilateral aid agencies improve coherence of international development system as opposed to just transferring resources • Citizens' report cards • Email promotes networks across and within institutions • **Poverty** increasingly accepted as multidimensional – beyond income and consumption and health and education to include the poor's definition of poverty (through PPAs, etc) Streamlining conditionality • Aid agencies give more **budget support** • Making globalization work for poor people on the	information disclosed (website); aid agency institutional language becomes less obscure (but still difficult to understand by outsiders); more discussion about past mistakes • Alignment of World Bank and IMF instruments begins to change Bank/IMF relations • English language even more dominant • Aid agency procedures and instruments moving towards more transparency; untying aid; in-country offices; national professionals; working with other aid agencies; making more room for government to lead; facilitating meetings between different local interests; learning local languages and culture; investing in people initiatives; personal and group behaviour and discourse encouraged to promote diversity and diminish

- US enhanced unilateralism; Kyoto Protocol without US; new worldwide polarization with increased alienation from the US

agenda
- Specific localized projects on the decline
- Increased aid by rich countries after 11 September 2001, with the recognition that poverty and misery can breed terrorism
- Aid agencies try to coordinate efforts in Afghanistan

hierarchy; trusting local people to manage aid agency financial resources; social audits

Source: based on a timeline produced at the Procedures, Power and Relationships workshop held at the Institute for Development Studies, University of Sussex, 8–12 May 2001 and comments from John Mitchell, Veena Siddharth, Greg Toulmin (World Bank) and Robert Chambers (IDS)

Index